AUSTERITY BLUES

AUSTERITY BLUES

[*Fighting for the Soul of Public Higher Education*]

MICHAEL FABRICANT & STEPHEN BRIER

Johns Hopkins University Press
Baltimore

© 2016 Johns Hopkins University Press
All rights reserved. Published 2016
Printed in the United States of America on acid-free paper

2 4 6 8 9 7 5 3 1

Johns Hopkins University Press
2715 North Charles Street
Baltimore, Maryland 21218-4363
www.press.jhu.edu

Library of Congress Cataloging-in-Publication Data

Names: Fabricant, Michael, author. | Brier, Stephen, 1946– author.
Title: Austerity blues : fighting for the soul of public higher education /
    Michael Fabricant and Stephen Brier.
Description: Baltimore, Maryland : Johns Hopkins University Press, 2016. |
    Includes bibliographical references and index.
Identifiers: LCCN 2015049916 | ISBN 9781421420677 (hardcover : alk. paper) |
    ISBN 9781421420684 (electronic) | ISBN 1421420678 (hardcover : alk. paper) |
    ISBN 1421420686 (electronic)
Subjects: LCSH: Public universities and colleges—United States—Finance. |
    Education, Higher—United States—Finance. | Government aid to higher
    education—United States. | Federal aid to higher education—United States. |
    Higher education and state—United States. | College costs—United States. |
    Student loans—United States.
Classification: LCC LB2342 .F34 2016 | DDC 378/.05—dc23
    LC record available at http://lccn.loc.gov/2015049916

A catalog record for this book is available from the British Library.

Special discounts are available for bulk purchases of this book.
For more information, please contact Special Sales at 410-516-6936 or
specialsales@press.jhu.edu.

Johns Hopkins University Press uses environmentally friendly book materials,
including recycled text paper that is composed of at least 30 percent
post-consumer waste, whenever possible.

To our grandchildren
Kioka, Amelia, Lucas, and Ariel
and
Nate
in the hope that a vibrant public university that was so important in their grandfathers' lives and careers will be there for them as well

[CONTENTS]

AUSTERITY BLUES

Introduction

For, while the tale of how we suffer and how we are delighted, and how we may triumph is never new, it always must be heard. There isn't any other tale to tell, it's the only light we've got in all this darkness.—James Baldwin, *Sonny's Blues*

Writing this book has allowed us to reflect on a time and place that made a decisive difference in both of our lives. College was unfamiliar to both of our working-class families, one on the West Coast, the other in the East. It nevertheless fueled aspirations and hope as a portal to a different life. One of our fathers said: "You will do better than me working with your mind and not your hands." The other said: "I didn't work all my life in a factory so you could work in a factory, too." What each of them did not say, but believed, was that college was a place where ideas mattered and their son's mind would be nurtured. And so our parents imagined that there were untold opportunities, economic and intellectual, hidden behind ivory towers and that those opportunities would transport their children to places unknown. In turn, we both held the deep belief that a university experience and a college degree would prove transformative in our own lives. Our parents' dreams and our own aspirations were not disappointed. Indeed, our university experiences altered our individual and collective experiences. It was so life-altering, both of us decided to organize our lives around university citizenship as faculty members. Needless to say, we have not been disappointed in our choices.

We both entered college as white, working-class men in a remarkable, all-too-brief moment in the history of higher education when dramatic growth brought the contemporary public university into being. During the long decade of the 1960s, anything and everything seemed possible, as social movements emerged to challenge political, economic, and intellectual orthodoxies. One of the centers of turmoil was public higher education. From Berkeley to Michigan to New York City, student ferment fed the larger social justice movement taking shape outside university walls. The conflict inside the public university was no less intense. The movement from the classroom into the community; the entry of subordinated knowledge of race, gender, and class into academic discourse; and the push to actively situate student and faculty voices in a university decision-making process increasingly dominated by administrators all turned out to be significant sites of struggle. In that consequential decade we were both very much engaged in the work of redefining and remaking public higher education. We made connections as students between the politics of the antiwar and antiracism movements and the public university as an epicenter of critical social struggles. We were shaped intellectually and politically during that era. Matters of race, class, gender, power, the public good, and the meaning of public education coursed through our academic work, our classroom teaching, and our political organizing choices. It was in the public university during that era where we learned that the external world of political economy and our own interior lives were inseparable. These worlds had to be linked to be understood. That struggle for unification has marked much of our academic work ever since.

The opportunities we had to choose lives of the mind and political agency, however, were not accidental. Our individual aspirations were linked to a political topography of intense class conflict dating back to the Great Depression. That struggle, led in large part by labor unions and leftist political parties, produced a shift in the roles and functions of the state. It was within this context that governmental institutions assumed more and more social responsibility for citizens. New programs were created and laws passed to protect working people from the negative consequences of the labor market (e.g., the National Labor Relations and Social Security acts). Substantially greater public investment was made in the postwar era, especially in education and health care, which rewarded veterans returning from World War II with a variety of benefits and, in turn, created a more productive workforce.

We have both been beneficiaries of those gains and the conflicts out of which they arose. We struggled, first as students and then as teachers and scholars, to carry forward the class politics of the 1930s by incorporating a vision of race, gender, and later, sexuality into our work. The successful progressive political struggles that preceded our entry into public higher education in the 1960s afforded us access to the full-time faculty necessary for positive classroom experiences and tuition that was affordable or even free, both made possible by substantial state subsidies.

No matter the historic contributions of public higher education, it is important not to romanticize either its intellectual risk taking or its academic independence. It remains firmly embedded in the apparatus of the state and the larger market-based economy. At its best, public higher education has had goals that were often contradictory. These tensions have been grounded in historical and contemporary academic discourse, employment opportunities, democratic participation, centralized administrative prerogatives, and finally, the scope and nature of dissent. What makes the public university unique is that such contradictions have been tolerated, if not always nurtured. The light shed by the contemporary public university on contentious issues—often defined by unpopular discourse, contradiction, political struggle, and dissent—is a flickering candle.

The same calculus of politics, public investment, and transformative opportunities is shaping and reshaping the public university today. We are increasingly troubled by the present policy drift that has rapidly become a strong undercurrent of disinvestment, growing student indebtedness, and fiscal starvation of public higher education. We fear for the future of public higher education, both nationally and close to home at the City University of New York (CUNY). Year after year, we witness the steady withdrawal of state funds and, in turn, restricted access for "the children of the whole people" (CUNY's original mission, as stated in the mid-nineteenth century) to a quality public higher education. Conversely, we have seen tuition at CUNY increase by 25 percent at the same time that about $500 million of public money has been withdrawn. Over the past forty years at CUNY, the ratio of tuition paid by full-time students to public funding has shifted from zero to about 50 percent for students, many of whose annual family incomes are below $30,000. Within that same time frame the proportion of classes taught by full-time faculty has diminished from almost 100 percent to less than 50 percent. We also see the continuing disappearance of young males of color, especially African Americans, in undergraduate education, with black women outnumbering black men in CUNY's community and senior colleges by a ratio of 3 to 2. These are not merely local but rather national trends.

The future of both public higher education access and the quality of the undergraduate education that our students, now and in the future, can expect to receive is in doubt. Even as we admit undergraduates in record numbers at CUNY (274,000 as of the 2014–15 academic year), we are concerned because their experience is ever more compromised by sharply diminished public fiscal underpinnings.

We are hearing a language of crisis, with concepts like "austerity" and "efficiency," what economist Paul Krugman has correctly termed "austerity ideology," applied to every public institution. As faculty members we believe the language of crisis is used at CUNY to legitimate bad policies of diminished public support; increased tuition; growing use of part-time faculty paid impoverished wages; and decaying physical facilities. The human toll of these policies is masked by declarations that efficiencies need to be extracted from available public resources because new or increased public resources are simply not available. Furthermore, we are told that only through such efficiencies can quality be achieved. We are indeed at a crossroads in public higher education. The choices are clear. Our personal experiences as undergraduates almost half a century ago offer a stark counterpoint to present policies as well as a reminder that increased and targeted public investment, not efficiencies driven by austerity, remains the best, most responsible way to increase the quality of public higher education, now and in the future.

The fiscal landscape of continuing disinvestment is neither preordained nor natural. It is a consequence of a politics of austerity that disproportionately denies the poorest students, especially those of color, quality higher education. We are faced with a series of political, economic, and structural choices regarding the future of public higher education.

In contrast to the austerity policies undermining public higher education and much else in the public sphere in the United States, China, with global economic and political ambitions, has significantly increased its investments, spending $250 billion to expand its human capital capacities. "Just as the United States helped build a white collar middle class in the late 1940's and early 1950's by using the G.I. Bill to help educate millions of World War II veterans," Keith Bradsher reports in the *New York Times* Business Section, "the Chinese government is using large subsidies to educate tens of millions of young people" (Bradsher 2013). China is specifically targeting its investments in building new higher education institutions (Nylander 2015). These investments recently yielded a rise in the global rankings of seven of China's universities, each of which is now ranked internationally in the top two hundred (Nylander 2015). While the United States continues to disinvest in public higher education, China has significantly ramped up its investment. The reasoning for China's increased expenditures is summarized by Keith Bradsher: "Increasingly, college graduates all over the world (*in a globalized economy*) compete for similar work, and the boom in higher education in China is starting to put pressure on employment opportunities for college graduates elsewhere—including in the United States. Importantly the objectives of the Chinese investment are largely economic" (Bradsher 2013). What is rarely discussed beyond higher education's economic impact, are the ways public higher education in China and the United States choose or not to reconceive the nature of citizenship roles or to foster innovation. Those critical functions are essential not only in resisting austerity policies but also in creating a more robust academic experience that deepens students' critical relationships to the world and enlarges their potential contributions to society. Later in the book we will sketch what we describe as emancipatory forms of education that must shape the ways we target increased public investment to create the most dynamic and successful forms of public higher education.

Levels and kinds of public investment are therefore not merely technical or fiscal exercises but rather the consequence of human and political choices. Those choices will be determined in the United States, as in the past, by the kind of struggles we are prepared to wage for a redistributive and emancipatory public higher education. The success of these struggles will be determined by linking public higher education's fate to other progressive campaigns for social justice in health care, policing, subsistence wages, the environment, and housing. Without a doubt, there must be independent advocacy for more fiscal support for public higher education. But that independent work, as in the 1930s and 1960s, must be linked to larger social movements for broad, redistributive justice and equity. Only the power and success of such social movements can provide the necessary corrective to forces presently pushing for policies of radical disinvestment, restructuring, and resource reallocation in public higher education.

We wrote this book to address the following questions that are too often either ignored or considered in isolation from each other:

- What is driving the present restructuring of public higher education?
- What are the incentives for disinvestment? What are the alternatives?
- Is there a history of reform that offers alternative approaches?
- How does austerity promote intensified forms of inequality?
- In what ways has technology influenced the ongoing restructuring of public higher education?
- How do we begin to chart a way forward, effectively challenging the present change agenda?

Present policy, especially the withdrawal of public resources, is designed to redefine the purposes of public higher education. Redistributive policies and politics are the antonyms to present policies of austerity. The historic struggle for a redistributive public higher education and other, largely public goods—however incomplete even in its most expansive moment in the 1960s—remains a site of critical contestation. The work of this book is to develop a more comprehensive understanding of what is changing and what is at stake. It is on this basis that we intend to show how the United States arrived at this moment of the unraveling of its justifiably admired public higher education system and what we can do to change it. The book tells two parallel stories: the first is about the systematic current assault on public institutions, particularly public higher education; the second is about the sparks of creativity, dedication, desire, desperation, and collective conviction that continue to make a vibrant public higher education essential to the health and soul of the city, the state, and the nation.

Austerity Blues is organized into three parts, encompassing seven chapters and an epilogue.

Part 1, "The Political-Economic Context of Public Higher Education," consists of three chapters. The first sets the current state of public higher education within the larger context of recent neoliberal attacks on a range of public goods, including the imposition of austerity measures in health care and K–12 education. The austerity regime currently confronting public universities is not unique to higher education; it affects all levels of social and public services and the quality of citizens' lives. We believe that any analysis of the current status of public higher education needs to be set within this larger political-economic context.

The second and third chapters set the larger historical context for understanding how public higher education systems across the country were fundamentally transformed in the three decades following the end of World War II. Chapter 2, "The State Expansion of Public Higher Education," traces the combined efforts of the federal government, individual states, and key political actors (focusing particularly on California and New York, the states with the three largest public university systems) to make significant investments in the expansion of public higher education institutions between 1943 and 1960. These investments were in large part prompted by the burgeoning needs of both the postwar economy and the massive influx of new college students spurred by the baby boom generation. Chapter 3, "Students and Faculty Take Command," explores the rise in the 1960s of what University of California (UC) administrator Clark Kerr famously called "the multiversity." The multiversity became a site of growing tension for many undergraduate and graduate students, who would launch an open rebellion in 1964 at UC Berkeley. They were soon joined by faculty and students at other public flagship and private universities. These struggles were fueled by student and faculty opposition not only to the multiversity's increasingly mechanistic and routinized culture but also to the Vietnam War and in support of the antiracist politics of the civil rights movement. The decade of public university-based student rebellion that followed would result in 1969 in massive student strikes and sit-ins at various CUNY campuses. The struggle to open CUNY's doors to students of color and to broaden the purposes of its curriculum generated fierce opposition, culminating in the system's contraction during the city's fiscal crisis in the 1970s. In turn this series of events helped to set the stage for early neoliberal battles to constrain and defund public institutions such as CUNY.

Part 2, "The State of Austerity" consists of three chapters that sketch the growth of neoliberal theories and policies as they have been applied to public higher education over the past three decades. Chapter 4, "The Making of the Neoliberal Public University," describes this process. In the first era, the twenty- to twenty-five-year period between the last decade of the twentieth century and the first decade of the twenty-first, public higher education was faced with a dilemma of accelerating disinvestment of public funds. This first era of austerity reform produced ever-greater reliance of public universities not only on increased tuition but also on expanding the number of undergraduate students to allow them to stay afloat financially. Since the onset of the Great Recession, public universities entered a second era of neoliberal policy making that focused on capping tuition increases, expanding "efficient" distance-learning/ technology, and promoting strategic public-private partnerships to bolster higher education in an era of declining public budgets as well as soaring student debt. These recent trends are radically altering both the basic purposes and the educational experiences of public higher education.

Chapter 5, "The Public University as an Engine of Inequality," explores the austerity policies that provide "cover" for ever more aggressive practices mirroring growing stratification and inequality in the larger society. Austerity policies have created a need for universities and other public agencies to develop "efficient practices" that do more with less because of drastically reduced state funding. Corporate and for-profit business practices are being imported wholesale into public university management, no matter their fit or misfit with higher education's core mission or larger contributions to the public good. One consequence of disinvestment is an increasingly tiered system of public higher education that produces differential levels of investment and access to high-quality public higher education by race and class. Stratification of the public university student body is mirrored at all levels of the university from community colleges to Research 1 institutions. The largest part of the undergraduate teaching workforce is now part time, low wage, and job insecure. The stratification of labor within the public university also includes the growing numbers and salaries of administrators when compared to those of the teaching labor force. The intensifying stratification and inequality within public higher education touch every stakeholder in the university, from students to faculty to administrators.

Chapter 6, "Technology as a 'Magic Bullet' in an Era of Austerity," explores the history of university administrators' and policy makers' fervent embrace over the last century of various forms of technology as solutions for all that ailed higher education. Technology was expected to solve a range of problems arising from the dramatic increases in college enrollments and expansion of public higher education. Early uses of radio and educational television were eclipsed by the historic rise of computer-based technologies over the past thirty years, fueling fever dreams of cost savings, mechanized instruction, and not coincidentally, visions of profit generation among university administrators and their private-sector enablers. We look at early academic instantiations of such profit-making digital projects at UCLA and at Columbia University as well as the parallel rise of the nonprofit open educational resources movement after 2001. We also explore the decidedly profit-seeking objectives of massive open online course (MOOC) providers such as Coursera and Udacity. This chapter ends with a look at Arizona State University, where heavy reliance on online instruction is the harbinger, we suspect, of the new twenty-first-century public multiversity. The widespread embrace of digital technology "solutions" at public universities has occurred at precisely the same time that tax funds in support of public higher education continue their sharp decline and growing austerity policies in turn define and reshape public higher education.

Part 3, "Resistance Efforts and the Fight for Emancipatory Education," consists of a final chapter and the epilogue. Chapter 7, "Fighting for the Soul of Public Higher Education," argues that only a bold reform platform, tied to and enabled by a similarly bold social movement, can successfully confront the austerity-driven policies and intensified stratification of the public university, part and parcel of larger social and economic trends of inequality. Some part of that platform is currently being developed by a cross section of groups across the country involved in struggles over a range of issues, including student debt, the equitable treatment of contingent faculty members, increased capital and operating cost investments in public universities, and development of more robust and technologically appropriate curricula. This concluding chapter describes, in a series of snapshots, the contested terrain in these critical areas, including examples of contemporary battles being waged by local, regional, and national alliances of student and faculty groups. Finally, in the epilogue we discuss what will be required to successfully change the national agenda for public universities, offer several contemporary examples of transformative campus-based struggles, and describe what an alternative future for public higher education might look like.

The overarching challenge facing all of us is to protect the public university as a democratic experiment firmly planted in the public commons. This can only be accomplished by creating a democracy that assures economic security, health, public education, a clean and sustainable environment, and robust citizen participation. For this to happen, we suggest in chapter 7 and the epilogue that policies must be crafted to enable the state to regulate and tax dominant private economic interests and make major public investments. These investments must enhance the intellectual development and critical thinking of large sectors of society otherwise deemed disposable. This brings us back to our personal experiences fifty years ago when such investments were made (differentially by race and gender, to be sure) and joined to an understanding that higher education should enlarge the lives of students as both citizens and workers. We argue that austerity policies have eroded the development of robust democracy by diminishing a variety of public goods. As Mark Blyth, the author of *Austerity: The History of a Dangerous Idea,* told the *New York Times*'s Jennifer Szalai, "austerity policies . . . turn an economic situation into a 'morality tale of saints and sinners' leading to punishment rather than problem solving." Blyth further suggests that austerity "relies on the poor paying for the mistakes of the rich" and that the "moral stays the same. Those with less are expected to be the ones to do without" (Szalai 2015, 13–15; Blyth 2013, 10). We argue throughout this book that such austerity policies are also robbing an increasing number of citizens of access to a quality and emancipatory public higher education and, in turn, their fuller enfranchisement as citizens and workers.

PART I

THE POLITICAL-ECONOMIC CONTEXT OF PUBLIC HIGHER EDUCATION

[1]

Public Assets in an Era of Austerity

The United States was once committed as a nation to broadening access to higher education, creating a path to social mobility for the nation's poor and working-class citizens. The 1862 Morrill Land-Grant Act provided individual states with a financial incentive to open public universities, which they did in great numbers and with remarkable success. In New York City, a unique municipal college system, founded in the mid-nineteenth century and expanded in the twentieth, provided tuition-free, publicly supported higher education for the city's immigrant and poor citizens. The 1944 GI Bill, the Higher Education Act of 1965, and the Higher Education Amendments of 1972 created a federal system of assistance that veterans and other citizens could use to attend public or private colleges.

This federal support of college attendance was joined to local higher education systems, like CUNY, which remained tuition-free to city residents until 1976; or to regional systems like the one in California, which promised perhaps the most democratic and generous system of public higher education in the country until the 1990s. Public dollars and expanding systems of higher education in the post–World War II era fueled not only easy access to college education but also rapid expansion in the number and size of public universities throughout the country. This "golden age" of US higher education produced unprecedented levels of college graduations, relatively rapid time-to-degree college completion rates, low or even free tuition, and an explosion in the number of graduate programs and graduate degrees, and high-end, federally supported research projects. Simultaneously, the US economy was rapidly growing, in large part because of the increased contributions and productivity of the nation's expanding higher education sector (Folbre 2010, 35–41; Mettler 2014, 7–9).

In 2015 these are fading memories, a faint echo with little resonance for eighteen-year-old, working-class and poor women and men struggling to build a future. For these young people the cost of austerity budget-cutting and shrinking opportunities in traditional portals of social mobility such as higher education is a frustrating fact of life. The citizenry is left to wonder about a collective future that no longer seems to include the vast majority of poor, working-class, and even middle-class Americans. As college completion and even initial attendance are increasingly out of reach for more and more women and men, and the marketplace offers reduced wages to an ever-expanding number of workers, the prospects for poor and working-class students to achieve some part of their dream seem more and more remote.

The diminishment of the state's facilitating role in redressing imbalances of wealth or income is a key factor in this downward shift in opportunity. The state is increasingly seen as an impediment to the "natural" and efficient mechanisms of wealth creation and income distribution that flow from the marketplace. This attack on the purposes and functions of the state as a drag on the market is part of the larger global project inaugurated by neoliberal economists, politicians, and ideologues in the 1970s that continues to this day (Giroux 2014, 5–8; Harvey 2003, 149–182). Neoliberal ideology argues that advances in human well-being can be achieved "by liberating individual entrepreneurial freedoms and skills within an institutional framework characterized by strong property rights, free markets, and free trade" (Harvey 2005, 2). One key goal of neoliberal policies is the further diminishment of an already partial welfare state. After four decades of neoliberal hegemony, ordinary Americans are left to wonder: What is our collective future as a nation if the state is less and less able to make leveling social investments in public education and public health? What motivates resistance to public investment on the one hand and a blind faith in privatization of public assets on the other, particularly in a period of intensifying global competition? These questions are not easily answered, but some part of the calculus of current choices appears to be embedded in the larger social and political crises facing nations across the globe.

Crises of employment, incarceration, disease, and, perhaps most important, ecological disaster can only be addressed through an educated workforce and a collective political will. The policy choices facing Americans during this political moment suggest either surrender in the face of mounting social problems or denial about both the magnitude and accelerating gravity of these challenges. Denial and policy indifference are especially acute in relationship to the growing environmental threat, with a major wing of one of the two dominant US political parties essentially claiming that climate change and its consequences are fictions perpetrated by dissembling scientists and their left-wing political enablers. We begin this book by using the policy silence about ecological degradation as both a metaphor and a policy referent to help understand our present course of action regarding public higher education. Clearly, this is an unorthodox starting point. However, the policy choice to abandon the environment to accelerating degradation while denying the biological consequences presently and in the future provides a powerful frame of reference for initiating a discussion about the transformations that are reshaping public higher education.

Deregulation, Disinvestment, and Degradation

With trend-line data indicating that ecological breakdowns are not only increasing in number but also producing a growing level of destruction, US policy makers remain more or less quiescent. The degradation of the state's autonomous policy-making role and the deregulation of centralized state authority have combined to diminish the capacity of policy makers to effectively intervene in the face of current and impending ecological disasters. More to the point, the long- and short-term planning role of state policy makers has given way in the face of the power of a cross section of powerful interest groups. These interest groups include but are not limited to energy-producing multinational corporations and industries dependent on fossil fuels (especially coal) that actively resist governmental regulation to reduce greenhouse gas emissions. This powerful web of economic and political power and interests is daunting in large part because it is able to render invisible or suspect important data about the destructive long-term impact of fossil fuel emissions. In the midst of these environmental changes, the role of government as a strategic planning mechanism, whatever its past limitations and contradictions, is diminished. Individual corporations, because of their primary responsibility to shareholders and profit making, are clearly not positioned to address this crisis holistically or systematically (Ghani and Lockhart 2008, 8–12). To the contrary, corporate power has worked to weaken regulatory and other reform efforts. The market cannot and will not save us from the unfolding ecological disaster. This crisis demands a collective, centralized decision-making mechanism, supported by necessary autonomy, resources, and power to make decisions regarding the short-term *and* long-term welfare of the entire population. And yet, in this era of neoliberalism, the capacity of the state—faced as it is with a rapidly changing landscape of increasing need and crises—to be able to manage even its most basic historical functions, much less invent new ones, is highly compromised.

At the same time, state social reproduction functions—the necessary goods and services citizens need to minimally function in society and the economy—have been significantly diminished in the United States over the past four decades. This has occurred as a result of policies of disinvestment and/or austerity affecting basic services ranging from health care to K–12 education. Student per capita public spending in higher education, for example, has declined over the past fifteen years. The reduction of investment has in turn had a significant impact on the quality of education as class sizes increase, pedagogy is mechanized, and academic content is increasingly standardized or watered down. The social reproduction of college students from one generation to the next is less likely as a result to promote the kind of classroom work and faculty engagement that sharpen students' critical thinking and writing skills. This shift in education quality also has negative consequences for many college graduates, who are increasingly unable to function as informed citizens and to take on challenging job roles.

This declension has reversed more than a century and a half of class tensions and social movements that produced a halting embrace of, and a heightened commitment to, social welfare legislation (Fabricant and Fine 2013, 35–54). Beginning with the emergence of tax-supported public schooling in the early nineteenth century, then expanding to encompass industrial and health regulation during the Progressive Era in the first decades of the last century, the state increasingly came to regulate the worst excesses of industrial capitalism and assume at least partial responsibility for the public's health and well-being, including assuring the quality and safety of the food and drugs it consumed and the health and safety of workers in its factories. Such guarantees of the American public's well-being expanded during the New Deal era with the growth of a partial welfare state that included employment programs, the federally assured right to organize labor unions, and unemployment and Social Security insurance programs (American Social History Project 2008, 2:444–94). The great expansion of government guarantees of a decent social wage for all citizens culminated in the era of the Great Society with the passage of the Medicare and Medicaid amendments to Social Security in 1965. It is important to remember that the state and dominant economic and political interests never accepted these redistributive policies willingly. To the contrary, reactive political resistance to progressive change was exemplified by opposition to New Deal and Great Society policies such as Social Security and Medicare, as well as repressive policing and the tamping down of dissent (Jansson 2012, 205–7; Piven and Cloward 1993, 84–86; Biondi 2006, 138). Nonetheless, between the 1930s and early 1970s, progressive movements were able to produce expanded state investment in collective social programming and individual entitlements.

Recently, however, the state's ability to socially reproduce a labor force that is physically healthy, sufficiently well educated, and emotionally and financially stable has dramatically diminished. This diminishment can be traced to the reduced role of progressive social movements, declining investment in the social wage, radical restructuring of the purposes and organization of government, and alignment of political and economic forces promoting "new market-based reforms" as a viable alternative to an expanded public sphere. The decline of state autonomy and authority during this era of intensifying ecological and economic crisis, and its resulting hobbled capacity to effectively meet the needs of the whole people, is vividly illustrated by the changing social reproduction function of the state (Frazier 2014; Katz 2001, 717–24). It is important to note at the outset that this analysis will not romanticize the historic social reproduction role of the US state. It has been largely defined, for example, by substantially less investment in African American and Latino communities. A cross section of services from health care to K–12 education was also allocated differentially on the basis of race and class. The *Brown v. the Board of Education* case was a concrete example of racial discrimination in public education, and the US Supreme Court's 1954 decision that called for the integration of public schools proved inadequate in realizing the decision's basic purpose of promoting equity in the allocation of a vital public good. Similarly, Medicaid and public hospitals have historically offered a lower quality of health services to the poor than that available to employed middle- and working-class citizens seeking services from for-profit or nonprofit hospitals. This stratification in the quality of services by race and class extends to public higher education, where flagship state universities frequently received a disproportionate share of public investment from their state legislatures while generally serving a largely white and/or middle-class student population.

The present moment of market reform and the monetization of all things public are creating even greater inequalities in the allocation of state resources and investment in social reproduction functions. Perhaps most important, the modest redistribution of public assets to the poorest citizens has been halted and even reversed, as evidenced by the recent successful efforts of Republicans in the US Congress to cut food stamp and unemployment insurance benefits. The capacity of legislative and bureaucratic policy makers to intervene as semiautonomous advocates for heightened public investment has been significantly eroded because the power and reach of progressive social movements have declined in the face of constant attacks. As noted earlier, these trends and the pace of change in reconstituting and reducing the state's social reproduction functions have substantial forward momentum. A number of parallels can also be drawn between changes in the state's function to assure social reproduction and its diminished environmental regulatory function (Hacker and Pierson 2011, 4).

Evidence of growing crises and ineffective state responses to breakdowns in the environment, health care, and K–12 schooling have largely been ignored by state actors. As these crises have deepened, the economic and ideological commitment of powerful interest groups to an agenda of privatization has intensified. This point is especially important because the market is almost universally viewed as the sole solution to degradation of both the environment and social reproduction (Harvey 2003, 149–82). The historically destructive impact of these market reforms on human and natural resources is widely embraced as an unfortunate but necessary by-product of the creative, disruptive processes of capital.

The packaging of public discourse and denial of the consequences of ecological deregulation and social disinvestment increasingly pockmark policy debates and undermine democratic decision making. On issues ranging from climate change—where major energy industries such as coal and oil create counter "evidence" to refute global warming—to public-school "reform" efforts that produce little tangible evidence of academic improvement, policies are being increasingly shaped by special-interest or corporate rhetoric, while objective, policy-informed data and arguments are more likely to be dismissed or buried (Fabricant and Fine 2013, 53; Henig 2009, 1–14; Morozov 2013, 262).

To understand breakdowns in basic state functions of strategic planning and social reproduction, we must examine the broader context that has spawned the increased paralysis and apparent policy-making irrationality of current state actors, both nationally and regionally. It is not the intention of this analysis to explore every aspect of state policy making. Rather, we will examine the transformative changes presently sweeping through higher education as a window on broader currents of state policy responses to emergent crises. We will argue that higher education represents a cutting edge of the present reassembly and hobbling of the state.

We have selected higher education for a number of reasons. To begin with, the most rapid and far-reaching policy changes in the public sector have recently been directed at public higher education. At the epicenter of these changes is the role of instructional technology, which promises to rapidly alter the content, financing, and teaching methodologies of the university (Selingo 2013, 86–104). Equally important, US public higher education has historically played a key role in developing a cohort of educated citizens capable of understanding and addressing problems as complex and persistent as a declining economy and a degraded physical environment. This transformative ability raises an elemental question regarding the purpose and function of higher education. As this site of knowledge and citizen production is altered, how will it affect the capacity of university graduates and the larger society to address present and impending crises we face as a nation? Public universities have long represented a point of entry for new immigrant groups and working people to the historic American dream of acquiring a college degree and becoming a productive citizen. As the very structure of the university changes, will it imperil not only this dream but also the attendant project of democracy?

Neither the outcome nor the level of struggle regarding the future of public higher education is preordained. The present direction, momentum, and content of change are increasingly clear, however. To better understand the current agenda to "reform" public higher education, we have developed a series of propositions to clarify the logic of that agenda. Before we turn the page of the narrative to these propositions, however, it is important to recall our opening discussion about environmental rupture. It is our contention that the present circumstance of public higher education offers an especially useful way to understand broader ecological and other policy issues. As we suggested initially, many of the themes regarding denial, evidence, action, and crisis overlap. Perhaps, most important, the conjunction between higher education and social as well as technical solutions to ecological disaster is clear. We will return to these points of conjunction of problems and struggles in our final chapter.

Six Propositions for Understanding the Restructuring of Public Higher Education

A series of basic propositions will help to frame our analysis and offer basic referents for the reconstitution of the state and more specifically the sphere of public higher education.

Proposition 1: We are faced with an epic economic crisis of global capital.

The current economic crisis has been richly described inside and outside of the academy. The most far-reaching analyses have described the present crisis as being highly correlated with ever-greater difficulties in producing historic levels of profit. This difficulty threatens the very foundation of global capital. As more and more surplus capital pours into the financial sector to produce new higher and quicker levels of profit, that sector accumulates an ever-greater share of both economic benefit and power. For example, the financial sector accounts for almost 50 percent of the profit produced by the American economy. This figure dwarfs every other service and manufacturing sector (Harvey 2005, 158; McCoy 2010). As large profits are made by only a few corporate entities, unequal distribution of the profits of the larger economy become even more pronounced, and the intensifying pressure on the finance sector to continue to record new and ever higher profit margins continues to mount (Piketty 2014). These dynamics have in large part accounted for substantial investment in subprime mortgage lending after the turn of the current century that, although highly risky, promised immediate and substantial dividends to investors. This speculative bubble exploded in 2008 in an economic meltdown of epic proportions. The consequent migration of a larger and larger share of the economy's capital and profit making to the financial sector has been described by David Harvey and others as powerfully illustrative of the decline of earlier engines of long-term economic growth and a sign that the American economy is in serious decline (Harvey 2003, 205–6).

The economic crisis of 2008, commonly referred to as "The Great Recession," also produced an intensifying attack on labor unions in general and public worker unions in particular. Over a four-year period a number of states, including but not limited to Indiana, Michigan, and Wisconsin, passed legislation that severely weakened public worker unions. This legislation included attacks on the agency shop clause in union contracts, eliminating automatic dues check off and the agency fee paid to unions representing workers at specific job sites, whether the workers chose to become union members or not. These measures required unions to engage in a continual process of membership renewal and dues collection. In turn, unions were forced to refocus attention from expanding membership to a struggle to maintain the shrinking union base. This antiunion legislation also deflected union leadership's attention from responding to cascading cuts in public budgets and substantial reductions in public workers' salaries and benefits. In turn, such legislative initiatives further hobbled public workers in their efforts to develop a collective counterforce to policies of public austerity as the economic crisis of 2008 further diminished public investment. It is important to note that although the economic crisis was real, the response of imposing state austerity policies was manufactured.

Proposition 2: The crisis of capital was used to promote intensified rationing and growing inequality in the distribution of public or state resources.

Over the past thirty years, the income tax structure of the federal government has become increasingly regressive. The ever-greater tax burden placed on the working and middle classes has been counterbalanced by reduced obligations for the wealthy and super wealthy. The taxing trends of the federal government have been replicated by a number of state governments, most notably New York and California. This shift has been accompanied by rising federal debt and in turn has increased calls for "balancing the budget" through cost cutting, especially of social support programs. Less frequently mentioned by policy makers in this era of public austerity is the possibility of increasing tax rates on the very wealthy and on corporate profits.

Cost-cutting measures as the natural and singular response to broad economic crisis and increasing public debt are essentially manufactured. The alternative of implementing a more progressive tax code is dismissed by dominant and other interests as counterproductive because, they assert, it would drive the migration of wealth and the wealthy from specific high-tax regions, and possibly out of the nation entirely. This assertion persists despite hard evidence to the contrary. The most salient outcome of this policy choice is that at precisely the moment that demand for public jobs, social services, health care, and education has grown, the state has a diminished capacity to meet either present or historic levels of increased need. The gap between demand for and supply of government services has in turn increased the rationing of public goods. This has produced longer waiting periods for health care and other social services and reduced access to the overcrowded public community colleges that are the essential first step for so many Americans in their pursuit of higher education.

From California to New York, state governments have been reducing their investments in public higher education. The shrinking public budget in New York State, for example, resulted in the CUNY system absorbing more than a 17 percent budget cut in real-dollar-per-student direct state investment between 2008 and 2015. Tuition for CUNY was legislated to increase significantly between 2010 and 2015 in part to counter this state disinvestment (Goldstein 2011). In California, between the 2009 and 2012 fiscal years, state support for two of its three major public higher education systems (UC and CSU) was cut by 8 percent while tuition and fees rose 33 percent (Brown 2013). These dramatic reductions in base aid levels have forced public institutions to search for other sources of revenue. These public institutions have had to fill yawning budget gaps with private dollars including, but not limited to, increased tuition charges and private donations from the wealthy.

The ever greater reliance on new sources of private revenue for public goods has had an especially deleterious effect on those least able to pay. This has been especially pronounced in public higher education. Almost 60 percent of CUNY students' annual family income is under thirty thousand dollars, and yet between 2011 and 2016, those families were required to absorb tuition increases of 38 percent at the four-year colleges and 45 percent at the community colleges without commensurate increases above the TAP (Tuition Assistance Program) reimbursement limit of approximately five thousand dollars a year. Increased tuition disproportionately levied against middle-class, working-class, and poor students is a national problem. The unequal impact of austerity policies is not limited to the pursuit of private tuition dollars to pay for public goods. Student access to public education is also increasingly segmented by socioeconomic and demographic factors. As higher education is starved, decisions are made about where to allocate increasingly scarce public resources. As a result, systems of public higher education are reorganizing themselves to sell both elite and "mass-consumption" learning, often to very different audiences.

The intensifying segmentation of higher education at CUNY, SUNY, the California systems, and other public universities is expressed through a continuum of options beginning with community colleges at the base, extending to comprehensive (undergraduate) colleges, and ending with elite undergraduate and graduate schools at the pinnacle. As more and more families search for bargains in an ever more unstable job market and stagnant economy, families, including many middle-class ones, are increasingly selecting elite public universities over private colleges. The choice of commuter schools for college-bound students also reflects a desire to further reduce college expenses in the face of the rising price of college room and board. This migration back to elite public colleges has intensified competition for scarce seats. The consequence is that as competition increases, the metrics or test scores required for admission to public universities such as CUNY, SUNY, and UC are rising. This dynamic threatens to radically recompose the student population at public colleges, making it increasingly white, Asian, and middle class at the expense of blacks, Latinos, and the working class and poor (Treschan and Mehrotra 2012; McDermott 2013; Carnevale and Strohl 2013, 7–14).

Urban students of color graduating from underfinanced K–12 public systems have historically performed less well on standardized forms of assessment of high school performance that remain key to securing entry into higher education institutions. Relatively affluent students increasingly attracted to public higher education are more likely to have higher scores on standardized tests such as the SAT and ACT. If such standardized testing remains the singular tool for assessing prospective student worth, the outcomes over time are reasonably clear. Inequalities reshaping the larger culture will be etched ever more deeply into the experience of public higher education. The poorest students of color will be redistributed out of elite public institutions into other sectors of the higher education system. Such rationing will also negatively affect poor students of color by charging them more tuition to attend the most under-financed, overcrowded, and challenged learning environments within the public higher education system (Mettler 2014, 19–50; Carnevale and Strohl 2013, 7–14). Rationing of higher education mirrors the growing inequalities in the social order as a whole, with income and wealth disparities in the United States as well as in the southern tier of Europe greater now than at any time since the Great Depression. And that poverty, as well as inequality, is consequently growing.

It is important to underscore the relationship between this reallocation and rationing of public resources and the growing, uncontested power of concentrated wealth. The political process is increasingly influenced, directly and indirectly (via foundations, philanthropy, and megacontributions to political campaigns), by the interests of concentrated wealth. The nexus between the economic and political elite and its impact on policy making is ever more transparent and naked in its self-interest. We will return to this important point later in the book.

Proposition 3: Intensified socioeconomic rationing has had a profound impact on the content and structure of public goods and the social reproduction of the labor force.

The development of public goods and services is increasingly embedded in market principles of choice, competition, efficiency, productivity, and measurable forms of accountability. Across the varied social reproduction roles of the welfare state, from the emergence of charter schools in the K–12 sector of public education, to HMOs in health care, and for-profit colleges in higher education, the trend is clear. In a world of dwindling public funding, the creation of more privatized competitors to public institutions is played out as a zero-sum game in the allocation of scarce public dollars (Fabricant and Fine 2013, 35–54). What the private competitors gain, the traditional public institutions lose. As an ever-greater share of public dollars is reallocated to charter schools, for example, the share of public dollars available to traditional K–12 public education shrinks. The dictum of doing more with less, in an increasingly more austere fiscal environment, is driven in part by this reallocation. What is unknown is whether this trend is intended as an adjunct to traditional public institutions or a wholesale replacement of them. If the recent rapid expansion of market alternatives is a signal of intention, we may be witnessing a widespread overhaul of the purposes and content of state social services (Morozov 2013, 7–9).

The privatization of public services, like the growth of charter schools, is dependent in part on the support of poor people of color, many of whom have lost faith in the public sector and its ability to provide necessary social and educational supports (Fabricant and Fine 2013, 62–64). The desperation in many poor communities about failed public schools, poor health care, and intensifying competition between different ethnic and racial subgroups has recently produced partial support for market and quasi-market alternatives such as charter schools to replace traditional public services. This tenuous support emerges out of a sense of scarcity of viable alternatives, the erosion and failure of public programming, and increasing desperation to try any alternative in an effort to overcome increasingly dire circumstances. A willingness to experiment with "new market policy fixes" is often focused on one's own children, not necessarily the children of others (Fabricant 2010; Warren and Mapp 2011). As the competition for scarce dollars intensifies, embrace of market-based solutions invariably is driven by self-interest. This approach peels off potential leaders of collective community responses to public problems and results in an increased focus on the maximization of individual and family benefit. This dynamic represents yet another adulteration of the promise of a public good (Fabricant and Fine 2013, 27–30). Equally important, these dynamics tend to intensify competition between oppressed subgroups that have experienced historical tensions (including Latinos, Africans, Caribbean Americans, and African Americans), further decollectivizing efforts to fight for greater investment in and improvement of public institutions.

The hot-wired circuitry legitimating austerity and privatization is accompanied by a new "science" or "metrics" of accountability for public institutions. For example, K–12 schooling increasingly emphasizes standardized testing measurements to assess student academic improvement and teacher effectiveness. Public higher education is being rated more and more on the basis of both time to degree and the stabilization of tuition costs. The Obama administration recently announced a plan to introduce a grading system (e.g., "A," "B," and "C") for higher education based on those metrics (Lewin 2013). Similarly, health-care workers' success is measured by the volume of patients or clients seen in a day and compliance with ever-changing requirements of eligibility or access to scarce services. The measurement of outcomes is viewed by some as an analog to profit making in the private sector. However, profit making and its quantitative analogs of accountability produce distortions in outcome and process when applied to state services (Field 2014; Blumenstyk 2014). It is hard to imagine how a college or university receiving a letter grade on the relative speed of its students achieving AA or BA degrees is going to improve the quality or availability of higher education (Stripling 2013). Moreover, technology and the streamlining of services are being "sold" through the federal government's new rating system as motors that will drive more effective and efficient forms of higher education delivery, in turn stabilizing tuition costs and reducing student debt. In fact, this frame obscures the real drivers of "reform": the push to rapidly reduce state expenditures in public higher education and the accelerating introduction of market-based initiatives monetizing course delivery and content (Folbre 2010, 99–122; McGettigan 2013, 17–24, 96–112).

As assessment measures increasingly shape the delivery of public goods, they reframe their meaning and content. If test scores are seen as the single measure of academic success and teacher effectiveness, K–12 classroom instruction will, by definition, change. More and more time will be devoted to reshaping classroom pedagogy and developing tools that raise test scores (Fain 2013). At the same time, any part of the curriculum that does not contribute directly to improved test scores will be reassessed and likely deemphasized—that is, if it is not deleted entirely from the course of study including, but hardly limited to, critical thinking, interpretive reading and writing, art and culture, and even physical education.

In this way, the very center of the social reproduction process shifts from the relationship between the student and teacher to a narrower link to a specific testing regime (Morozov 2013, 9–13). As the complexity and dynamism of the social reproduction process are rendered flatter and simpler, so too are the skills, knowledge, and potential of students and their teachers. As a result, the graduating student may be a better test taker but a poorer writer and a diminished critical or imaginative thinker. It is important not to romanticize the historical contributions of K–12 education to critical thinking or writing. In general, public education has not been structured to develop writers, critical thinkers, thoughtful artists, and cultural critics with robust expertise, especially in the poorest communities of color. Yet, whatever the flaws of traditional forms of public education in the past, the present testing culture within public schools further degrades the relationship between the student and the teacher, compromising the student's ability to engage in complex learning and to develop a critical understanding of the larger world.

Diminished public investment is changing higher education. Part-time and full-time faculty, for example, have less and less time to respond to the learning needs of the growing number of students enrolled in their classes (US Senate 2012; *New York Times* Editorial Board 2014). Standardized multiple-choice tests are increasingly relied upon in place of more rigorous writing assignments. These assessment tools take less time to grade than essays, for example, especially when linked to computerized grading tools. Trade-offs of increased course loads and larger classes are also embedded in such austerity policies. These trade-offs raise a number of troubling questions. As the assessment obsession focuses on tiny bits of information and not on a more holistic, interpretive, and clearly articulated analysis, what is lost in college students' learning? For example, does classroom pedagogy increasingly emphasize static forms of lecturing and learning while deemphasizing vigorous interactions around ideas between students and teachers, and among the students themselves? Equally important, how has the exchange between instructors and students outside the classroom changed? The answers to these questions will significantly influence the ways in which students are changed or socially reproduced through their experiences within public higher education (Morozov 2013, 7–9).

Public disinvestment and the diminished quality of public higher education differ by class and race. It is more likely that poor students of color will be channeled into nonelite public colleges, usually comprehensive and community colleges. In general, these colleges have less public support, fewer full-time instructors, larger classes, and a greater emphasis on standardized testing as a basis for evaluating student work than elite public or especially private senior colleges and universities. In precisely this way, the higher education experience mirrors K–12 education for the vast majority of students of color. The consequence is that the poorest students are twice betrayed, first in their often inadequate academic K–12 preparation, and subsequently in higher education as they have diminished access to the resources, learning environments, and skills development needed to advance their academic and intellectual capacities.

Affluent students, on the other hand, are much more likely to be exposed to the complex learning demands of critical thinking and writing precisely because they achieve higher test scores and thus do not require the regimen of test-based curricula to reach appropriate assessment targets. The already-advantaged are therefore further advantaged by enriched learning environments typically not available to poor students. This segmentation of social reproduction by class and race has powerful implications for the slotting of graduates into a stratified labor market. Which students are most likely to be selected for the relatively complex, interpretive work of financial decision making, legal argumentation, medical diagnosis, or entrepreneurial start-up projects—the ones immersed in rote learning for sixteen years, often failing to achieve rudimentary writing and reading skills, or the male and female college graduates exposed to critical thinking, uses of analytical or conceptual imagination, and writing skills? Such differing opportunities and outcomes affect income and employment options over an individual's lifetime. We will return to this nexus of social reproduction, class, race, and the changing labor market later in our analysis.

This part of the discussion would be incomplete if we failed to mention that the social reproduction processes associated with "doing more with less" are touted as socially just by new reformers, for example, advocates for charter schools. The argument is rather straightforward: increased competition and choice will produce more effective practices for those who need them the most, namely, poor children of color (Simon and Banchero 2010; Klein 2014). This imperative is seen by market advocates as linked to the need to roll back if not eliminate job protections such as tenure and unionization for teachers. The intention is to "liberate" public schools from the teachers' "self-interest," which is seen as conflicting with the fundamental learning needs of students. This dichotomy between student and teacher/union interest is fundamental to dominant policy discourse that blames teachers for the present crisis of public education. Never discussed is that the policy push for privatization and diminished job protections, joined to measureable, uniform services, is embedded in a simultaneous reduction of short-term and long-term investments in education and public goods more generally. This disinvestment may, in fact, produce more high school and college graduates. Such reforms may also produce modestly higher test scores and the increased productivity of seeing or serving more people in less time. Those outcomes, however, must be counterposed to the following questions: Are the needs of graduates and communities being better met in the aftermath of these market reforms? Are poor students more likely to meet basic literacy or numeracy standards? Are poor people with health problems more likely to have their basic medical needs met?

Proposition 4: The reassembly of the welfare state and its social reproduction processes are tightly aligned with the effort to legitimate the capitalization of public assets during a moment of economic crisis.

During moments of economic crisis in a market economy, new forms of technology are developed and disseminated by business leaders and policy makers to reduce labor costs and increase profits. This dynamic of replacing labor by deploying new technologies to reduce costs is driven by the effort to restore or increase historic rates or margins of productivity and profit. Continuing declines in profit margins threaten the very existence of capitalist or market economies and spur investment in technology.

The economic crises of the past fifty years have unleashed many new forms of labor-saving, productivity-enhancing technologies. None of them, however, has proved as important as computers and virtual forms of communication. The introduction of these technologies into various sectors of the marketplace has stimulated increases in labor productivity and displacement of substantial numbers of workers, for example, secretaries, printers, print journalists, dock workers, and assembly line workers (Braverman 1975, 327–47; Lanier 2013, 35). The circuitry of this technological innovation, which has cycled through various economic sectors, is now being routed through the public sector to yield greater efficiency and productivity (Morozov 2013, 9–13, 35). Other market principles applied to public services include increased choice and competition, as well as administrative and organizational innovations.

It is on these bases that technologies of online learning and innovative programming such as charter schooling are offered as alternatives to traditional public schools and public universities. These reforms are also legitimated as producing cost savings and thus are aligned with the sharp decline in public funding for traditional public schooling. The crisis of funding is linked directly to the need to create an ever-leaner, more efficient service sector that will be realized through the introduction of new technologies, programming, and market principles. Politicians and policy makers offer no alternative to this austerity reform agenda.

Neoliberal advocates see the privatization of all things public as part of a naturalized landscape without alternatives. They present privatization as the only fiscally viable and effective way to reassemble public services. This legitimating discourse from businesses, foundations, the state, and the media to downsize and privatize public agencies offers a powerful argument for restructuring public services in ways that mimic the marketplace and over time reallocate public resources to profit-making enterprises.

The "redistribution of public resources or assets" to private entrepreneurs is also legitimated as part of a necessary second stage of aligning public services with market principles. The reallocation of public dollars to private firms is seen as necessary to produce a greater yield or return through increased competition, choice, and innovation. Profit-making services are legitimated on the basis of promoting a more equitable distribution of services. It is anticipated that the efficiencies of the market will yield an improved "product" to be delivered to a greater number of people. Profit-making charter schools and testing infrastructures are seen, for example, as providing poor students of color with greater academic rigor and preparation that are traditionally not available through public education systems (Klein 2007, 3–26, 29–49; Toch 2009).

In the brave new world of for-profit higher education, colleges are described as reaching students who otherwise would not be able to achieve an associate's or bachelor's degree. The reach of higher education is further extended by global online learning through the promotion and development of MOOCs and other online forms of instruction, which are seen as benefiting very poor students here and abroad who might otherwise not have access to university courses.

Ironically, the monetization or capitalization of public goods is heralded as the social justice movement of the twenty-first century. The joining of the market with social justice aspirations is, perhaps, the most powerful legitimating discourse in the drive to privatize and monetize all things public and provides privatizers with a race and class fig leaf to cover their profit-making aspirations.

Empirical support for privatization is largely linked to illustrations of exemplary programming. From charter schools to test-driven curricula

and online learning, exemplars are offered as proof that market principles, incentives, and structures are viable solutions for the crisis of public
services and, more specifically, education. The refiguring of the exemplar
as the norm allows advocates to more easily make the argument that
excellence in both service provision and positive social outcomes can only
be achieved through privatization. This line of argument helps to conceal
the sharp redirection of public resources to private gain, the radical restructuring of the social reproduction of families, the unequal distribution of scarce public resources, increasingly regressive tax structures, and
ever more abundant examples of failed experiments in privatization.

The legitimating discourse of faith in market principles and magnifi-
cation by the media of the exemplar as the norm effectively represents a
closed loop of argument about reform, effectively a tautology that privatization is the only reform path worth pursuing. Conversely, public goods
and services are systematically denigrated as having failed. This discur-
sive shaming of the public sphere is generalized over time so as to make
the argument that the welfare state, even in its partial form, is a failed
experiment. This popular discourse further reinforces general public
understanding regarding both the inevitable failure of public services, particularly in the poorest communities, as meager public resources decline
and the circular logic that privatization is the only way forward.

As public resources are redirected to the marketplace, state agencies
shrink in the face of declining budgets. Equally important, the quality of
services is stratified by class and race. In the poorest communities, services are being radically restructured to emphasize less direct contact by
ordinary citizens with providers, uniformity of and more limited encounters with professionals, the dilution of services, and reduced access. It is
within this context that the expansive disposability of large segments of
the population needs to be examined.

*Proposition 5: The starvation of public agencies and reallocation of public
resources to privatized experiments results in dramatic disinvestment in
poor and working-class citizens of color and their communities, effectively
defining these populations as disposable.*

As the phenomenon of public-sector reform is complex, so too is the
impact of social disposability on the general citizenry. These experiences
of disposability occur across multiple dimensions. As public institutions
are starved and privatized, the social reproduction experience of very

poor citizens is altered. This restructuring most concretely results in cheapened services, ranging from more constricted encounters with service providers in health care to a testing regimen in public schools devoid of the skill development and critical thinking essential to securing well-paying jobs and an informed citizenry. Cheapened service is also a hallmark of public higher education's increasingly overcrowded and technologized classrooms that pockmark university learning experiences (Marcus 2009; Moltz 2009; Kolowich 2013).

Social reproduction in straitened public institutions is especially pronounced in the very poorest communities of color. These trends result in diminished confidence that health care and public K–12 and higher education institutions can meet even the most basic intellectual, job market, or medical needs of the poor communities they serve. More to the point, the circuitry of disposability wired into social reproduction in starved public institutions leaves very poor communities increasingly marginalized and neglected.

The dilution of social reproduction supports in state welfare agencies is braided with a range of specific policies promoting social disinvestment and disposability. For example, in public higher education, as the proportion of public to private investment shrinks, there is greater reliance on increased tuition charges from those least able to pay (Quinterno 2012, 12; Eaton et al. 2014, 1–3; Desrochers and Kirshstein 2012, 1–4). In K–12, the loss of experienced teachers in schools where students have complex and challenging learning needs represents a profound mismatch of need and resource allocation. Finally, from health-care systems historically unable to meet basic medical needs (although the recent implementation of the Affordable Care Act has already addressed some part of this neglect by assuring greater access for millions of previously uninsured citizens), to courts that have waiting periods for trials of up to five years, poor communities experience a dramatic disjuncture between needed investment and intensifying austerity policies. This gulf is also expressed in the lack of a public jobs program for the chronically unemployed that might focus on rebuilding the nation's increasingly tattered and decaying infrastructure. This systematic neglect and the disinvestment in the public sector create an ever more pervasive sense that both poor individuals and their communities are disposable. This linking of social disinvestment and disposability has been underway for over fifty years. It has accelerated over the past decade as policies of austerity have intensified.

Experiences of disposability are also linked to the growing income and wealth gaps reshaping the larger social order. As the real dollar value of incomes in working-class and poor communities declines and the wealth as well as the incomes of those in the top tier of the economy grow disproportionately, estrangement at the bottom is likely to intensify, as we have already begun to witness (Wilkinson and Pickett 2009, 49–62; Hacker and Pierson 2011, 1; Piketty 2014, 21–35). This gap marks a growing segment of the population as having diminished value. These trends also relegate an increasing proportion of the population to the very margins of the economy. The combination of a growing wealth gap and the economic marginalization of a growing proportion of the population is dangerously dry social tinder. It contributes to escalating resentment as it shreds basic forms of economic enfranchisement. Whether such resentment can be collectivized into a progressive political response is unknown, though we can see inklings of a populist response in the Occupy, Black Lives Matter, and the climate change movements and the 2013 landslide victory of Bill de Blasio as mayor of New York City after campaigning on a well-articulated "tax-the-rich" platform. It is clear that rapidly diminishing wages for the largest segment of the population in a moment when a very small minority is leveraging extraordinary growth in its personal wealth contributes to economic marginalization and disposability and a concomitant desire for economic and political change.

Proposition 6: As wealth and income gaps grow and uneasiness about potential social and political turmoil spreads there is an increased public and private investment in surveillance, control, and outright repression.

It is on this basis that "stop-and-frisk" tactics by the police against people of color are instituted; ever more sophisticated technologies of detection and apprehension are implemented in schools; the incidence of incarceration grows, especially in very poor communities of color; and police violence against young men of color escalates. For the wealthy, largely white, upper-middle classes, there is a simultaneous retreat to cocooned housing fortresses with walls of geographic separation, enhanced policing, and the latest technologies of personal and property security. As the economics of the class divide grows, so too does the social divide of separation, distrust, and flight. Flight may be the most powerful metaphor for the present reassembly of the public sphere and the larger social order. This flight most palpably expresses itself in a retreat from collective social responsibility. It is expressed through a diminishment of social investment coupled with a continuing attack on as well as weakening of a redistributive state apparatus. This ecology of flight and denial is incubated by a series of interlinked developments:

- a hot-house political system that favors the interests of the very wealthy while enacting austerity measures to reduce public programs (Hacker and Pierson 2012);
- a regime of increasingly regressive taxation and tax cutting insisted upon by concentrated wealth (Stiglitz 2013, 47);
- an arid landscape of diminished economic and social opportunities for an increasing proportion of the population, understood as a necessary price for sustaining and even increasing present levels of wealth accumulation; and
- growing resentment, fear, and policies of control, as well as increased electronic and other forms of citizen surveillance.

The messages of disposability of poor people of color are particularly vivid when heightened control measures of detection, surveillance, and incarceration result in an expansive encroachment on personal dignity and individual freedom (Alexander 2010, 5–15). Disposability reached its nadir in the escalating number of deaths over the past several years of young men of color at the hands of local police forces across the country. Especially important to this discussion is that control policies have demanded a greater share of tax dollars as fear and social neglect become a more dominant emphasis in political discourse and drain on the public purse.

Economic Crisis and the Capitalization of Public Goods

The crisis of the global economy reached an apex during the 2008 meltdown of financial markets internationally. The years since have provided ample proof that not only is the crisis still very much alive, but it is in fact deepening and extending despite frequent public pronouncements by politicians and business leaders that it is over. Historically low interest rates in the United States have helped to finance cascading public debt, but the slowing rate of growth of China's superheated industrial economy now threatens global economic stability. Europe's spreading virus of economic slowdown in Spain, Cyprus, Portugal, and, most especially, Greece has destabilized the Euro and threatens other parts of the continent's economic and social structures. These signs are powerful reminders that the international economy remains especially fragile and interconnected.

David Harvey's (2003) prescient analysis forecasted this deepening crisis. He argued a dozen years ago that the increasing concentration of profit making in the financial sector indicated that manufacturing and service sectors of the economy would be unable to produce historic rates of profit and that capital migrates from other parts of the economy to the finance industry and circulates at ever greater speed in its search to recapture historic rates of profit, both domestically and internationally. The continuing growth of profit margins over time is a predicate for sustaining not only the market, but also the very structure of international capitalism.

The financial sector's increased role in sustaining and increasing profit margins for the entire social order produces greater rewards and pressures on hedge-fund managers and other financial risk takers and decision makers at the center of the restless movement of trillions of dollars of capital. The pressure to rapidly produce profit and the growing difficulty in locating such investment opportunities helps create a dynamic of ever riskier investments to promote the desired large returns. More to the point, risk triggers the sort of increased speculation and profit bubbles that were evidenced in the subprime mortgage crisis in 2007, which was preceded by the technology bubble of the late 1990s, which was itself preceded by the savings and loan crisis of the late 1980s and early 1990s. These are not aberrant events, but rather cyclical crises gestated by the larger instability of capital. Rather than exceptions, bubbles may define the new normal of contemporary finance-engorged capital.

It is within the context of this profit-making crisis and the continuing search for new sites of investment and return that the private sector has cast its steely gaze upon public-sector resources. The public sector in the United States expends trillions of dollars annually. Equally important, it is a relatively secure site of investment because of both the steady flow of tax dollars into public coffers and the continuing, albeit reduced commitment of the social order to invest in a range of public services. At least one of the short-term fixes for increasingly insecure and declining rates of profit is the appropriation of public assets and services by private entrepreneurs. In New York City alone, the annual budget for the public school system, admittedly the largest in the United States, now totals more than $25 billion (New York City Department of Education 2014). One need not go much beyond Willie Sutton's famous response to the question of why he robbed banks—"Because that's where the money is!"—to understand why private entrepreneurs and hedge-fund managers want to underwrite their charter school and public higher education experiments with public money.

The ideology and economics of austerity, although an independent force, are influenced by the intensifying privatization and monetization of public services. Although austerity dampens the growth of public dollars and is interlocked with regressive taxation policies, it also provides a political platform for "doing more with less." As noted earlier, the ideology of doing more with less is a tight fit with a business fundamentalism that preaches efficiency, productivity, and technological innovation. Business ideology and practices promise to reduce costs by producing savings. These savings accumulate as labor is replaced by technology, increasingly uniform practices are instituted to reduce the cost of producing services, and quality is rationed on the basis of capacity to pay or other individualized metrics. It is within this context that the private sector suggests it can create programming that will live and thrive within a framework of austerity by doing more with less. What is never measured or assessed is the degree to which services and the social reproduction function are profoundly changed by this new calculus.

This shift raises a number of compelling questions that to date remain unaddressed. Does a shift toward the private offer a basis for hope in responding to emerging public problems such as global warming, or a political system increasingly dominated by money in both its electoral and policy making processes? Can that privatized system offer the same promise of quality to the poor or working classes that it does to the wealthy who have priority access to more privatized or publicly enriched forms of service? These questions are not simply rhetorical. They are at the heart of what it means to provide a collective public good.

Universal access to quality public services that improve the life circumstances of the poor and working classes has been a core hope and aspiration of the public good from the Progressive Era, through the New Deal and the civil rights era, to the latter part of the twentieth century. That aspiration and, in turn, the meaning of the public good in its production and consumption functions, is being transformed. So too is the unfulfilled promise of the link between the state and notions of redistributive justice.

This struggle for redistribution was especially vivid in moments when social movements advanced an agenda of progressive taxation and welfare-state programs that included health care, education, old-age pensions, and social services to meet the basic needs and hopes of working-class and poor citizens. The struggles to create these public agencies and public services were part of a larger fight for enfranchisement and emancipation through political mobilization, economic redistribution, and the development of necessary social supports. The new "reform" agenda that monetizes, privatizes, and shrinks public services threatens nothing less than the hope for continued enfranchisement of the broad mass of the citizenry within a democratic society.

The Radical Restructuring of Public Higher Education

In the conjunction between economic crisis and the welfare state's reassembly, public higher education is also being transformed. Higher education is the public good most susceptible to globalizing trends. New online technologies create a basis for faculty and university programs to reach a growing mass audience nationally and internationally. Online students represent a new potential revenue stream in an unstable economic moment. The incentives for administrators to monetize this opportunity are substantial.

The private entrepreneurs who created and populate Google and Goldman Sachs as well as Coursera and Udacity are investing in the technology and instruments of higher education profit making. At the present time, the real basis for extracting profits from online learning technologies, for example, remains decidedly unclear. Capital has been unable to fully solve this part of the puzzle. Yet, the necessary technology exists, potential consumers have been identified, private entrepreneurs are positioned to capitalize on the opportunity, and academic "products" are being developed to mass-market distance-learning solutions to higher education "problems." This offers an unparalleled opportunity to turn public and nonprofit higher education alike into sites of increased profit making in which public universities are forced to do more with less. Equally important, it is a moment in which the very meaning of public higher education may be fundamentally rewritten (Welen 2013).

The enormity of the convergence of political and economic factors poised to transform higher education was underscored at the 2013 World

Economic Forum in Davos, Switzerland. International leaders gathered to strategize about the progress and future of the world's economy. *Time* magazine noted that the three most important "takeaways" from the meetings were that currency wars will rage, the Syrian conflict must end, and online higher education is gaining traction in the marketplace (Foroohar 2013a).

Time's third takeaway is a powerful reminder of the increasing importance of higher education to the global economy, the centrality of short-term restoration of profit making, and private entrepreneurs' and financiers' relentless search for new investment sites. The *Time* report went on to note that "websites like Coursera and Udacity may one day transform education worldwide, but questions remain over what business models will ultimately emerge to finance these courses" (Foroohar 2013a). Although the Davos event is part of "the factory in which conventional wisdom is manufactured," it underscored the continuing and deepening global crisis contributing to the monetization of higher education. Axel Weber, UBS chairman, noted that "[as] central bankers we can buy time but we can't fix the world's underlying economic problems.... We're buying short term fixes at the expense of future generations" (Foroohar 2013b). Apparently, one such short-term fix is the monetization and capitalization of higher education.

Another important piece of the architecture of capitalizing higher education is the marketing of colleges and universities as products. In the brave new world of online education, rankings are important to maximizing revenue streams. As the *New York Times* recently reported, "[t]he appeal of an arbiter of educational quality, however subjective, has spread across the globe as students [and universities] become ever more mobile ... [and] look even farther beyond their borders" (Guttenplan 2013). The conjunction between reputation and choice is influencing the migration destinations of students to virtual and nonvirtual sites of higher education.

Higher education is a relatively healthy sector of the American economy. More to the point, in a comparison of international higher education systems, "while American dominance has slipped slightly, from 45 schools in the top 100 two years ago to 43 this year, no other country comes anywhere close. Second-place Britain fills just 9 of the top 100 places; Australia, in third place, has only 6" (Guttenplan 2013). If some part of what is needed to restore global economic stability is a restoration of American competitiveness and profit making, higher education is a site with enormous immediate promise. The combination of fiscal crisis, the financial sector's search for profit-making sites, globalization, emergent forms of technology, and restoration of American competitiveness are cohering and pointing to higher education as a locus for massive reassembly and monetization.

To fully understand the present trend in public higher education, the contradictory set of policies and developments embedded in the recent history of investment in and expansion of US public universities must be examined. Past public policies, beginning during World War II and extending over the next three decades, targeted strategic investment and consequent social reproduction practices of enlarged access, public subsidization of tuition, low-interest loans redeemed for public service, growth of full-time faculty, and the emergence of knowledge and course offerings that developed broader analytical lenses emphasizing race, class, gender, and sexuality as a basis for restructuring both democratic inquiry and public higher education itself. To imagine a future for higher education that disrupts present trends, we must first reconstruct a past that offers at least a partial compass to chart a new direction. It is to that task that we turn in the next two chapters.

[2]

The State Expansion of Public Higher Education

Beginning during World War II, the federal government and various state governments conceived and financed the dramatic expansion of the nation's public higher education system. Many federal and state policy makers, driven largely by economic and political concerns, determined that higher education opportunities needed to be more broadly available to America's citizens. As early as 1943 (well before Allied forces had decisively won World War II), state legislators across the country, prodded by ambitious governors, began developing long-range plans and committed significant levels of funding to create and expand statewide public higher education systems. Many states focused increased funding in the postwar years on community colleges, perhaps the most important expansion of higher education in the twentieth century. The growth of community colleges at the state and municipal levels was often accompanied by ambitious thinking about how to build a structure of public higher education, from community colleges that granted associate's degrees through professional schools and research-intensive doctoral programs. The 1960s witnessed the most dramatic growth in higher education in US history, with expenditures more than tripling to $27 billion, college enrollments more than doubling to 8.6 million students (two of five of whom were women), and instructional staff also doubling to almost 600,000 (Halstead 1974, 1; National Center for Education Statistics 1993, 65).

The ideology that helped explain and justify this dramatic expansion included an uneasy mix of politically pragmatic (sometimes opportunistic) and visionary beliefs. A dominant ideological orientation was utilitarian, articulating the need to prepare a new and rapidly growing generation for the technical and service jobs essential to the transformation and expansion of American capitalism in the postwar era. Second was the need to "do right" by the millions of servicemen (and a far smaller number of women) by giving them access to publicly funded education and training. A third ideological justification for public university expansion focused on enduring democratic ideals and values that had come to the fore in the war against Nazism and fascism that had defeated the forces of racialism and anti-Semitism. All three justifications—offered by national and state-level political and business leaders, university officials, trade union leaders, and pundits—also underscored the need to create an informed democratic citizenry. Well-educated citizens, many of whom would now be veterans, were expected to enhance American society while also bolstering US global dominance in the postwar era. These largely complementary yet sometimes conflicting ideologies about the meaning of higher education in postwar America would soon be challenged by the dramatic upheavals that roiled college campuses throughout the "long" decade stretching from the early 1960s through the mid-1970s. In those years, students and faculty members across the country questioned traditional verities about whom colleges and universities were intended to serve and the broader purposes of higher education in a democracy.

This chapter explores the dramatic expansion of American higher education in the decade and a half following the end of World War II. It analyzes the sometimes conflicting political, economic, and ideological rationales that justified that expansion, as well as the social forces that spurred on and challenged these emergent policies. The dynamic, often contentious relationship between these social forces would fundamentally reshape public higher education in the United States in the final quarter of the twentieth century.

The GI Bill

Prior to the 1930s and 1940s, the federal government's role in the nation's colleges and universities consisted of providing grants of income-generating federal land to old and new states in the Union to help underwrite the establishment and maintenance of public colleges. The rationale for public financing via land grants tended to emphasize the practical aspects of public education. For example, the 1862 Morrill Land-Grant

Act's stated purpose, according to Maine's senator Justin Morrill, was to provide "colleges for the benefit of agriculture and the Mechanic arts." The University of California, Cornell, the University of Nebraska, the University of Wisconsin, and many other major university systems and smaller colleges—north and south, east and west—exist today because of seed funding of "land scrip" provided by Morrill Land-Grant Acts.[1] With the exception of the provision of land grants, the federal government's role in higher education throughout the nineteenth and early twentieth centuries remained passive.

The Great Depression changed the federal government's involvement in higher education, especially its relationship with public universities. New Deal policies increasingly looked to higher education, and especially the colleges and universities supported by land grants, to extend the government's fight against unemployment and to create the college work-study program, as well as an array of new social services, public works projects, and agricultural reforms through the federal Cooperative Extension Service (Loss 2012, 12–13, 53–87).

As early as 1933, for example, the federal government financially supported the establishment of emergency collegiate centers (ECCs), prototypical junior colleges providing two years of college for unemployed adults and young people while also giving jobs to unemployed college teachers and other white-collar workers. The state-level ECCs, in the words of their New York State director, served "to whet the appetite of parents and students for *free* college instruction near home" (Carmichael 1955, 32–33; Abbott 1958, 144–145, italics in original). With federal financial support New York State by 1938 established a total of twenty-two ECCs sited at private colleges as well as at the City College of New York (Gilbert 1950, 35–43). Their rapid expansion demonstrated the unmet need in New York State before World War II for tuition-free, public higher education.

The federal role in public higher education dramatically escalated during World War II. This was true even before the passage of the Servicemen's Readjustment Act (the famous "GI Bill of Rights") in June 1944. The Roosevelt administration agreed by 1940 with university leaders that colleges should play a key role in helping to train scientific and technical personnel essential to the war effort. US entry into World War II prompted a dramatic expansion of federal funding for university-based research programs and projects deemed essential to the war effort. By

December 1942, the federal government also established nonmilitary training programs at a number of colleges and universities (Cardozier 1993, 4–8). These federally funded research and teaching programs helped stave off bankruptcy for many public and private universities, which faced drastic wartime reductions in their student bodies as a result of enlistments and the compulsory draft (Cardozier 1993, 211–12). The Roosevelt administration extended higher educational opportunities to enlisted or soon-to-be-drafted soldiers and sailors, opportunities they believed were "essential for the exercise of citizenship in a democratic society" (Mettler 2005, 16). "We must replenish our supply of persons qualified to discharge the heavy responsibilities of the postwar world," President Roosevelt stated in October 1943. "We have taught our youth how to wage war; we must also teach them how to live useful and happy lives in freedom, justice, and democracy" (Mettler 2005, 17; FDR Library, n.d.).

By 1944, public and private universities across the country were educating several hundred thousand GIs drawn from all branches of the military in specialized courses in engineering, medicine, dentistry, law, mathematics, physics, and foreign languages (Loss 2012, 101; Cardozier 1993, 40, 75). Many soldiers embraced these newly expanded educational opportunities as a means to improve their future employment prospects after the war. But for many other GIs, the army university centers—set up in England, France, Italy, and Hawaii near the war's end—offered the democratic experience of a racially, ethnically, and religiously integrated education (Cardozier 1993, 168; Loss 2012, 108). "Military leaders looked to education as an instrument to create the soldiers the army most wanted to have," historian Christopher Loss concludes, "while soldiers gravitated toward education because it offered a pathway to becoming the citizens they most wanted to be" (Loss 2012, 93).

From this unprecedented expansion of higher educational opportunities for GIs during the war, the US government quickly pivoted in 1944 to education planning for the peacetime era. National and state political and business leaders expressed concerns about the impact of the demobilization of 16 million soldiers and sailors and the need for their rapid and orderly return to civilian life (Aronowitz 2000, 27). The civil and political unrest that had occurred at the end of World War I (a short twenty-five years earlier) was still vivid in many people's minds. That unrest included armed veterans who had participated in urban labor disturbances and race riots across the country in 1919, as well as the violent suppression in 1932 by US Army troops of the "Bonus Army" of World War I vets, who had marched on Washington to demand long-deferred military service bonuses (American Social History Project 2008, 2:320–27, 414–16; Nasaw 1979, 173; Cardozier 1993, 223).

With fear of such militant veterans' protests as a backdrop, the Roosevelt administration decided in 1943 to support a bipartisan congressional coalition's early draft of the GI Bill. The powerful and reactionary American Legion had endorsed the draft bill because it assured that individual states would exercise a measure of control in the allocation of the bill's benefits to their citizens, assuring segregationist policies would prevail in southern states (Katznelson 2005, 123–24; Cardozier 1993, 222). A similarly cautious approach to justifying educational benefits for GIs was evident in the final legislation. The GI Bill featured a heavy emphasis on the obligation of the government to support citizen-soldiers who had exercised their civic duty by serving in the military, rather than a broader social commitment to educating citizens for democratic participation and world citizenship. It was the latter perspective that had shaped the Roosevelt administration's ideas and policies about higher education earlier in World War II (Mettler 2005, 17, 22, 61).[2]

No matter the political motivations of the ungainly coalition that supported the GI Bill, its passage in June 1944 ultimately allowed almost half of the total number of vets who had served in the military (7.8 million in all, seven in ten of whom were discharged between August and the end of December) to pursue training or educational opportunities financed by the federal government. Of this number, more than two million attended higher education institutions in the dozen years immediately after the war. After several modifications and liberalizations, pushed by members of Congress concerned with economic stability and potential social unrest, the GI Bill provided funding to help pay tuition and fees (at both public and private colleges and universities), up to $500 a year, for individual service members who served a minimum of ninety days; veterans also received monthly living stipends.[3] And unlike earlier New Deal programs that emphasized creation of socially progressive institutions, the GI Bill provided federal grants-in-aid to individual veterans to expend in the education and housing marketplaces, public or private, as they saw fit. By 1948, 15 percent of the entire federal budget was being spent on GI Bill benefits. Within the first decade following its passage, the federal government spent $14.5 billion (almost $125 billion in 2013 dollars); of that amount, $10 billion went for subsistence allowances and $4 billion to pay tuition and fees to colleges (Mettler 2005, 6–7, 61, 85; Katznelson 2005, 113).

The GI Bill had a leveling effect politically and educationally, albeit one stratified by race and, to a lesser extent, gender. The bill opened higher education to many demographic groups whose previous access was either severely restricted or entirely blocked. "The social rights offered by the G. I. Bill," Suzanne Mettler argues, "broadened educational opportunity to veterans who were Jewish or Catholic, African American, and immigrants as well as those whose families had struggled in the American working class for generations" (Mettler 2005, 11, 55–57; Frydl, 2009, 308). Ira Katznelson argues that the inclusion of black vets among the GI Bill's beneficiaries is "misleading," however. Despite its color-blind intentions, the GI Bill was unable to overcome entrenched racial barriers and quotas, especially in southern states. Although large numbers of black vets used the GI Bill to pursue higher education across the South, their attendance was largely restricted to historically black (and segregated) colleges, which quickly became overcrowded (Katznelson 2005, 121–22, 129–31; Frydl 2009, 240–47). The surge in the number of male veterans taking advantage of GI education benefits in the early postwar years temporarily drove down the percentage of enrolled female college students nationally (from 36 percent to 30 percent) before the percentage rebounded to 40 percent after 1960 (National Center for Education Statistics 1993, 65).[4]

It should be noted that the United States was unique during the postwar era in making access to a college education *broadly* available to its citizens, and especially its veterans. No other Western nation followed a similar path, though many did make efforts to expand their higher education systems. One reason was that few industrialized nations had previously embraced the idea of widely available, publicly supported education, which by 1945 had been a hallmark of US historical development for more than a century. It is also significant that, with the exception of the British Dominions, the United States was alone among Allied and Axis nations in avoiding the devastation of its physical infrastructure and national economy during World War II.

The Presidential Panel on Higher Education

The passage and implementation of the GI Bill explain much about the expansion of US higher education in the postwar era. To adequately address this dramatic spike in demand, however, the supply side (i.e., where these hordes of new college students were going to sit and study) had to be simultaneously addressed by policy makers. The college classroom supply problem, profound by the war's end, was considered by the twenty-eight-member Presidential Panel on Higher Education, popularly known as the Zook Commission, that President Truman convened in 1946.[5] Truman charged the commission to identify "the best means of providing educational opportunities to all able young people" (Zook 1947, 17). Its work was paralleled over the next few years by state-level and regional commissions and reports ordered by governors and legislators in key states such as California and New York (Rudolph 1962, 483). Such state and national analyses of higher education were expected to determine how best to meet the anticipated growth, thanks to the GI Bill, in the number of new students clamoring for entry into colleges and universities.

The Zook Commission's six compact reports, issued seriatim between December 1947 and February 1948 under the title "Higher Education for American Democracy," had a heavily Progressive cast (in a John-Deweyan sense). The reports argued that college education needed to be extended to all citizens "without regard to economic status, race, religion or color" (Zook 1947, 17). "No one who senses the spirit of America today," George Zook wrote, "can fail to see that we are undergoing a social revolution in the sense that we are attempting to give a greater vitality to the moral commitments that lie at the base of the American way of life" (Zook 1947, 17; Schrum 2007, 277–301). The Zook Commission's grand vision of public higher education joined expanded access with increased economic opportunity, as well as greater citizenship rights and obligations.

The commission was quite clear that those "moral commitments" had crystallized in the successful wartime struggle against Nazi and fascist racialism. Describing long-standing discriminatory practices in the United States such as the quota system as "un-American," the report described such practices as "European in origin and application, and we have lately witnessed on that continent the horrors to which, in its logical extension, it can lead" (Zook et al. 1947, 1:35). Wartime policies and ideological statements had reshaped national discourse about fundamental issues of democracy; racial and religious freedom; equality of opportunity; and eradication of racial, religious, and ethnic discrimination (Denning 1996, 419). This support for the development of an inclusive postwar public higher education system was erected on the foundation of the New Deal's broadly social democratic ethos and the federal government's perceived commitment during the war to defend and extend democratic rights.

The Zook Commission detailed the "specific ingredients" of a robust democracy, which included "the right of all men to equality of opportunity, the equal right of all citizens to vote and hold office, the rights of religious liberty, freedom of speech and all forms of expression, freedom of association, freedom from want and from fear and ignorance" (Zook et al. 1947, 1:11). While this list of rights might seem unexceptional in our own time (except perhaps for the inclusion of FDR's "Four Freedoms," which no doubt would sound like socialist propaganda to today's right-wing conservatives), it is important to remember that seventy years ago, when the Zook Commission argued for these democratic rights, the country was still roiled by especially intense expressions of racism that included a decades-long era of de jure and de facto segregation and Jim Crow across the North and the South. That segregation extended to the military, despite the numerous examples of heroism demonstrated by black troops, sailors, and airmen during the war.[6] The Zook Commission report specifically embraced racial justice in its call for an end to discrimination in the US educational system. The report not only anticipated the US Supreme Court's landmark decision in *Brown v. Board* seven years hence; it also went one step further, suggesting that white and black students *alike* were negatively affected by segregation (Zook et al. 1947, 1:34–35).

The Zook Commission argued that community colleges were foundational to the expanded architecture of higher education:

> To make sure of its own health and strength a democratic society must provide free and equal access to education for its youth, and at the same time it must recognize their differences in capacity and purpose. . . . [To achieve] the expansion of educational opportunity and the diversification of educational offerings it considers necessary, this Commission recommends that the number of community colleges be increased and that their activities be multiplied. (Zook et al. 1947, 1:67)

This ringing support for "free and equal access to education" was built on the historic foundation of tax-supported public education, with the right to public education now extended from K–12 to encompass public colleges and universities.

The Zook Commission report was criticized at the time for offering utopian and impractical designs for higher education reform (Harlow 1953, 17–24). While an element of utopianism ran through the report, the commission also offered a pragmatic blueprint for the next stage of the nation's development. The report joined a utilitarian view of building national and regional systems of public higher education as America entered the postwar era with the goal of offering greater access and consequently creating a more democratic citizenry. The report further challenged and inspired many Americans—state policy makers, business and education leaders, and ordinary citizens alike—to rethink the meaning and purposes of a taxpayer-supported, public higher education system in a modern democracy. Sadly, the commission's public embrace of these egalitarian ideals and the expansive democratic discourse it inspired were ascendant for only a few years. The Zook report's rhetoric was soon overwhelmed by the fear, insularity, and deformation of political discourse sparked by the vicious anti-Communism that swept across so much of the Western world—especially the United States—in the 1950s (American Social History Project 2008, 573–78).

Public Higher Education in California, New York, and Beyond

Similar debates about the purposes and functions of public higher education also occurred at the state level over the three decades following World War II. The remainder of this chapter examines the expansion of state-level higher education systems in these decades, focusing primarily on California and New York, the two states (along with New York City) that would develop the largest and most comprehensive public university systems in the country. We detail the dramatic and very different growth of the public higher education systems in these two states, which were emblematic of state-level public higher education growth across the country in this period.

Building on the work of the Zook Commission, California's and New York's political leaders in the immediate postwar years—led by

Republican governors Earl Warren and Thomas Dewey, respectively—determined that their states needed to expand and rationalize their public higher education systems. Substantial tax funds were dedicated in both states to that task. And despite both governors' national political aspirations, their commitment to public higher education was not simply an outgrowth of narrow calculation. Each governor, and the coalitions they commanded, accepted the Zook Commission report's basic premises that public universities made sense economically, politically, and educationally. The two governors also hoped their state-level policy initiatives would serve to inspire a broader expansion of public higher education regionally and nationally. These postwar, state-level higher education initiatives proved extraordinarily successful over the course of the next fifteen years. Today, the California and New York public universities constitute the three largest public higher education systems in the country, becoming, in the process, national exemplars, albeit distinct from one another. Each offered a unique approach toward integrating an enlarged public higher education system with their state's rapidly expanding and diversifying economy and citizenry. California and New York would choose starkly different approaches to structuring and funding their incipient systems.

The evolution of public universities across the country in the postwar era was differentiated by the particular histories, economics, politics, and demographics of each state. We are not suggesting in what follows that New York and California represent the only two possible paths that public universities could or did follow. But a quick overview of the growth of a number of other state university and community college campuses and systems in the postwar era, especially the major state systems in the Midwest (Illinois, Indiana, Michigan, Ohio, and Wisconsin), suggests that other states generally followed California's (and, to a lesser degree, New York's) example (Ingraham 1975, 74). Outsize growth of college enrollments in the 1950s and 1960s, stimulated by the GI Bill, led most states to dramatically expand the capacity and function of their public university systems, dwarfing the private universities and colleges in many of those states. "The state universities began to grow toward gigantic size," concludes Frederick Rudolph, arguing that "emulation of the chain department store would in the end offer a way out of the problems created by an almost insatiable popular appetite for higher education" (Rudolph 1962, 463–64). Embracing one of the Zook Commission's key arguments, local communities in states across the country, but especially in the Midwest and Far West, would also build out their community ("junior") and technical/vocational college systems in the 1950s and 1960s in order to rapidly expand access to higher education (Katsinas, Johnson, and Snider 1999, 3; Snider 1999, 107–28). By 1980 almost 80 percent of all US undergraduates would be enrolled in public colleges and universities (Mettler 2014, 7).

The University of California (UC) was founded at Berkeley in 1868 as the state's land-grant institution. It was established as a public trust governed by a separate board of regents, and was supported from the outset by state tax dollars (in addition to the income generated from the sale of the federal land grant). Over the fifty years following UC's founding, California slowly built out its public colleges in response to growing citizen and bipartisan political demands for the establishment of more tax-supported, public higher education institutions across the state. On the eve of World War II, California's higher education system had already achieved its modern tripartite shape and nomenclature: the UC system consisted of three campuses; there were nine state colleges, which had taken on their new identity as liberal arts institutions (rather than narrower teacher-training institutions) by 1938; and thirty-eight junior colleges had been established throughout the state by 1932. California already possessed arguably the most robust public university system in the country on the eve of World War II.

New York's higher education system, unlike California's, was dominated for a century and a half prior to World War II by private colleges. The state founded the board of regents[7] in 1784 to oversee the operation and functioning of the state's private colleges. The regents were disinterested in the possibilities of establishing a public university *system* in New York State. Rather than use land-grant income generated by New York's share of the Morrill Act to set up a free-standing public university, Ezra Cornell, a member of the New York State legislature, convinced his legislative colleagues in 1865 to found the eponymous university that would be the beneficiary of the substantial income generated from the state's land-grant allocation (Abbott 1958, 45–48; Carmichael 1955, 14; Connery and Benjamin 1979, 295).[8]

The city of New York, unlike the state, enthusiastically embraced a unique public, tuition-free, and municipal taxpayer-supported higher education relatively early in its history. The all-male Free Academy was founded as a secondary school in 1847, becoming the College of the City of New York (CCNY) two decades later; Hunter College was founded in 1870 as a "normal school," a teachers college, for women.

By World War I there were still only three tuition-free public universities in the entire state educating several thousand students in total. Yet, as late as 1936–37, a regents' study of public education in New York State concluded that despite strong interest in college attendance among its citizens (evidenced by the spread of the emergency collegiate centers in the same years), New York State was "adequately supplied with private colleges, universities, and public and private professional schools" (Abbott 1958, 177). On the eve of World War II, the state of New York had the dubious distinction among the forty-eight states of having failed to establish any kind of public university system.

World War II disrupted New York State's long-standing resistance to a more expansive and widely available public higher education system. The regents felt compelled to develop a plan to meet the postwar needs of what they estimated as one hundred thousand new college students (compared to the slightly more than eighteen thousand enrolled in the state's private and public colleges in 1939–40). The regents' December 1943 plan included expanded scholarship aid for New York State residents (to be spent at private colleges) and the establishment of twenty-two new junior college prototypes across the state, including New York City. Governor Dewey, at this stage, embraced the regents' cautious approach to public university expansion (Abbott 1958, 201, 206–10).

In sharp contrast to the state's caution, New York City continued to invest substantial city tax dollars in public higher education in the four decades prior to World War II. By war's end New York City was spending $10.5 million annually (more than 90 percent of the municipal system's total operating budget) to support its four tuition-free municipal colleges.[9] By comparison, the state was spending only one-third of that amount ($3.6 million) on its eleven public teachers colleges (Carmichael 1955, 35; Glazer 1981, 154). In 1945 New York State ranked forty-seventh in state expenditures per college student, while its college students paid a disproportionate share of higher education instructional costs. Equally telling, private tuition costs drove thousands of New York residents (almost twice as many as those who entered the state to attend college) to pursue higher education opportunities at cheaper colleges outside of the state (Abbott 1958, 209).

New York policy makers, including Governor Dewey, were thus caught in the contradictory position of trying to respond to emergent economic and political postwar realities while simultaneously maintaining their primary allegiance to the state's private colleges. This posture was unsustainable in both the short and the long term. Attitudes toward public higher education in Albany clearly lacked a coherent vision, especially when compared to New York City's or California's, which featured expansive state planning and fiscal roles in enlarging public higher education opportunities for their citizens.

The Founding and Expansion of SUNY and the Status of New York City's Municipal Colleges

A "tidal wave of returning veterans," seizing on the generous education benefits provided by the GI Bill, overwhelmed Dewey and the regents' cautious and measured approach to expanding state-supported higher education (Abbott 1958, 212). The rapid escalation of demand for public higher education was breathtaking. Half a million New York State veterans were demobilized in the first six months of 1946, with one hundred thousand seeking college enrollment in the state that year alone. By November 1946, New York State colleges and universities had already enrolled 270,000 full-time students, almost three times the anticipated demand; nearly half were veterans. As a result New York colleges could not find sufficient space to accommodate this welter of new students (Abbott 1958, 214–21; Glazer 1981, 163).

Yet, even in the midst of this transformative demand, New York State political and educational officials remained unwilling to entertain even the modest public university solutions proposed and implemented by other states, most notably California. J. Hillis Miller, associate commissioner for higher and professional education of the New York State Board of Regents, argued that the state's higher education emergency should "not be resolved at the expense of free enterprise in higher education in the State, nor in such a way as to impair the independence of the private colleges and universities." Syracuse University's chancellor, William Tolley, went even further, arguing, "We do not want [to create] an embryo of a state university" (Abbott 1958, 220–25).

In the face of this entrenched opposition to the establishment of new public colleges, New York City leaders adopted a counterstrategy. They focused public attention on the racial and religious discrimination (especially experienced by African Americans and Jews) endemic in the state's private higher education institutions and across much of New York's economy, culture, and society in the first half of the twentieth century. Anticipating the Zook Commission, in 1946 Mayor Fiorello La Guardia's Commission on Unity, created after the 1943 Harlem race riot, held public hearings and uncovered examples of racial and religious discrimination in private college admissions (Wechsler 2010, 32; Abbott 1958, 227). One analyst has suggested that only about one half of 1 percent of New York State's college student population in 1946 was African American and that Jews were limited to 10 to 15 percent of admissions at major private universities such as Cornell and Columbia and fewer than 5 percent at smaller private colleges such as Colgate (Ottman 2010, 19). A number of groups, led by the NAACP, the American Jewish Committee, and the Anti-Defamation League of B'nai Brith, as well as mainstream Protestant organizations, formed an antidiscrimination campaign. This progressive coalition focused on linking a legal struggle to end discrimination in higher education with support for the creation of a publicly funded state university. Their approach included political pressure mixing traditional lobbying of the state legislature with newspaper coverage of discriminatory practices and sponsorship of a series of marches and sit-ins in Albany. These tactics generated broad support among the public (Carmichael 1955, 326–27; Ottman 2010, 20). Similar linkages between discrimination and political struggles occurred during the civil rights era and in more recent broad-based, progressive coalitions fighting discrimination based on gender, race, and sexuality.

Despite determined opposition from private and Catholic college officials, advocates for public university expansion continued in late 1946 to press the need for a state university supported by public funds. The Democrats, encouraged by the state AFL-CIO, proposed a bill in the 1946–47 legislative session to create such a system (Abbott 1958, 231–32). This effort was supported by New York City political and business leaders because of growing concern about the long-term financial viability of the city's municipal colleges. There were even some postwar discussions among the city's higher education policy makers about imposing tuition, a position that ran counter to the century-long commitment to what political scientist Judith Glazer has called "a sacrosanct act of political faith" to maintain free tuition in its public colleges (Glazer 1981, 226).

The suggestion to charge tuition was dismissed as heretical by the New York City Board of Higher Education (Glazer 1981, 173–74).[10] In any case, the growing support in New York City for a state university helped push Albany policy makers to take the first steps in launching a statewide higher education system.

Taking note of the political prestige being garnered by President Truman from the publication of the Zook report, the charges of discriminatory admissions practices by private universities, and growing calls for expansion of state university systems in New York City and across the country, Dewey finally became more assertive late in 1947. He presented a plan that included the founding of the State University of New York (SUNY), creation of new community colleges across the state, and development of two medical centers (one upstate; one downstate in New York City) (Abbott 1958, 263). True to form, the regents and the private universities opposed Dewey's bill. Despite their opposition, the state legislature passed the SUNY bill, and Dewey signed it on March 12, 1948. Simultaneously with passage of the SUNY authorization bill, the legislature passed the Fair Education Practices Act (FEPA), which banned racial, ethnic, and religious discrimination in college admissions, a significant victory for the state's progressive forces, especially in New York City.[11]

In April 1949, SUNY launched five Institutes of Applied Arts and Sciences (i.e., community colleges, only one of which was sited in New York City), plus seven new specialty colleges, which were "contracted out" to private universities, including Cornell (agriculture) and Syracuse (forestry) (Clark, Leslie, and O'Brien 2010, xviii). In the end Dewey had managed to secure little more than an administrative scaffolding for a state university system (creation of a central SUNY administration and a board of trustees to oversee it), without conceiving of, let alone building, a single new senior college campus (Abbott 1958, 306). Despite these limitations the governor had managed to launch an entirely new SUNY system. By the time Dewey left office in 1954, SUNY's total state budget allocation was $43 million, not quite half of the $97 million California appropriated for its UC and state college systems in the same year.

Like SUNY, the New York City Board of Higher Education (BHE) governing the four municipal colleges demonstrated little interest in community college development. This indifference contrasted sharply with the burgeoning movement reshaping higher education in the rest of the country during the postwar era. The BHE remained largely passive, worried more about how the city would underwrite the growing operating costs of its municipal college system (including its free tuition program for full-time students) than about expanding entry-level higher educational opportunities for students with a broad range of academic capabilities (Gordon 1975, 53–59).[12]

The BHE finally opened the city's first community college in 1955 on Staten Island (the only borough without a municipal college campus); two additional community colleges—one in the Bronx and the other in Queens—soon followed. Enrollment in the three New York City community colleges remained initially modest, totaling no more than three thousand students as late as 1960 (Gordon 1975, 81). While New York City's full-time, four-year municipal college students continued to receive their education tuition-free, full-time, two-year community college students initially paid full tuition. This disparity stemmed from an explicit decision by the BHE to use the community college tuition revenue stream to help defray the public expenses of the four-year colleges. "What was perceived [by the BHE] as necessary for the four-year colleges," Sheila Gordon concludes, "was of little concern for the two-year institutions in the 1950s" (Gordon 1975, 71–72). Community college tuition charges would end in the mid-1960s, but that determination and the political calculation that made it happen were still five years in the future, a future that included the rise of a robust civil rights movement in the city.

A decade after SUNY's creation and on the eve of the 1958 state election, the university system remained largely an empty shell. Despite the availability of state capital funding (the legislature passed a \$250 million bond issue in 1957), SUNY had no plans to undertake any new construction or program expansion—nor did New York City's municipal colleges. However, Nelson Rockefeller's election as governor changed that go-slow attitude. Following the old regents/Dewey playbook, Rockefeller proposed that the expansion of the state's higher education system be accomplished by building out, or expanding SUNY, offering state scholarships to individual students to attend colleges where they wished (including private colleges) and providing direct aid to the state's vast private higher education sector, which in 1958 still enrolled 60 percent of all students in the state (Connery and Benjamin 1979, 294). Like Dewey, Rockefeller was not about to spend, at least initially, enormous amounts of operating funds to expand SUNY. He intended instead to impose tuition on all students attending New York's public colleges, a plan decidedly at odds with California's plans for its state universities and colleges.

At the end of 1959 Rockefeller and the board of regents established the Committee to Review Higher Education Needs and Facilities, chaired by Henry Heald.[13] The Heald report called for an expansion of SUNY into "one of the major systems of higher education in the country." It also advocated an end to New York City's free-tuition policy in its municipal colleges, public aid for private colleges and universities, and increased state scholarships. The report proposed to double the state's college attendance from four hundred thousand in 1959 to eight hundred thousand by 1970. It was anticipated that this growth could only occur if existing public higher education systems in the state (i.e., SUNY and the municipal colleges in New York City) absorbed the lion's share of the projected increase of new college students.[14]

Following the release of the Heald report in November 1960, state higher education policy makers, including the regents, reasserted the need for a public commitment to the private sector. The regents immediately called for a state legislative allocation of $18.2 million in the form of grants of $100 per semester to students to help pay their *private* college tuition charges. In order to blunt the opposition of the private colleges to its expansion, SUNY's board of trustees supported the regents' plan to use public funds to help pay for private college tuition. Opposition to state subsidies for private colleges, especially sectarian ones such as Catholic schools, was strongest in New York City among Jewish and Protestant groups, the NAACP, and other progressive organizations.

Rockefeller stepped cautiously into this political minefield. To begin with, he did not support direct grants to private institutions, but rather assistance through the indirect revenue conduit of tuition subsidies to college students. He also insisted that no matter how poor a student's family, the subsidy should not reduce his or her annual tuition payments below $200. He remained adamant in his desire to charge tuition in state-supported institutions of higher education as a means of generating a steady and predictable income stream to underwrite high-grade state capital construction bonds, a position in marked contrast with California's. The Scholar Incentive Bill passed the state legislature and was signed into law by the governor in April 1961 (Connery and Benjamin 1979, 306–12). After 1961 a breathtaking expansion of both the SUNY and the soon-to-be-created CUNY systems would occur, as we will see in chapter 3. This turn of events would thrust New York, along with California, into the top rank of public university systems in the United States and even the world.

The California Master Plan for Higher Education

As in New York, political actors in California became concerned about the capacity of the university system to handle the anticipated post–World War II flood of new students, particularly veterans. But, unlike New York, California had a substantial and well-developed public higher education system already in place: the UC campuses, the state colleges, and three-dozen junior colleges.

Many of the two million demobilized veterans migrating to California, the largest number in the nation, quickly took advantage of the educational and training benefits of the GI Bill. The state also used its bulging tax coffers, bolstered by an economic boom spurred by wartime production, to undertake an unprecedented public works program, constructing highways, housing, and public buildings as soon as the war ended. Between 1945 and 1950 state expenditures, including a massive expansion of the state's public university systems, had more than tripled. Governor Earl Warren and other state policy makers hoped that increased spending on higher education would help to spur the growth of California's postwar economy. "Public higher education could absorb the huge number of veterans as it helped industry in California," John Aubrey Douglass notes. "Junior colleges could provide vocational and credential programs, while the state colleges could increase their role in training technical professionals, including engineers." At the top of the state's public higher education pyramid, the University of California system (which had expanded to three campuses during the war) would provide the necessary high-end research work and professional credentialing in anticipation of the state's postwar economic expansion, as UC Berkeley had during the war when it hosted the Manhattan A-Bomb Project (Douglass 2000, 175, 195–96).[15]

The chief hindrances to the efficient enlargement of the state's higher education system were, as in New York State, local politics and political self-interest. Many state legislators demanded that a branch campus of the state higher education system be built in their home districts. Despite these relatively parochial interests, a broader plan was laid out by the Strayer Commission, established by Governor Warren and the state legislature. The 1948 Strayer report, which called for dramatic expansion of all three branches of the state's higher education system, especially the junior and state colleges, formed the basis a dozen years later for the landmark 1960 California Master Plan (Smelser 1974, 27; Douglass 2000, 184–85).

The Strayer report, like the earlier Zook Commission recommendations, argued that junior colleges should not only provide technical training but also "general education," thus better preparing California's students in the postwar era for their dual roles as workers and citizens. The authors of the report concluded that to "function effectively as a member of a family, a community, a state, a nation, and a world" required a general education in addition to a technical one. The report also suggested California's state colleges move beyond their traditional focus on teacher education to encompass "a wide variety of curricula" leading to both bachelor's and master's degrees in selected fields. Perhaps most important, the report called for more stringent criteria for admissions, focusing on a three-tiered grades and class-rankings structure that would become a fundamental underpinning of the California Master Plan a dozen years later (Douglass 2000, 186–88; Smelser 1974, 27). The Strayer report assigned the UC system "exclusive responsibility" for training for the professions (e.g., medicine and law), for doctoral-level graduate work, and for high-end research and scholarly publication.

By 1947 more than 130,000 vets were attending public and private colleges and universities in California (including the state's fifty-five public junior colleges, the largest state total in the nation). Fewer than 40,000 of these students were enrolled in the state's private colleges, contrasting sharply with New York State's enrollment trends during this period. The Strayer report predicted a total college enrollment in California of more than 300,000 by 1965, a dramatic expansion that necessitated further building out of the higher education system (Douglass 2000, 190–93).

California and New York were thus at the forefront of a national movement to expand public higher education opportunities for citizens from the late 1940s through the early 1960s by providing expanded college access, supported by state and federal funds and at little or no cost to students. These policies, sustained by public investment, were endorsed by a consensus of political decision makers across the country as the best way to address the growing number and variety of jobs generated by the postwar economy and to produce a sufficient number of qualified workers to fill those positions. Considering this broader context, Douglass concludes,

> Leaders in state government increasingly saw the need to equalize educational opportunity, to essentially lower the economic and social barriers to attending a higher education institution, and to provide a greater geographic distribution of colleges and universities. State governments, it was believed, needed to guide and shoulder a significant new financial burden to expand higher education (199).

The lofty goals for US higher education articulated in the Zook report ten years earlier had focused on the creation of well-informed citizens of the world. That humanist rationale contrasted with California's more pragmatic political calculation to expand the state's economy by providing low-cost or even free higher educational opportunities to a growing number of its citizens.

No matter the policy intention or calculation, higher education was understood by the vast majority of US citizens as well as decision makers as an essential public good. But this expansive public commitment provoked rapid, often uncoordinated growth of public university systems across the country. University expansion clearly demanded greater coordination and consolidation to secure necessary cost efficiencies, especially when the economic boom years immediately following the war waned. It was on this basis that New York State, California, and twenty-four other states—including North Carolina, Indiana, Michigan, Ohio, and Wisconsin—established "super" boards and commissions to coordinate higher education planning. It was expected that such coordination would wring cost savings from public university budgets (Glenny 1965, 86–103; Douglass 2000, 217, 265; Nasaw 1979, 207; Snider 1999, 117–18; Fellman 1975, 105).

In fact, California privileged growth over cost savings in the early 1950s as its public higher education system expanded dramatically in both rural and urban areas, especially in the major site of population growth, Los Angeles. By 1955, UC Berkeley, UCLA, and UC Santa Barbara were joined by UC campuses in Riverside, Davis, and San Diego. Four of the six campuses were located in Southern California, supporting the booming aeronautics and defense industries there. Three new state colleges were also authorized by the legislature in 1957, two in Southern California and one in Northern California, reflecting the political clout of the powerful Republican state legislators representing those major population areas (Douglass 2000, 227–33; Smelser 1974, 29).

This intensely political process to determine where new public higher education institutions would be built in California was exacerbated by several interconnected factors. First, powerful tensions were increasingly evident between the UC system, which saw itself as the jewel in the state's higher education crown and thus worthy of the largest share of state higher education spending, and the state and junior colleges, which argued that they were relatively underfunded given the large number of students they educated. Intensified competition for resources between tiers of university systems also occurred in several other states, including Wisconsin.[16] The less elite parts of the California higher education system argued that they should be allocated the bulk of new state resources because they were educating a far larger share of the undergraduates now flocking to colleges across the state. A second key factor threatening to slow the expansion of California's public higher education system was the perilous condition of the state's economy, which resulted in major budget shortfalls in 1957. The huge expansion of state services left California in that year with its largest level of public debt since the Great Depression (Douglass 2000, 246).

Simultaneously, Cold War politics were reshaping higher education policy nationwide. The Soviets' successful launch of the Sputnik satellite in October 1957 unsettled politicians, business leaders, education officials, and ordinary citizens across the Western world. Sputnik, according to one educational analyst, "shocked our citizens and our government out of their complacent faith . . . in the superiority of our educational program" (Douglass 2000, 234). In terms of public higher education policy debates, Sputnik spurred Americans at all levels to reexamine higher education plans and priorities across the nation and within their own states, pushing many to call for even greater state and federal expenditures to overcome the technological advantage that the Soviets apparently possessed.

It was within this context that California's state legislature ordered a series of hearings to reevaluate "the primary purposes, tools and techniques of our public education system." Early the following year, the legislature concluded that the state's education system, from primary schools to PhDs, was insufficiently coordinated and therefore needed to be fundamentally reshaped. A new master plan for higher education in

California was gestating, one that built on California's past successes. Its emphasis on the system's greater efficiency and differentiated functions would reverberate across the next six decades in California and beyond. Equally important, the nature of such efficiencies and, in turn, the larger meaning of public higher education would soon be redefined in response to broader political and economic forces at play nationally and internationally.

As in New York under Republican Governor Nelson Rockefeller, with the election of Democrat Edmund G. "Pat" Brown as California's governor in fall 1957 and the appointment at that same moment of Clark Kerr as president of the UC system, the political and organizational stars aligned to effect a reconfiguration of public higher education in California. Within a year of taking office, Brown succeeded in securing tax increases and bond issues to launch new public works programs that the Warren administration had planned but failed to implement a decade earlier. Brown's financial reforms, according to John Aubrey Douglass, "returned activist state government to California" (2000, 247). It is important to reiterate that even with Democratic control of both houses of the state legislature, political and budgetary realities continued to constrain state policy makers. They were therefore forced to implement efficiency measures that conflicted with a number of the activist promises made by state leaders.

It was within this context that UC President Clark Kerr convinced the statewide Liaison Committee on higher education to appoint a study commission to develop yet another plan for reforming the state's higher education system. He also called on the UC Board of Regents and the state board of education, which had oversight of the state colleges and junior colleges, to hold joint meetings. At the second such meeting in 1959, the participants decided to proceed with the development of a master plan for higher education expansion (Douglass 2000, 260–64).

Negotiations regarding the content of the plan occurred against the backdrop of dramatic growth in college enrollments across the state. In 1960, several years before the first wave of baby boomers would enter the state's higher education system, California colleges already enrolled almost a half million students, with more than 70 percent of that total enrolled in the state's community colleges (Smelser 1974, 45). The most dramatic enrollment growth—annual double-digit increases in all three college-university sectors—had begun in 1953 and continued unabated for half a dozen years. Higher education policy makers agreed that the junior colleges now needed to handle an even greater percentage of entering undergraduates.

The authors of the Master Plan proposal, therefore, quickly settled on a schema for distributing high school graduates across the tripartite structure, proposing that the UC system admit the top 12.5 percent in the state, the state colleges admit the top 33.3 percent, and the remainder (approximately 54 percent) have unlimited access to two-year junior colleges. Douglass concludes that this rejiggered division was "a choice heavily conditioned by the need to reduce costs to taxpayers" since educating undergraduates in community colleges was understood as being considerably less expensive than in state colleges and, especially, at UC campuses (Douglass 2000, 280–84; Smelser 1974, 48). Kerr later characterized the Master Plan as a "desperate attempt" to prepare for the even larger tidal wave of new students that would soon batter the doors of the state's public higher education institutions (Bowen and Tobin 2015, 227).

The draft Master Plan, released in December 1959, projected that California's public college enrollments would increase 230 percent by 1975. Throughout the 1960s all three sectors in fact experienced almost double-digit enrollment growth *annually*. Even more dramatically, over the next fifteen years the total increase in the number of students was almost five-fold, in part because of the rapid expansion of junior college enrollment. This was a trend that the Master Plan had not quite envisioned or anticipated (Douglass 2000, 317; Smelser 1974, 49).

Kerr and State Superintendent Roy E. Simpson sent the *Master Plan for Higher Education in California: 1960–1975* to the state legislature for approval. Despite inevitable political maneuvering and principled opposition expressed by some groups, the Master Plan was approved by the legislature and signed by Governor Brown on April 14, 1960. Each of the three levels of California's higher education system enjoyed substantial gains: three new UC campuses were approved in San Diego, Irvine, and Santa Cruz, as well as their continued monopoly over doctoral education, which holds to this day; four new state college campuses were authorized as well as creation of an autonomous board of trustees; and twenty-two new community college campuses were approved. Equally important, the community colleges were promised an increase in the state's contribution to their operating budgets from

30 percent to 45 percent by 1975. And, in a win for broadened access to higher education, prospective public college students and their parents saw the no-tuition policy, except for "incidental fees," reaffirmed (Douglass 2000, 286, 310).

In retrospect, Governor Brown argued that by adopting the Master Plan California had "developed a unique system of tuition-free education, from kindergarten through graduate school, for all qualified students. . . . [I]t is the result of the determination of the people to make a massive investment in an educational system which cuts through all barriers of race and socioeconomic background" (Brown 1965, 104). The decision to invest in public higher education occurred because of the commitment of California's citizenry to the idea of a largely free public higher education system. This political understanding between citizens and state policy makers lasted for more than two decades following the Master Plan's adoption. California higher education historian John Aubrey Douglass largely agrees with Brown's assessment of the Master Plan's importance, while also describing the racial and ethnic myopia of its original political calculations:

> With a largely homogeneous population, the primary barrier to higher education, thought the authors of the [Master] plan, was economic class. There was little concern about the role of race and inequities in local schools. Low costs for students and their families and a wide geographic distribution of public institutions, they believed, would provide the primary basis for equitable access to all students who could benefit from a higher education. (Douglass 2000, 297)

The "largely homogeneous population" that Douglass refers to was the overwhelmingly white (more than 91 percent) composition of the state's population in 1960, according to the US Census (the 91 percent included a substantial number of Latinos, however, who were not counted separately in the census until 1980)—only 5.6 percent of the total population was identified as black (US Census Bureau 2014). As we will see in the next chapter, New York City's racial and ethnic profile was quite different from California's in these years. The city was in the midst of a dramatic demographic transformation from 1945 through 1960 as more than one million African Americans and Latinos, one in eight city residents, migrated to New York City from the South and from Puerto Rico. That demographic differences between New York City and California would have profound consequences on the ways in which public higher education struggles played out in each place from 1960 through 1975.

The confluence of California's particular political, demographic, and economic factors made the historic expansion of its higher education system seem almost inevitable. "[T]he rapid growth of the California system of higher education in the 1950s and 1960s was in many ways over determined," UC Berkeley sociologist Neil Smelser has argued.

> By virtue of their commitment to the values of competitive excellence and egalitarianism, the leaders and citizens of the state *wanted* the system to grow; because of great demographic and economic pressures, it *had* to grow; because of the availability of substantial financial resources from many quarters, it *could* grow; and because the political forces regulating the growth were found, in the long run, in the state's representative bodies, the state was not very well equipped to *prevent* the system from growing. (Smelser 1974, 33, italics in original)

The significant, unanticipated political consequences from this planned, frequently "overdetermined" growth of California's public university system accounted at least in part for later student resistance to the growing corporatized practices of the university. The rapid expansion of public higher education after 1960 would pose significant challenges to faculty and students whose emergent and changing roles within the public university system were fraught with contradiction and tension.

[3]

Students and Faculty
Take Command

The fifteen years following the passage and implementation of the 1960 California Master Plan witnessed a fundamental transformation of public higher education, not only in California, but also in New York State, New York City, and across the country. This chapter explores the political and cultural forces unleashed by the expansion of public higher education after 1960 and the ways in which students, faculty members, and ordinary citizens responded politically and ideologically to that expansion. We focus on the student and faculty upheavals at public universities in California and New York in the 1960s and the ways they fundamentally transformed each state's public higher education system. The chapter concludes with the 1976 fiscal crisis in New York City and its role in undercutting the egalitarian possibilities and hopes of a unique public university system, the City University of New York (CUNY). The New York City fiscal crisis and its aftermath signaled an early battle in the austerity regime that launched the fundamental restructuring of public services and institutions across the country for the next four decades. And, critical to our analysis, these and similar attacks would lead to a dramatic reshaping of public higher education, the effects of which continue to reverberate in our own time.

New York State, CUNY, and the Struggle
for Open Admissions

The year 1961 proved to be important in the history of public higher education in New York State, as 1960 had been in California. Following many of the recommendations in the Heald Committee's report, Governor

Nelson Rockefeller launched a campaign that succeeded in consolidating and expanding public higher education across the state over the course of the next decade. The growth of the SUNY system in these years was nothing short of remarkable. New senior and community colleges were opened in nearly every county. By 1967 there were fifty-nine campuses in the SUNY system, thirty of them operated directly by the state, with a total enrollment of 138,000 full-time and 83,000 part-time students. These numbers dramatically increased by 1975 to more than 350,000 students. The SUNY budget, which had totaled $44 million when Rockefeller took office, swelled to $280 million by 1967, a more than six-fold increase in less than a decade. The Heald report projected that SUNY should double its enrollment between 1961 and 1970, a goal it in fact achieved a year early. Rockefeller, according to one of his biographers, considered SUNY "his crowning achievement as governor," having turned a "string of teachers colleges" into "the largest system of higher education in the world" (Persico 1982, 201).

In order to create new SUNY campuses and construct additional academic buildings on older ones to accommodate the expanding student enrollment, Rockefeller extended the functions of the state's public benefit corporations. These quasi-independent entities allowed him to avoid having to go back to the state legislature every year for continuing funding for previously approved construction projects. The state legislature endorsed the State University Construction Fund (SUCF) as a public-benefit corporation in 1962; the fund ultimately carried out more than $700 million in SUNY capital projects. However, the governor insisted on imposing tuition on state residents. This cash flow was required to underwrite the private bonds that funded his dramatic building plans (Connery and Benjamin 1979, 313; Axelrod 1974, 131–45).

The governor's shrewd economic and political calculation (capital money to build out public colleges in exchange for the imposition of tuition) contradicted the state's, and especially New York City's, more than century-long commitment to free tuition at its handful of pre-1948 public colleges.[1] In the first few decades of the post-1945 economic boom the profile of New York City's municipal college students had begun to change. Still overwhelmingly Jewish, the family economies of undergraduates enrolled in the late 1950s and the early 1960s at CCNY and at Hunter, Brooklyn, and Queens colleges were becoming more prosperous, even middle class, at the time that admissions requirements to qualify for the scarce seats in the municipal colleges were becoming ever more stringent (Wechsler 1977, 264–65). By 1965 it reportedly required a 92 or A– high school average to gain admission to City College because of high student demand combined with limited space. Increased competition occurred as the system, largely reliant on city tax funds to underwrite operating costs, strained to educate a relatively small number of students (fewer than forty thousand undergraduates in 1960–61) (Gordon 1975, 98). As late as 1967, CUNY's census revealed that 82 percent of its students were white, 10 percent black, and 3 percent Puerto Rican (Glazer 1981, 276, 306).

It was within this context that the Heald Committee and the governor in 1960 and 1961 recommended that the city streamline and rationalize its municipal college system. These state decision makers advocated combining the four senior colleges and three community colleges under the aegis of a single, new entity, the City University of New York, and forming an administrative infrastructure, headed by a new CUNY chancellor, to coordinate and rationalize the new system. In return, the governor promised increased funding to expand the new system's capacity to meet the burgeoning demands of a rapidly diversifying citizenry.[2] The substantial fiscal resources offered by the state constituted an enticing incentive, a kind of velvet glove, to restructure the municipal colleges.[3] The iron fist that it cloaked was the demand by Rockefeller that CUNY impose tuition on all of its students, as he had done at SUNY in 1962, as a quid pro quo for financing a dramatic expansion of the state and city systems he envisioned (Glazer 1981, 223–24). This measure was formally approved by the state legislature and signed into law by the governor in April 1961.

Rockefeller assumed that he had won the battle to abolish free tuition at CUNY. He further assumed that the state's economic leverage would ultimately allow him to absorb CUNY into the newly expanded SUNY system. But both calculations proved wrong. His politically aggressive effort to enact tuition served to awaken the CUNY BHE, powerful municipal college alumni associations (especially CCNY's), and the city's political and business elites. An aroused and empowered BHE refused the imposition of tuition and, at the same time, determined that it was an appropriate moment to produce its own master plan—"A Long-Range Plan for the City University of New York" (Butt 2014).

The BHE's long-range plan called for more flexible admissions policies to respond to the growing number of city high school graduates and to establish community colleges to absorb the expected increase in the numbers of undergraduates. The proposed goals of the plan, a staggering sixty-three in total, were to be realized at a distant future date—1975—thus giving the newly formed university system a dozen years to evolve and grow. Three of the goals are especially relevant to this discussion: first, to expand enrollment by creating a more flexible admissions policy, targeting as many as half of all public and private high school graduates in the city for recruitment to CUNY; second, based on the California model, to build or acquire more community colleges; and third, to maintain free tuition across the CUNY system. Within two years CUNY created the Borough of Manhattan Community College and Kingsborough Community College in Brooklyn, both of which opened in 1964. In that same year, the BHE acquired the New York State Institute of Arts and Sciences—one of the original, Dewey-era technical institutes—which it renamed New York City Community College (Gordon 1975, 85–88, 138–41).

Perhaps most significantly, the BHE committed itself, in Sheila Gordon's phrase, to extend "the hallowed principle of free tuition" to CUNY's community college students, despite Rockefeller's and the New York State regents' determined efforts to impose tuition on *all* SUNY and CUNY students. Mayor Robert F. Wagner Jr. agreed with the BHE's plan and was actively supported by a progressive coalition of religious and civic organizations. Consequently, free tuition was extended by the city of New York, beginning in the 1964–65 academic year, to all full-time students attending CUNY's community colleges, the same privilege its full-time senior college students had enjoyed for more than a century. This defense of the free-tuition policy rested on the invocation by the BHE's and the municipal colleges' numerous and powerful alumni of a meritocratic ideology that saw free tuition as a policy that on the one hand rewarded academic accomplishment and on the other assured wide (but not universal) access to undergraduate public education (Gordon 1975, 89; Glazer 1981, 220, 250–52; Butt 2014).

While the BHE and CUNY won the free tuition battle with Rockefeller in 1961–62 for at least the next fifteen years, they gradually lost the much larger war with New York State to expand the number of campuses and faculty to handle its swelling number of undergraduates. Commenting on this lost opportunity, CUNY administrator Ted Hollander told historian Judith Glazer:

CUNY missed the golden age of the sixties when college construction was booming everywhere and campuses were being overbuilt. Its growth was stunted by a recalcitrant Legislature and an unsympathetic Governor, all because of an anachronism—free tuition. The environment (at CUNY) would have been different today if it had moved faster, and had assured the state more of a role in its development. (Glazer 1987, 257)

As we will see, the fervent embrace of free tuition at CUNY in 1961–62 would have profound political consequences for CUNY and the city at the end of the decade.

Despite these constraining influences, the BHE's plans for the new CUNY took a fortuitous turn in 1963 when Albert Bowker, a mathematician and then dean of the Stanford University graduate school, was hired as CUNY's second chancellor. The BHE was quite fortunate to snare Bowker, a man of great vision who also possessed a taste for and requisite skill in the intense, high-stakes political infighting that characterized the struggle to reimagine New York City's public higher education sector in this formative era.

Bowker understood immediately that he would have to find the necessary financial resources to build out the newly formed and rapidly expanding CUNY system, especially its community colleges. He further understood that resources were no longer going to be provided exclusively by New York City taxpayers. Bowker also anticipated that the CUNY student population would grow rapidly in a short period of time and look very different, demographically and culturally, from previous municipal college cohorts. An expanding number of students of color would need to be educated in CUNY's community colleges in future years to fill the growing number of semiprofessional administrative and service jobs across the city as traditional manufacturing jobs in the city receded. Bowker quickly concluded that these new students would need significant remedial support to succeed, which had not been as much of a concern in the smaller and more elite traditional municipal colleges in years past. Finally, Bowker understood that he was going to have to pry power and authority away from an "old school" BHE and the traditional academic leaders at the four older senior colleges. In turn, he worked to have part of this power and authority transferred to a new, centralized CUNY bureaucracy to assure coordinated and systemic oversight of the system's expansion, enlarged access, and impending demographic changes. To Bowker's credit and in realization of CUNY's larger purposes and goals, he succeeded in each of these critical tasks by the end of the decade.

Bowker's success in centralizing administrative authority resulted in the BHE approving in 1966, at least in principle, the idea of open admissions (though the policy was not planned for full implementation until 1975). Open admissions guaranteed any New York City high school graduate admission to a CUNY community or senior college. This achievement alone would have marked Bowker's chancellery as a major success, but Bowker's greatest achievement can be traced to his fight for increased state funding. In exchange for state support the chancellor expressed a willingness to rethink New York City's hallowed commitment to free tuition.[4] He understood the paramount need to leverage state funds to expand the entire CUNY system (Glazer 1987, 286; Butt 2014). Bowker and his colleagues were animated by a compelling need to respond to the expected dramatic shifts in the demographics of CUNY. They anticipated that unlike the earlier Irish, Italian, and especially Jewish working-class migrants to New York, whose children had been able to take full advantage of the city's highly regarded public secondary schools in the 1920s, 1930s, and 1940s, the children of the nearly one million African Americans and Puerto Ricans who poured into the city in the 1950s and 1960s entered and exited an increasingly dysfunctional public-school system that simply did not and could not meet many of their intellectual and cultural needs. In the absence of state funding CUNY would likely fail to provide sufficient seats for these new students as well as the academic supports necessary to prepare this new cohort of students to undertake college-level work. It was within this context that Bowker focused on the importance of securing expanding revenue streams to finance and dramatically enlarge remedial education programs across the CUNY system.

It would be reasonable to assume that this anticipated wave of underprepared and educationally challenged new students would be funneled to CUNY's half dozen community colleges, where, like their California counterparts, they could be helped to succeed at their academic work while pursuing associate's degrees. But unlike California, CUNY's community colleges, according to Sheila Gordon, were almost as restrictive in their admissions requirements as the senior colleges by 1965, which set their admissions bars very high. Moreover, as late as 1964 CUNY's *total* undergraduate enrollment remained relatively small at forty-nine thousand students. This level of enrollment contrasted sharply with the demand for college entry, which was significantly greater. "The public rhetoric of the University may have been toward easing access," Gordon notes, "but it was not until 1970, with the introduction of open admissions, that any broad changes were made" (Gordon 1975, 91–92).

To respond to CUNY's still-restrictive admissions policies, even in its new community colleges, Bowker supported the launching of two path-breaking remedial education programs: College Discovery, begun in 1964 for new CUNY community college students, and SEEK (Search for Education, Elevation, and Knowledge), which was implemented in 1966 to assist academically underprepared senior college students. Both College Discovery and SEEK—the latter inspired and led by CUNY writing pioneer Mina Shaughnessy, and in which famous poets and writers such as Adrienne Rich, Toni Cade (Bambara), June Jordan, and Audre Lorde taught at CCNY—helped the university respond to students attending old and new CUNY campuses who may have otherwise been unsuccessful in their academic endeavors (Wechsler 1977, 275–80; Jordan 1989, 20).

It was within a context of rapid expansion and demographic shifts in the CUNY student body that Bowker was able, after 1967, to secure a commitment from the BHE to open three additional CUNY community colleges to relieve overcrowding. This commitment was in part a consequence of several existing CUNY campuses operating at more than 135 percent of capacity. Unfortunately, the three new community college campuses (Medgar Evers in Brooklyn, La Guardia in Queens, and Hostos in the Bronx) were not slated to open until after 1970. During the same period, three new senior colleges—John Jay in Manhattan, Richmond in Staten Island, and York in Brooklyn—and a graduate school were also authorized. The Hunter campus in the Bronx (Lehman) and CCNY's downtown campus (Baruch) were also repurposed to accommodate the large influx of new students.

CUNY—which had assumed it had until 1975 to enlarge its physical plant and hire new full-time faculty to manage the expected significant spike of open admissions students—had in fact miscalculated. Breakdowns and friction between growing student demands and the deficient supply of instructors as well as physical facilities occurred well before the end of the decade. These tensions flared and exploded, as we will see below, across the multicampus CUNY system in 1969 as it became one of the nation's primary battlefields in the decade-long fight for the soul of public higher education.

The Multiversity and the Student Movement

Though impressive, the 1960s expansion of SUNY and CUNY did not vault either system to the top of the public university pyramid, as Nelson Rockefeller might have hoped. Rather, the public university system in California and its widely admired tripartite university structure set the standard for public higher education nationally. UC president Clark Kerr, who later claimed grandiosely that he had "initiated and guided the development of the California Master Plan," now presided over the restructuring of the UC system (Kerr 1991, xvii). That restructuring was designed to respond to the anticipated arrival of a "tidal wave" of baby boom teenagers, which would have a profound, two-decade impact on higher education across the country. The Master Plan had mandated that the largest part of the undergraduate baby boom expansion would be handled by California's state colleges and community colleges. Together they were expected after 1960 to admit seven of every eight high school graduates seeking college admission. While the California system under the Master Plan indeed guaranteed all high school students entry into a public college, the system was structured along meritocratic lines of grade tracking, admitting only one out of eight high school graduates to UC schools. It was this elite group that Kerr focused on, overseeing the development of three new UC campuses in the 1960s (Santa Cruz in the northern part of the state; San Diego and Irvine in the south). As anticipated, enrollments at the two oldest UC campuses, UC Berkeley and UCLA, quickly approached their mandated limit of 27,500 students each (a third of whom would be graduate students), with Berkeley's student population increasing more than 30 percent between 1960 and 1964 and UCLA's by more than 50 percent between 1960 and 1967 (Smelser 1974, 51; Bowen and Tobin 2015, 228). Doctoral education and professional credentialing, still the exclusive province of the UC system, also expanded on every UC campus, with especially robust growth occurring at the newer ones (Smelser 1974, 80). To handle this sharp increase in undergraduates during the 1960s, the UC system hired a large number of new, young faculty members. The flagship Berkeley campus was an exception. Older, tenured UCB professors lent their institution considerable prestige through academic publications and grants, supplemented by a growing cadre of graduate teaching assistants (their numbers had in fact tripled between 1953 and 1964), who, as we will see, maintained much of the face-to-face contact (one estimate indicated half) with the campus's rising population of undergraduates. Undergraduate education at UC Berkeley and UCLA, as a result, suffered from a kind of neglect (Kerr's word). This model of two-track teaching would soon be emulated in large public higher education systems nationally (Smelser 1974, 82–87, 95–99; Bowen and Tobin 2015, 229).

The expansion of the UC system in the 1960s, and its continued preeminent role in high-end research and professional credentialing, rekindled tensions with the state college system. In general, the state colleges' faculty did not enjoy the same academic prestige and grant-supported research available to their UC counterparts. Beginning in 1967, state college faculty and administrators pushed to change their institution's name from the California State *College* system to the California State *University*. They believed that altering their "brand" would bolster institutional prestige and aid in faculty recruitment. That it took until 1972 to convince the state legislature to approve this modest name change suggests how dominant UC's voice and political hegemony remained in California higher education affairs during this era (Smelser 1974, 69–74).

The power and prestige of the UC system were also made possible by a major expansion in the size and authority of the Kerr-led central UC administration after 1960 (Smelser 1974, 76–77). Kerr wholeheartedly supported the centralizing tendencies of academic administration in the age of the "multiversity," the term he coined to describe the modern university system: "As the institution becomes larger . . . as the institution becomes more complex, the role of administration becomes more central in integrating it; as it becomes more related to the once external world, the administration assumes the burden of those relationships" (Kerr 1963, 28; Smelser 1974, 112).

The growing bureaucratic power of the UC system accreted not only to the UC administrative structure led by Clark Kerr, but also to the board of regents, a twenty-four-member governing body with a strong business orientation.[5] The power of the regents (who had selected Kerr as the system's first president in 1958) significantly increased after 1960.

The regents controlled more than $400 million in public funds. The chairman of the board of regents in 1964 was Edward Carter, a department store magnate and also a trustee of the Irvine Foundation, which donated the land for UC's new Irvine campus in Orange County that opened in 1965.[6] While major politicians (including the governor and lieutenant governor), a labor leader, educational officials (including the UC president), and lawyers held seats, the UC board was dominated, as were many other state university system boards in this period, by corporate interests. Underscoring this point, thirteen regents (led by Carter) out of twenty-four hailed from the business world. "The corporations do not merely buy the University's products and hire its graduates," UC student activist Marvin Garson argued in 1965, "they reproduce in the heart of the University itself their own bureaucratic power system, their own goals and values" (Garson 1965, 3–11, 20). Despite their concentrated economic and political power, the regents left the day-to-day operation of the institution and much of the long-range planning to Kerr and his chosen team of system and campus administrators. As we will see, campus events in 1964 caused the regents to take more aggressive and controlling actions.

Clark Kerr's reconceptualization of the modern public university in California provided a template that a number of other states followed. Rather than seeing the university as an intellectual community or a living organism, as educational reformer Abraham Flexner famously did in 1930, Kerr, true to his roots as a labor mediator, instead defined it as "more a mechanism—a series of processes producing a series of results—a mechanism held together by administrative rules and powered by money" and as having "many 'publics' with many interests" (Kerr 1963, 20, 27). The multiversity is "the child of middle-class pluralism," in Kerr's conception, managing in that revealing phrase to elide the public university's longstanding commitment to and engagement with its working-class students and their families (118). This middle-class pluralist vision demanded that the leader of the multiversity above all else function as a mediator, the essential attribute, in Kerr's mind, of a successful contemporary university leader.[7]

The dramatic increases in federal funding of university research projects and institutes made possible the rise of the multiversity, which nearly resulted in the federalizing of American higher education during the Cold War years. Kerr characterized this massive infusion of federal funds in the postwar era as effectively turning the multiversity into a "federal grant university," a status that many of Kerr's fellow state university presidents and chancellors aspired to achieve for their institutions. By 1960 20 percent of the operating income of the nation's colleges and universities and 70 percent of all university research funds were fully provided by the federal government (Rudolph 1962, 490). The obvious upside of receiving increased federal funding was eroded for the inhabitants of the multiversity by disciplinary jealousies between the haves (the scientists) and the have-nots (the humanists), as well as a deemphasis on the instruction of undergraduates (barely discussed at all by Kerr in his magnum opus, *The Uses of the University*[8]) in favor of instruction by graduate students. The public university was thus less driven by academic or pedagogical necessity, as Kerr openly admits, than "by the external environment, including the federal government, the foundations, the surrounding and sometimes engulfing industry" (122).

Kerr concludes that the multiversity is now the "focal point" of a new "knowledge industry" that is driving national economic growth in the postwar era, an analysis still referenced a half century later by public university administrators and trustees and continues to inform contemporary debates about the purposes of public higher education. The growth of the multiversity, according to Kerr, is often driven by the "mad scramble for football stars and professorial luminaries" to burnish the institution's national reputation as well as brand and bolster continuing contributions from successful alumni (Kerr 1963, 87–90). He critiques the faculty's fierce defense of its prerogatives against administrative encroachments as part of the deep strain of liberal/radical politics, concluding, "The faculty member who gets arrested as a 'freedom rider' in the South is a flaming supporter of unanimous prior faculty consent to any change whatsoever on his campus in the North. The door to the faculty club leads both in and out" (99).

In *The Uses of the University*, Kerr became (and remains for many) the exemplar of the modern public university president or chancellor in late twentieth-century America. To be successful, the multiversity administrator must be able to placate the meddling external powers wanting to control how the university operates in the world while simultaneously searching for ways to rationalize and impose efficiencies on educational services and research deliverables, thus mediating among and between constituencies. So, time-tested academic calendars need to be jiggered and instruction mechanized by television and other new educational technologies; excess supplies of PhDs better managed; and new academic fields, such as interdisciplinary science, seeded (Kerr 1963, 109–12). In order to accomplish all of this and justify its very existence, "the university as producer, wholesaler and retailer of knowledge" must embrace its service role within the larger society (114; Lustig 2004, 51–53). If the "Captain of the Bureaucracy" (Kerr's chosen descriptor) is unable to balance these conflicting demands and constituencies, chaos will indeed reign (Kerr 1963, 33). In a telling and prescient sentence written a year before the Free Speech movement, Kerr suggested that "When the extremists get in control of the students, the faculty, or the trustees with class warfare concepts, then the 'delicate balance of interests' becomes an actual war" (39). It is important to remember how far removed Kerr's depiction of the multiversity in 1963 is from the Zook Commission's arguments in support of public higher education barely fifteen years earlier. In the next era of public higher education, the Zook Commission's analysis of the purposes of public higher education in large part would be revived by students and faculty members.

Kerr could little imagine that "an actual war" was about to break out on his flagship campus one year after first publishing *The Uses of the University*.[9] The UC administration, in response to local political pressure, had issued several new regulations in September 1964 as the fall semester began, banning political advocacy and solicitation of funds in Sproul Plaza, the main public entrance to the Berkeley campus. That decision adversely affected student activists seeking financial support and student volunteers for racial struggles unfolding in the South. Jack Weinberg, a civil rights activist, was placed under arrest for defying the UC ban on political solicitation in Sproul Plaza. He was dragged from the campus and placed in a police car, which was quickly surrounded by several thousand UC Berkeley students who spontaneously sat down for what turned out to be thirty-two hours to block the car's exit.[10] Very quickly, Mario Savio and a dozen others who would end up leading the new student movement at Berkeley stood on top of the police car and launched a long and intense discussion with other student protesters about political advocacy, the purposes of the university, and, foremost, the principle of freedom of speech. Students, who had barely appeared in Clark Kerr's vision of the multiversity, had suddenly thrust themselves center stage in a battle of and for the public university.

So began the Free Speech movement (FSM), which launched more than a decade of college student activism that would help reshape the nature and function of higher education, both within the United States and internationally. The 1964 Berkeley uprising would culminate in a mass sit-in by one thousand FSM supporters at Sproul Hall two months later on December 2. The sit-in—likened by Clark Kerr to KKK lawlessness and condemned unequivocally as "an attempt at anarchy"— resulted in the mass arrests and jailing the next day of more than eight hundred protesters followed by a strike by teaching assistants and students that lasted nearly a week (Cohen 2009, 209; UC Berkeley Bancroft Library, 2014).

While the immediate causes of the 1964 Berkeley student revolt were fundamental freedoms of speech, assembly, and political advocacy that the university administration had tried to squelch, the FSM also managed to surface simmering discontents among students and supportive faculty members about the nature of the contemporary public university. In the year before the strike, Kerr's flagship multiversity, UC Berkeley, often felt like a large assembly line to many of the students and faculty members who studied and worked there. UC Berkeley was jam-packed with an unprecedented number of students in 1964. Many required undergraduate classes were extraordinarily large. The introductory American history survey course, for example, met in Wheeler Auditorium, which seated one thousand, one of Berkeley's largest classrooms. But student demand for the history survey (a required course for undergraduates) required five hundred additional seats. These students were required to view live lectures on television monitors in adjacent rooms in Wheeler Hall, an early instance (though by no means the first or only one, as we will see in chapter 6) of simulcasting in US higher education. The twice-weekly lectures by the single faculty member responsible for the course were supplemented by a passel of history graduate students who taught dozens of fifteen-to-twenty-student discussion sections.[11] Kerr estimated that graduate teaching assistants and nontenured faculty made up 61 percent of UCB's teaching personnel in 1964 (Bowen and Tobin 2015, 82).

No wonder, then, that when the student strike paralyzing campus operations erupted after the arrest of more than eight hundred FSM supporters on December 2, undergraduate and graduate student picketers alike wore IBM punch cards around their necks on which they had hand-written "I am a student. Please do not fold, spindle or mutilate," which mimicked the warning text printed at the bottom of every IBM punch card.[12] The FSM was therefore for many students as much about the growing size and mechanization of public higher education in the era of Clark Kerr's multiversity as it was about fighting for the right to protest, to speak out, and to organize against social and racial injustice. Mario Savio, in his famous December 2 speech on Sproul Hall's steps encouraging the assembled mass of FSM supporters to sit-in and thus stop the administration building from functioning, used familiar industrial-production imagery (much as Kerr had done in *The Uses of the University*) to criticize the functioning of Kerr's multiversity:

> There's a time when the operation of the machine becomes so odious, makes you so sick at heart, that you can't take part. You can't even passively take part. And you've got to put your bodies upon the gears and upon the wheels, upon the levers, upon all the apparatus, and you've got to make it stop. And you've got to indicate to the people who run it, to people who own it, that unless you're free the machine will be prevented from working at all! (Cohen 2009, 178–79)[13]

The UC Board of Regents did not take the FSM or the support that it garnered among the majority of UC Berkeley faculty lightly. The regents soon dismissed the bumbling UCB chancellor, Edward Strong. President Clark Kerr, the master builder of the UC multiversity, would suffer the same fate several years later, fired by the regents in 1967 in the wake of Ronald Reagan's 1966 victory in the California gubernatorial race. The governorship was Reagan's first elected office, which he secured, in large measure, thanks to his unrelenting attacks on university student radicalism.

The 1964 free speech fight at UC Berkeley proved to be the opening shot in a much larger set of political and ideological battles on college campuses across the nation. The student movement at Berkeley was quickly propelled forward by the much larger struggle against the Vietnam War. Antiwar teach-ins, a particularly academic form of protest, blossomed at universities and colleges all over the country throughout the 1960s and 1970s. Over the next several decades the commitment to an engaged public scholarship launched the transformation of a number of social science disciplines—including history, sociology, political science, geography, and anthropology—from the pluralist consensus that had shaped much postwar social scientific work into deeper engagements with "bottom-up" analyses of the nation's social, economic, and political assumptions. This transformed scholarship asked new and difficult questions about the role of workers, women, African Americans, colonized peoples, immigrants, nonheteronormative individuals, and many other "subordinate" groups, within the United States and beyond. Equally important, it challenged the prerogatives of dominant social, political, economic, and intellectual groups and institutions, the last holding special significance for universities. As historian Roderick Ferguson has argued, the appearance of Kerr's *Uses of the University* in 1963 had a decidedly unintended consequence, helping transform the public university into "the center of discussions around minority difference and democracy, and the laboratory that might integrate these two institutional identities" (Ferguson 2012, 84). In 1969 alone there were more than 250 protests nationally, many of them at public universities, calling for the creation of separate racial and ethnic studies programs (5).

The rise of college-student radicalism after the mid-1960s had a similarly disruptive impact at other California public universities, including UCLA (1968–69), San Francisco State College (1968–69), and UC Santa Barbara (1970). The student movements in California were replicated at a cross section of public colleges across the country, including, but not limited to, the University of Michigan (1967–68), CUNY and SUNY (1969), the University of Wisconsin (1970), Kent State University (1970), and Jackson State University (1970). But these progressive developments inside universities also stirred up an empowered opposition. College uprisings contributed to the national revitalization of powerful conservative forces, which traced its roots to a California-based opposition not only to the radical forces of mass student protest occurring across the state but also to rising tax support for public institutions, particularly public universities, that was vital to their survival and growth. Ronald Reagan, one month after assuming the governor's office in 1967, used the state's fiscal crisis to argue for sharp cuts in the public higher education budget. Reagan justified these cuts by telling reporters that "[t]here are certain intellectual luxuries that perhaps we could do without" and that taxpayers shouldn't be "subsidizing intellectual curiosity" (Berrett 2015). It is no coincidence that the antitax austerity politics Ronald Reagan rode to national political prominence and that has maintained its iron grip on national and state policy four decades later had its origins in the attack on public higher education in California at the end of the 1960s. It is difficult to overstate how central this ideological confrontation was in triggering the sustained erosion not only of the public university but also of basic state functions, as well as the rise of austerity policies in America.

The Fate of Open Admissions

The "best-laid schemes" of senior university administrators often go awry, to paraphrase Scottish poet Robert Burns. Much as they had in the case of the UC system's Clark Kerr, so too were Albert Bowker's "schemes" for the measured expansion of the CUNY system overtaken by political events and CUNY student actions on the ground. As noted above, Bowker had persuaded the CUNY BHE in 1966 to institute a plan that would culminate in 1975 with a full rollout of open admissions at CUNY for all New York City high school graduates. Bowker also had tried to take steps to meet the needs of an increasingly academically unprepared high school student population through the creation of two innovative remedial education programs, SEEK and College Discovery. However, despite Bowker's and his fellow CUNY administrators' good intentions, even as late as 1968 SEEK managed to admit only 1,100 students of color to City College, Brooklyn College, Queens College, and several other CUNY senior colleges (Molloy 2015). Brooklyn College was 96 percent white in 1968, while City College, a bit more integrated, had a student body that was 91 percent white.

The orderly 1975 transition to open admissions at CUNY would not happen on Bowker's and the BHE's planned schedule. Rather, this target date was overtaken by political events much like those in Clark Kerr's UC system. Urban tensions boiled over into widespread racial violence and rioting in African American communities during protests launched in response to the April 1968 assassination of the Reverend Martin Luther King Jr. New York City managed to avoid overt racial conflict thanks to Mayor John Lindsay's community outreach efforts (Wechsler 1977, 278). Simmering beneath New York's surface calm, however, was an ongoing political and ideological struggle over community control of New York City's public schools, which erupted in the fall of 1968. This struggle dominated much of the city's political and intellectual attention for the rest of the year.

Early in 1969, the city's focus turned to CUNY. Students of color across the CUNY system, inspired by the community-level struggles to improve public schools in poor and working-class neighborhoods and by a wider embrace of black power, ethnic pride, and grassroots activism, had mobilized. Early in the spring 1969 term students of color organized to defend their modest toehold in CUNY and bolster special programs such as SEEK that supported minority student success in the university. The most immediate fiscal threat was to SEEK. It had been slotted for elimination in Nelson Rockefeller's proposed 1969 state budget at the same time CUNY administrators were struggling with severe, system-wide problems of overcrowding, as three new CUNY campuses would not be opened until the early 1970s. The growing gulf between the increased demand for higher education and the supply of classrooms, buildings, and faculty at CUNY could be traced, in part, to the ongoing resistance by New York State and New York City to the allocation of additional public monies to accommodate the needs of CUNY's rapidly changing student body (Wechsler 1977, 279). In response to this crisis, in February 1969 African American and Puerto Rican students, organized officially as the "Black and Puerto Rican Student Community" (BPRSC), presented five demands to the CCNY administration:

1. establishment of a Black and Puerto Rican studies school;
2. creation of a separate orientation program for Black and Puerto Rican freshmen;
3. save the SEEK program and give SEEK students a voice in its ongoing operation;
4. the racial composition of all entering classes at CCNY should reflect the actual representation of Black and Puerto Ricans populations in the New York City high schools;
5. classes in Black and Puerto Rican history and Spanish language for all education majors. (CCNY Libraries 2009; Dyer 1990, 93–94; Wechsler 1977, 280–81)

Each of these demands called for CUNY to meet the needs of the city's changing population. Of particular concern was realignment of CUNY's academic programs to create a better fit with the educational and cultural identities of students of color who would, and, by right, should, soon be transforming the racial and ethnic composition of CUNY's student body.

A series of negotiations, mass rallies, and confrontations over the next two months between students and administrative decision makers culminated on April 22 in a two-week occupation of the South Campus of CCNY by the BPRSC and its multiracial supporters drawn from every sector of the college. Political scientist Conrad Dyer has described the CCNY takeover as "one of the largest and longest student occupations of an American University campus" (Dyer 1990, 1). At this time, New York City was in the midst of a hotly contested mayoral campaign, with Mayor Lindsay running for reelection as the Liberal Party–Fusion candidate. When one of Mayor Lindsay's Democratic Party political opponents managed to secure a court order in early May to force CCNY's reopening, New York City police arrived on the campus on May 5 to retake the student-occupied buildings by force. A battle with black, Puerto Rican, and white student protesters ensued. The campus finally reopened but operated with a substantial police presence for the remaining few weeks of the spring term, punctuated by a boycott of classes by students and faculty supporters and a series of fires, vandalism, and physical attacks against both black and white students. Faculty, CUNY and CCNY administrators, and protesting students continued their negotiations during the course of these tumultuous weeks.

Similar struggles were occurring at the same time at campuses across CUNY, including sit-ins by hundreds of students at Queens College to protest the firing of radical professors and at Borough of Manhattan Community College to demand black and Puerto Rican studies programs. At Brooklyn College, militant black and Puerto Rican students organized an alliance and issued a set of eighteen demands in the spring of 1969, paralleling the five demands CCNY students had put forward. They called for the immediate expansion of black and Puerto Rican enrollment and the creation of black studies and Spanish-language curricula (Biondi 2012, 114–40). As at CCNY, the Brooklyn College students of color, led by the Black League of Afro-American Collegians (BLAC) and the Puerto Rican Alliance (PRA), escalated their tactics to get the administration and faculty to respond to their demands. Again paralleling the CCNY experience, allied black and white militants occupied several Brooklyn College buildings in early May, one of which included the president's office. When the police were called in on May 12 by Brooklyn College administrators, twenty leaders of the militant student groups were arrested and charged with major felonies (charges that were dropped a year later). A faculty and student strike immediately ensued, with one hundred police officers stationed on the Brooklyn College campus for the remainder of the spring term. CUNY in spring of 1969 was beginning to resemble university campuses in Europe and Latin America, similarly wracked by political conflict, violence, and military and police occupation.

The entire CUNY system was under siege. Its central administration and the political leadership in the city in turn felt pressured to respond immediately. Increasingly worried about racial unrest on the campuses and in the larger city, Mayor Lindsay and Chancellor Bowker announced their support for the protesters' specific demands for increased access to CUNY by minority students. Largely in response to the intensifying protests, the BHE decided on July 9, a short two months after the CCNY and Brooklyn College student occupations ended, to accelerate its original timetable and implement the CUNY open admissions plan in the fall of 1970, a full five years ahead of schedule (Dyer 1990, 93; Wechsler 1977, 283–86). All prior barriers to and requirements for admission to CUNY were lifted. Every New York City high school graduate was guaranteed a place in CUNY at either a senior or a community college, depending on his or her high school class ranking. This decision also assured entering students access to remedial and other support services. The primary goal of open admissions, in the words of the BHE's resolution, was nothing less than "the ethnic integration of the university." This policy shift essentially remade the system overnight from one that prized very selective admissions and narrow access to a CUNY now more fully and completely open. The rapidity of the policy shift and the breadth of CUNY's commitment to full access were unprecedented in the history of American higher education. However, these steps toward open admissions were also especially difficult to implement given CUNY's historic lack of space, insufficient budget, and relative scarcity of faculty members. The transformative policy directive for open admissions and access was therefore not aligned with the need to provide quality public higher education. The choice to provide broad access while resisting investment of public funds necessary to assure a quality education continues to define New York City and national higher education policy making to this day.

The demographic impact of this policy decision was immediate and undeniable. The first "open admissions" entering class in the fall of 1970 was 75 percent larger than the previous year's. In 1971, black and Puerto Rican enrollment in CUNY's senior colleges represented 24 percent of the total student body as contrasted to half that percentage a year earlier. To handle this dramatic increase in students of color and to meet their academic needs resulting from inadequate high school preparation, the SEEK and College Discovery programs were also expanded.

White, working-class students also benefited from CUNY's new open admissions policy. One of the reasons that Bowker and Lindsay were able to push the BHE to accelerate open admissions was the strong support offered by the New York City Central Labor Council (NYCCLC). Its leaders realized that CUNY's restrictive admissions policies prior to 1969 not only had succeeded in restricting access for black and Puerto Rican undergraduates but also had limited access for the children of the city's Irish and Italian working class, who made up the largest part of the membership of the unions affiliated with the NYCCLC. It was largely on the basis of expanded opportunities for the children of their white, black, and Puerto Rican working-class members that the New York labor movement endorsed accelerated implementation of open admissions at CUNY. It is within this context that the number of Italian Americans entering CUNY doubled from 1969 to 1971 (Freeman 2000, 231–33).[14]

By 1975, the original date for the start of open admissions, CUNY had created a more racially and ethnically diverse pool of 253,000 matriculating undergraduates—a 55 percent increase in total enrollment since 1969. As sociologist David Lavin noted, 78 percent of first-year students entering CUNY in 1969 had been white; by 1975, that percentage was 30. CUNY had also agreed to the development of a series of ethnic and black studies programs and centers at several of its campuses, including CCNY, Brooklyn, Hunter, and Queens colleges. In turn, this pioneering effort contributed to the evolution of more diverse university curricula nationally (Biondi 2012; Ferguson 2012, 5, 96–97). CUNY had thus put itself at the forefront of national efforts to make tuition-free public university education available to any high school graduate who wished to attend, a long-deferred dream first fully articulated in the 1947 Zook Commission report and embodied, albeit in a compromised form, in the 1960 California Master Plan.

But just as the FSM and the educational transformations it inaugurated in California birthed a staunch conservative opposition, so too did open admissions. That opposition took many forms, including long-standing CCNY faculty members who feared that open admissions, in the words of SEEK teacher and poet June Jordan, "would catapult the University into a trough of mediocrity" (Jordan 1969, 20–21). These older faculty members nostalgically harkened back to CCNY's "high standards" and reputation as the "poor man's Harvard" (Traub 1994). These lamentations resonated with conservative politicians and business leaders in New York and across the country who worried about increased public expenditures and radical new pedagogies and new fields of study. The emergence of conservative voices was soon amplified by breakdowns in the implementation of open admissions across CUNY. These ruptures could largely be traced to two factors: the need for more resources because of the acceleration of the open admissions timetable and the persistent inadequacy of public funding to meet the educational needs of a much larger and often more academically challenged student body.

The BHE's accelerated open admissions timetable proved chaotic during the first few years, with long registration lines, closed courses, insufficient classroom seats, and a scarcity of textbooks. In addition to a frenetic building program requiring substantial capital funds, the CUNY administration needed to secure additional operating funds to expand its faculty. CUNY administrators, despite the many challenges of launching the open-admissions experiment five years ahead of schedule, did hire thousands of new, younger faculty members. This infusion of new faculty helped revitalize CUNY's teaching workforce when it was most needed.

The pressures, however, that CUNY experienced were made all the more difficult when, in 1971, Albert Bowker agreed to return to California as UC Berkeley chancellor. He was replaced by Robert Kibbee, a private university administrator with no previous public university experience, who, in his own words, can best be described as "doing the best he could" under increasingly difficult circumstances to protect CUNY in the troubled decade that followed (Newt Davidson Collective 1974, 72).

Despite many immediate challenges, open admissions was indeed a triumph. It transformed CUNY into the most open and perhaps most envied higher education system in the country in the early 1970s. That triumph was articulated beautifully in a valedictory speech delivered by thirty-three-year-old Dawn Harris at the Borough of Manhattan Community College in 1973. She thanked "the brothers and sisters at

CCNY for deciding that five more years was just too long to wait for open enrollment." Harris also thanked "those who tried to stop me and tried to discourage me because they have made this day even sweeter. I wanted to make sure that they didn't count over-thirty, underprepared women with children out. I think I did it. I know we did—1,595 votes for Open Enrollment!" (Newt Davidson Collective 1974, 18).[15]

Despite the triumph of implementing open admissions, CUNY continued to suffer enormous constraints and deficits, both instructional and budgetary. The rapid rollout of remediation at the senior and community colleges severely limited the quality and effectiveness of these efforts. Neither the city nor the state, which remained jointly responsible for underwriting the operational costs of CUNY in the early 1970s, committed sufficient funding to support the required expansion of SEEK and College Discovery. A by-product of this underfunding was that two-thirds of the students entering CUNY in the early 1970s under the liberalized open admissions policies were leaving the system within four years of admission without graduating. Faculty workloads varied widely among CUNY campuses, and the number of part-time adjuncts hired across the system also increased dramatically. By 1974, adjunct faculty already comprised one in three CUNY instructors (Newt Davidson Collective 1974, 19–20). The use of adjunct faculty was more pronounced at the newer senior and community colleges in CUNY than it was at the older senior college campuses in Queens, Brooklyn, and Manhattan, which had many more senior, tenured faculty.

These fault lines and tensions on CUNY's increasingly diverse campuses intensified as city, state, and national budgets were further constrained by public-sector decision making. Rockefeller continued his quest to get CUNY to impose tuition charges on its undergraduates as he had required at SUNY. These additional tuition charges had resulted in a dramatic and well-financed expansion of the state system. While the BHE held firm on the municipal colleges' age-old commitment to its no-tuition policy for full-time students, Mayor Lindsay, worrying about the city's increasingly straitened finances at the end of 1971, was pressed to try to offload some, if not all, of CUNY's operating expenses onto the state. The battle between the state and city forces over CUNY's budget seesawed for several years without clear resolution.

As often happens, solutions to such political and budgetary problems are dictated externally. The worldwide economic crisis that began in fall

1973 with the OPEC oil embargo soon quadrupled the price of oil, wreaking havoc on the US economy (American Social History Project 2008, 685–86). These economic shock waves had cascading effects on the New York State and City economies. The US economy in 1974 had entered the worst downturn since the Great Depression, and, as the cliché goes, when the US economy caught a bad cold, New York City contracted fiscal pneumonia. For three decades following the end of World War II, the city had supported an extraordinary social democratic experiment with its tax dollars that led to a dramatic expansion of its public institutions, including municipal hospitals, housing, schools, and colleges, all staffed by a heavily unionized and relatively well-paid municipal workforce (Freeman 2000, 55).

Abe Beame, a Democratic Party regular and former city controller, replaced Lindsay when his second term as mayor ended in 1973. Despite various fiscal sleights of hand, Beame and his staff were unable to independently solve the city government's budgetary woes. Failed appeals were made to the big banks to continue to buy city bonds. Later, city and state officials appealed to Washington for help, but President Gerald Ford and Treasury Secretary William Simon, a former Salomon Brothers bond trader, turned them down cold in May 1975. Simon's economic rejection included a political attack on CUNY's free-tuition policy, among other New York City progressive policies. The next month the state legislature finally agreed to surrender the city's financial independence for a three-year period to the Emergency Financial Control Board (EFCB), in part managed by the banking industry. The EFCB immediately dictated the city's workforce be reduced by 15 percent (a loss of more than forty-seven thousand workers) over a seventeen-month period beginning in January 1975. And although the city cut CUNY's budget in the summer of 1975 by tens of millions of dollars, the BHE still resisted imposing tuition on CUNY's students.

Despite the EFCB's stringent controls, the city's red ink continued to flow, and the deficit grew larger in early 1976. New York State governor Hugh Carey finally stepped in, setting up a municipal assistance corporation, or "Big Mac," to sell new city bonds in return for Mayor Beame agreeing to drastically cut city spending. The mayor announced massive layoffs and targeted, in historian Joshua Freeman's words, "the social democratic achievements of working-class New York," of which an expanding CUNY system and the now 130-year-old free-tuition policy were especially vulnerable (Freeman 2000, 261). In June 1976, with CUNY's budget in tatters, the BHE could no longer resist and approved the imposition of tuition on CUNY students in exchange for a full state takeover of senior college finances (the community colleges would still largely be carried by New York City's budget). Nelson Rockefeller's dream of a unified SUNY-CUNY system had not quite come to pass. That said, the state did finally agree with the argument city politicians had made for years that CUNY should receive state financial support comparable to that of SUNY and even the private colleges. Despite the state takeover, all capital construction at CUNY was halted, and almost five thousand faculty and staff members were laid off. These policy initiatives in turn constrained and eroded the quality of a CUNY education. CUNY never fully recovered from this diminishment of its full-time instructional workforce. While open admissions at CUNY remained in place, at least officially, the decision to charge tuition and tighten admissions standards, especially at the senior colleges, dramatically eroded the underpinnings of a truly open admissions policy. The abandonment of free tuition resurfaced obstacles to access to public higher education, including straitened public support and growing poverty in the city. It is within this context that CUNY suffered a decline of sixty-two thousand students in its total enrollment by the end of the 1970s, with 50 percent fewer black and Latino freshmen among CUNY's entering class in 1980 (Tabb 1982, 49–50; Freeman 2000, 271; Demac and Mattera 1976, 132).

CUNY's decline would continue for two more decades as conservative politicians and business leaders used neoliberal arguments to malign its contributions and further cut public investment in its operating budget. These political attacks reached a fever pitch in 1999 under the Giuliani administration with the formal end of remedial instruction at the CUNY senior colleges. It is widely acknowledged that CUNY and other New York City public services and institutions were canaries in the coal mines of the global neoliberal offensive launched in the mid-1970s. That offensive began, as we have seen in this chapter, with the demonization and defunding of public services. As we will soon see, neoliberalism opened a second front in its war on public institutions with the lionizing of, and increased public funding for, private-sector solutions and institutions. It is to that larger national story that we now turn.

PART II

THE STATE OF AUSTERITY

[4]

The Making of the
Neoliberal Public University

The New York City fiscal crisis and the imposition of tuition at CUNY in the 1976–77 academic year signaled the end of the three-decades-long era of sustained growth in public higher education detailed in chapters 2 and 3. Declining public investment over the next four decades led public universities across the country to make a host of financial and administrative adjustments, dramatically reengineering the experience of higher education for teachers and students alike. The continuing restructuring of US higher education noted in chapter 1 is part of a much larger neoliberal agenda to promote privatization, disinvestment in the public sector, and a range of austerity measures.

For many citizens, the consequences of neoliberal policies are all too familiar. The multifaceted shift away from the public sphere to an increasingly privatized domain is the dominant trend in neoliberal reform. As noted earlier, neoliberal policy has produced diminished levels of public funding, shifts in the locus of funding, and monetization of public services, all in the name of austerity or "doing more with less." Equally important, neoliberal ideology has seeped into the governance and practices of most public agencies, where it has borrowed strategies from the business sector that focus on efficiency, increased productivity, and metrics of accountability and measurable outcomes. The culture of public agencies is rapidly changing as practices of austerity are more sharply aligned with broader policies of privatization and contraction of public funding. These shifts in the practice and organization of the public sphere produced radically changed modes of production and consumption of public goods.

Neoliberal Reform 1: Corporatizing University Culture

It is within this context that public higher education has been transformed in the latter part of the twentieth century and the early part of the twenty-first century. The changing ratio of public to private investment in higher education is an especially critical bellwether that signals the direction of recent transformations. The real dollar value of per capita student funding that states provided to public colleges and universities declined 2.3 percent between 1990 and 2010. The US inflation rate over that twenty-one-year period averaged 2.7 percent *per year*, totaling more than 56 percent over the course of the two decades (Statista 2015). "If states had provided the same level of funding as in 1990–1991," educational researcher John Quinterno concludes, "total appropriations in 2009–2010 would have equaled approximately $102 billion, an amount 35.3 percent greater than the actual one" (Quinterno 2012, 15).

CUNY experienced a 40 percent drop in state funding per student between 1992 and 2012 (Kamenetz 2013). These declines have accelerated over the past decade. New York State per-student funding for CUNY decreased by 17 percent between 2008–9 and 2015 in real dollars. These statistics, although dramatic, do not tell the more troubling story of steep declines in public funding for public university systems across the country. The universities of Minnesota, Illinois, and Washington, and Ohio State University, for example, presently receive less than 10 percent of their total operating budgets from tax levy or public dollars. The rest of their budgets must be raised largely through tuition; private fundraising; income derived from copyrights, patents, and "tech transfer" fees; and grants.

Between 1990 and 2010, college tuition more than doubled nationally at four-year public universities, rising by 112.5 percent after adjusting for inflation, while the cost of a community college education jumped by 71 percent (Quinterno 2012, 21). Tuition has risen 28 percent annually between 2008 and 2014 at four-year public colleges (Mitchell, Palacios, and Leachman 2014, 2–3). As tuition fills the financing gap, the amount of student debt is predictably rising to unprecedented levels. The total amount of student indebtedness passed the trillion-dollar mark in 2012, a figure now larger than total individual credit card debt in the United States. Other revenue sources are also being tapped to offset accelerating disinvestment in public higher education. Some public universities are also being sustained by expansion of their student bodies. For example, "full time equivalent" (FTE) student enrollment at CUNY increased 40 percent between 1990 and 2013 and 12 percent since 2001 (Professional Staff Congress 2014, 3). Other state university systems, notably those of Michigan and California, are rationing the sizes of their in-state censuses of new students to create a greater number of slots for higher-paying out-of-state applicants.

Public disinvestment in public higher education has affected the quality and conditions of learning. It has resulted in the rationing of high-demand courses, major disruptions and delays in degree completion and time to degree, overcrowded classrooms, decayed physical plants, and a rapid expansion in the number of part-time faculty. The quality of the public higher education experience is clearly being systematically diminished.

The effort to reduce public higher education costs has taken particular aim at the composition of the faculty. Austerity measures have resulted in a majority of the courses at public universities being taught by part-time teachers, the number of which grew by more than 300 percent between 1975 and 2011. Adjuncts now represent three-quarters of the instructional workforce nationally (House Committee on Education and the Workforce 2014, 3). The incomes of many part-time faculty are often well below the federal poverty line. The presumption is that part-time faculty members supplement their incomes by finding other kinds of full-time or part-time work. Increasingly that assumption is belied by the reality of the labor market, especially in the academy or other fields of public service, where full-time work is harder and harder to find. In addition, about 16 percent of CUNYs part-time faculty members rely on instructional income as their primary if not exclusive wage (Professional Staff Congress 2014).

In a survey recently conducted by *Academe*, the median rate of pay for part-time faculty teaching a total of 17,035 college courses nationwide was about $2,500 per course. Significant pay disparities existed between elite private universities and public universities. The report concludes by noting that "part time faculty members are paid unacceptably low wages and the extent of this inequity—together with the situation of full time tenure track faculty . . . forms a very real . . . multi-tier academic labor structure" (Curtis and Thornton 2013, 10). A recent article on contingent labor illustrated other indications of the degradations of invisibility and acute inequality experienced by adjunct faculty by noting, "It is no surprise that when 76% of professors are viewed as . . . disposable and indistinguishable . . . they are listed in course catalogs as 'Professor Staff'" (Kendzior 2013).

Expanding inequality within higher education is also a growing aspect of the student experience. For example, black PhD recipients carry twice the debt burden of their white counterparts, and undergraduate students who are poor experience significantly higher dropout rates (Kendzior 2013; DeParle 2012). There are also growing disparities on the basis of income, race, and wealth in terms of access to quality public higher education. A 2012 article in the *Chronicle of Higher Education* indicates that these inequalities are encoded in an array of local and federal policies. Exorbitant interest rates on student loans, for example, have a disproportionate impact on higher education access opportunities for the poorest students (Leef 2012). Anthony Carnevale (2012) notes that higher education is becoming a passive participant in the reproduction of economic privilege. Especially germane to this discussion is that as enrollments increase, especially among students of color, an increasingly stratified hierarchy of separate and unequal tiers has grown within four-year colleges and between senior and community colleges. Carnevale suggests that as enrollments in higher education increase, access for individual students may improve, but inequality among students as a whole widens. The relationship between public disinvestment and intensifying segmentation of the academic experience by race and class is increasingly a basic feature of the restructuring of public higher education (Bound, Lovenheim, and Turner 2007, 48).

Jason DeParle of the *New York Times* reported in December 2012, "With school success and earning prospects ever more entwined, the consequences carry far: education, a force meant to erode class barriers, appears to be fortifying them" (DeParle 2012, A1). The degree to which colleges are passive or active participants in the phenomenon of growing economic inequality will be more fully examined in chapter 5.

The first stage of neoliberal reform of higher education has resulted in growing debt for students (Wellman 2006, 1–2; Supiano 2013). As noted earlier, while public funding for higher education has been slashed, there has been a corresponding increase in tuition rates and, in turn, the indebtedness of students. In 2012, the level of aggregated student debt in the United States surpassed $1 trillion for the first time. This represents a 150 percent increase from 2004 to 2012 (Blow 2013). A report by the nonprofit State Higher Education Executive Officers Association found "that student loan debt as a share of household income was 24 percent for families in the lowest income quintile. That was at least twice the share of any other quintile." This gap has been growing despite the fact that "such households are less likely than those in other groups to attend college" (Blow 2013). As debt has ballooned, profit making by banks and the federal government from student loans has correspondingly grown. Profit increased following the August 2013 "reform" of the student loan program, signed into law by President Obama, which tied student loans to market rates with a higher interest rate cap (Equal Justice Works 2013). Terry Hartle, senior vice president of the American Council of Education, argues that "if the numbers are accurate, the government will make more money on student loans than Ford makes on automobiles. . . . Using student loans to create a profit center is not what anybody intended" (Lewin 2013, A-12). At the same time, the federal government is turning to an army of debt collectors to control rates of delinquency and defaults on loans. Private companies working directly for the federal government and through state agencies received commissions of approximately $1 billion on student loan payments for the nine-month period from January through September 2012 (Hechinger 2012).

Growing student debt has significant implications for students' short-term and long-term life prospects. Lauren Asher, president of the Institute for Student Access and Success, notes that "things like buying a home, starting a family, starting a business, saving for their own kids' education may not be options for people who are paying off a lot of debt" (Lewin 2011). The effort of students to minimize or avoid loan debt frequently results in their seeking to combine both part-time employment and a student status. In turn, these choices have consequences as students take longer to graduate and are less able to fully dedicate themselves to academic study. Asher's point has recently been confirmed by the *New York Times*'s Annie Lowery, who suggested that "student loan debt is not only constraining young adults, but also, at least in the near term, holding back the recovery itself. . . . The shadows might remain even as the economy picks up, by making workers more cautious when it comes to decisions about their careers and their finances" (Lowery 2013, B1). Thus, austerity policy making, in addition to its negative impact on higher education, is inhibiting present and future growth of the economy.

The debt carried by students is but one element of this. Lack of sufficient investment in students to accelerate their progress to graduation is another example of the short-sighted policy making embedded in austerity decision making.

Higher education during this first epoch of neoliberal policy making has also been marked by the ascent of for-profit institutions, led by the University of Phoenix, Kaplan University, and Corinthian Colleges. These schools offer a greater proportion of their curricula online. Their checkered history, however, is underscored by the US Senate Health, Education, Labor and Pensions Committee report on for-profit colleges entitled *The Failure to Safeguard Federal Investment or Ensure Student Success*: "For profit colleges are rapidly increasing their reliance on taxpayer dollars. In 2009–2010, the sector received 32 billion dollars, 25 percent of the total Department of Education budget" (US Senate Health, Education, Labor and Pensions Committee 2012, 2). However, for-profit higher education only accounts for 11.8 percent of all students attending college (Lederman 2010). In 2009, for the fifteen publicly traded for-profit colleges, 86 percent of revenue was derived from US taxpayers. For-profit colleges also invest substantial amounts of resources in noneducational spending, including marketing, recruiting, executive compensation, and profit taking. "Publicly traded companies operating for-profit colleges," the US Senate report notes, "have an average profit margin of 19.7 percent, generated a total of 3.2 billion in pre-tax profit and paid an average of 7.3 million dollars to their chief executive officers in 2009" (US Senate Health, Education, Labor and Pensions Committee 2012, 2). Finally, we also know that the record of for-profit colleges in terms of graduation and job placement is clearly deficient, with 54 percent of the students enrolled in for-profit colleges in 2008–9 having "left without a degree or Certificate by mid-2010" (US Senate Health, Education, Labor and Pensions Committee 2012, 4). For-profit education, in sum, is a burgeoning profit center producing limited results in terms of student success during a moment of economic crisis.

The monetization of higher education is not limited to for-profit schooling. The introduction of online curricula and large-scale management information systems also offers significant opportunities for profit making by private companies. For example, "CUNYfirst," an "enterprise resource planning" business software solution developed by

Oracle's PeopleSoft for CUNY to coordinate and "systematize" all university academic and administrative functions, will have a reported cost of more than $600 million in capital expenditure. That is not to mention the tens of thousands of unreported hours of CUNY staff time spent over the past decade of its implementation learning the complex procedures, time that could not be devoted to CUNY student and faculty needs. It is important to reiterate that this large cost has been incurred during a period of substantial student tuition increases and public-sector disinvestment. Equally important, CUNYfirst is an "off-the-shelf" system that has been plagued by many operating problems and obstacles, thus delaying its full implementation.[1]

In addition to using technology to wrest administrative efficiencies, a number of universities, especially Research 1 institutions, have also come to rely on "technology transfer," the monetization of patents and intellectual property (usually developed by individual research faculty) as a way to further bolster straitened budgets. Two of the oldest and most famous public university "tech transfer" successes were the sale by the University of Florida (UF) of the formula for Gatorade (developed by a team of UF faculty half a century ago), which has netted UF more than $150 million in royalties since the product's commercialization, and the development by a University of Wisconsin faculty member and subsequent patenting in the 1940s of the anticoagulant drug warfarin (sold commercially as Coumadin). The royalties collected and administered by the Wisconsin Alumni Research Foundation (WARF), the UW's tech transfer office, from numerous patents developed by its faculty yield an annual "contribution" of $70 million to the university's overall research budget (University of Wisconsin–Madison 2014). Diminishing state budgets for public university operations over the past two decades have further driven university administrators to intensify the pressure on faculty to develop commercially viable products that can generate substantial royalty income for their universities. UW, for example, has recently been described by the *Business Insider* as being a "patent savvy university" and WARF a "patent troll" for its aggressive efforts to use the courts to extract royalty payments, filing almost three-dozen lawsuits since 2000. WARF's recent lawsuit against Apple over alleged violations in use of technologies in its iPhones and iPads yielded a jury prize of $234 million to WARF (Chung 2015). As public university budgets tighten further we can expect expanding efforts at commercialization of intellectual property as well as aggressive use of the courts to extract substantial royalty payments.

Finally, the management structures of public universities have been reconfigured during this first stage of austerity reform. University administrators have been willing partners in this restructuring, pushing university staff to speed up and do more with less. It is within this context that new command-and-control information systems that centralize the work of the university have grown. These systems manage costs by emphasizing increasingly rote practices in everything from support services to remedial education, serving to intensify management's reach into matters historically governed by faculty, especially curricula and instruction. In a moment of austerity policy and practice these corporatizing tendencies have resulted in a significant rise in the size and cost of the administrative labor force. This has occurred as the proportion of full-time faculty has declined (Moser 2014; Newfield 2008, 159).

The reorganization of the university has significantly altered the makeup of the administrative workforce as well. The upper levels of public university administration are increasingly populated with managers drawn from business and government and certified by their MBA or JD degrees. This business ethos and its imposition on public universities during a period of austerity have also contributed to a cultural shift away from a traditional mix of qualitative and quantitative indices of what it means to be an educated college graduate to an exclusive reliance on test scores and time-to-degree metrics as measures of success (Folbre 2010; Giroux 2014). External factors such as federal and state policy directives have also clearly influenced definitions of institutional and student success.

The corporatization and commercialization of higher education also threaten historic understandings of faculty roles, institutional security, privacy, and learning. These trends have only intensified over the past ten years even as diverse organizations inside and outside of the academy have tried to slow the momentum of austerity policy making. The failure to slow, no less stop, this juggernaut of disinvestment and privatization has carried over in recent years into a second era of neoliberal threats to public higher education. It is in the second stage of neoliberal change that these forces are gathering and will rapidly alter the meaning and content of higher education as a public good (McGettigan 2013, 10–11; Brown, Lauder and Ashton 2011, 65).

Neoliberal Reform 2: The Perfect Storm of Online Technology and the Commodification of Knowledge

The conventional narrative of globalization is all too familiar. The economy of the United States and every other nation must fit into a global architecture of economic development. There is no alternative to this scaling up; the only two options are to fit in or die. It is on this basis that US public higher education is especially susceptible to increasing demands for profit making on public goods in the new global marketplace.

Higher education offers a market that some believe, in this era of austerity and privatization, must be reassembled and distributed through the circuitry of emergent online technologies. Consistent with this belief, higher education is especially well positioned to develop partnerships with the private sector in online knowledge dissemination, with a particular emphasis since 2012 on massive open online courses or "MOOCs." Venture capitalists have largely been responsible for underwriting, distributing, and marketing these online higher education products. Their investments were predicated on an assumption of large revenue streams and profits generated by MOOCs and other distance-learning "solutions," even as they were originally touted to the public as making higher education more broadly accessible by serving hundreds of thousands of students online.

Various high-profile efforts to employ MOOCs at colleges and universities across the country illustrate the tactics of marketplace entrepreneurs to monetize public higher education. Like K–12 charter schools, privatized online forms of higher education cast the experiences of exemplars as normative. MOOCs were described as maximizing the prospects for positive learning outcomes while they were intended to legitimate the transfer of public dollars to privately managed profit-making ventures in online education.

The momentum for this rapid redistribution of public money into private, corporate online learning has consistently grown over the past decade. What accounts for the growing support for this explosive, rapid change in agenda? Locating and exploiting new sites of profit making in a moment of economic crisis is one of the driving forces for the long-term transformation of public higher education. As noted in chapter 1, the 2013 Davos conference specified higher education as an especially important and emergent profit-making center globally. The fit between higher education and global profit making aligns with the expansive "consumer reach" of a growing raft of distance-learning courses and programs. Equally important, the transformation of some national economies into global knowledge centers such as Singapore and Abu Dhabi elevates the importance of universities in the further commodification of knowledge. Finally, the hunger for elite degrees—particularly within emergent international economic powers like India and China—makes US distance-learning course offerings especially attractive (Alonso 2010).

The commodification of higher education has particular salience for the United States. The US economy has few sectors that have remained internationally competitive. Certainly, technology and higher education are two areas that remain robust. High-tech corporations are a growing part of the US economy, but 47 percent of all profits are earned by the financial sector. These trends do not bode well for the overall economy. In effect, too much profit making is located in an essentially unproductive sector of the economy. The commercialization of higher education, however, does represent an important corrective for the economy. It promotes profit making in a sector of the US economy that is recognized internationally as dominant, as the United States can still claim 47 of the 100 "best" universities worldwide (Guttenplan 2013).

Another spur for the restructuring of public higher education is heightened uncertainty regarding its financing in an era of austerity (Selingo 2013; Giroux 2014). Over the past decade, public university systems in New York and California have shouldered a disproportionate share of state budget cutbacks. Increases in tuition and in the numbers of enrolled students have provided a partial corrective to this revenue decline. Increased revenue provided by tuition is imperiled by both shifts in policy making and demographics. President Obama, in his 2013 State of the Union address, pointed his audience to a college scorecard of universities and their relative cost or tuition alongside graduation rates (College Affordability and Transparency Center 2014). The president has subsequently proposed a ratings formula for higher education that emphasizes positive outcomes based on these metrics as a precondition for continued federal funding, including student financial aid programs such as Pell Grants and student loans. These metrics may prove as important in redefining public higher education as standardized testing has been in restructuring K–12 public schools (Field 2013).

Present trends suggest that as a matter of policy, public universities will increasingly be assessed on the basis of their ability to contain tuition increases while graduating a greater percentage of their undergraduates more rapidly. That is a recipe for both fiscal and curricular degradation, especially if the tuition caps are not accompanied by increased infusions of public operating funds. The lack of access to increased dollars from tuition will create ever more desperate fiscal circumstances for public universities. When combined with the decline of particular demographic cohorts of students producing some of the expanded enrollments in public universities in the recent past, the situation is exacerbated. Within this context, alternative sources of revenue from fully online, stand-alone courses, which also promise to increase both the geographic reach of the university and, in turn, the number of enrolled students, take on increasing importance. The opportunity to reduce costs by having one teacher, rather than two or even ten, instructing ever-larger numbers of students is especially attractive to academic managers and corporate profit seekers. The combination of reduced costs and increased revenue in a parched fiscal environment is accelerating the movement of public universities into privatized partnerships, often involving distance learning.

Public higher education is faced with increased competition for a stable population of students with little wiggle room on tuition costs alongside intensifying public disinvestment. The growing stratification or differentiation of elite from nonelite universities across the globe will continue to affect funding. Elite universities are likely to be the most popular choices for mass consumers and producers of online curricula. Where does this leave nonelite public higher education institutions situated in the second and third tiers? In all probability, these schools will increasingly find themselves struggling simply to sustain their operations. Higher education will no longer be insulated from Schumpeter's dictum regarding the creative destructive properties of capital (Alonso 2010; Collini 2013; Chomsky 2014).[2] As market dynamics create conditions for the rapid proliferation of various forms of online technology and education profit making, for example, these forces of change will simultaneously destroy (or at least undermine) traditional methods of communication and instruction. It is within this context that the rapid disappearance of traditional sources of revenue, when combined with the more pronounced competitive disadvantage of nonelite schools in the higher education marketplace, will result in accelerated closings and mergers of greater numbers of schools (Selingo 2013). Like Rust Belt industrial towns and cities of the Midwest in the 1980s, colleges and universities are more likely to be abandoned because of a lack of resources and an absence of political will to redefine and sustain public institutions in a period of rapid change.

We have outlined a very bleak political and economic landscape of intensifying scarcity, competition, privatization, rapid technological change, and recalculation of the meaning and value of a college degree. We are in a new moment of massive change in public higher education. It is the new K–12, the primary battlefield in the reconstitution of the public sector. Change—rapid disruptions and privatized attacks on public higher education as a public good—will increasingly be the new normal. How can or should university faculty and staff respond to these changes? What roles can or should we play to slow or alter the present direction or momentum of change? Many vexing questions animate the thinking of those interested in preserving access, public investment, complex learning, sustained commitment to the needs of challenged learners, and investment in faculty. What we do know, however, is that this more muscular, steroid-fueled form of convergent neoliberal policies is rapidly transforming both the learning culture and economic underpinnings of public higher education.

Elite Politics and Economics

Jane Wellman, the director of the Delta Cost Project, has indicated that by 2008 the 50 percent mark had been passed in public four-year institutions, with student tuition comprising more than half of operating expenses (Desrochers and Kirshstein 2012; Lewin 2011, A18). As public financing rapidly declines, the privatized costs of increased tuition and personal debt have soared. Ordinary American families are required to pony up more and more of their meager incomes to acquire the necessary certifications that public higher education provided for little or no tuition in the past.

Across the mainstream political spectrum there is growing consensus that tuition hikes are no longer a viable political or economic option. Articles in the *Wall Street Journal*, *Time* magazine, and the *New York Times* have lamented increases in student tuition and debt. The story lines consistently cite the experience of the middle class as having greater and greater difficulty meeting the cost of tuition. Consequently, there is an ascendant policy discourse emphasizing fixed or limited increases in tuition. Simultaneously, the pressure to graduate more public university students increases. This policy conversation ignores, however, the economics of debt, greater student need for part-time employment, and investment in college readiness as external factors affecting time to degree and graduation rates. It is instead assumed that rates of graduation can be inexpensively accelerated in an austerity environment through internally devised, efficient business models promoting greater productivity on the part of faculty and staff (Kelderman 2013). Like the prior policy discourse about K–12, the goal is to limit costs while achieving simple quantitative indices of success. For public higher education leaders, the metric of choice is graduation rates. Although this metric has significant legitimacy, it has been uncoupled from continuing disinvestment in public higher education. How can spikes in graduation rates be achieved in the absence of policies that attend to the learning and financial needs of students? And yet that is precisely what is being recommended through both college rating schemes and political rhetoric. As with K–12 testing reforms, the desired collegiate outcomes—whether through testing or faster graduation—are expected to be driven by efficiencies achieved through some combination of market principles, digital technology, and/or outsourcing of teaching labor, all of which are expected to increase productivity. This argument leaves no room for actual public investment or discussion of larger contexts. The Lumina Foundation, one of the most powerful and influential higher education charitable organizations, publishes analyses and recommendations each year and has had a significant influence on regional and national policy making. It has consistently endorsed higher and more rapid graduation rates but remains silent on the attendant necessary social investments to make that possible (Kelderman 2013; Eaton et al. 2014, 1–3; Fischer and Stripling 2014, A-36–A-37).

Reducing time to degree and increasing graduation rates are clearly laudable goals. No one wants students to take longer to complete their degrees or to drop out. However, public higher education is facing ever-starker revenue generation choices. According to US Department of Education projections, enrollment in colleges will continue to grow until 2021, although the increases will be flatter than the steep climbs seen in the previous decade (Schnoebelen 2013). The greatest declines will be among students from eighteen to twenty-four years old and least for those over thirty-five. Consequently, public higher education is in a fiscal vise, as it is being asked to manage the contraction of its most stable and expansive sources of privatized revenue-tuition increases and historic rates of expansion of student enrollments while continuing to endure public disinvestment.

This fiscal picture is accompanied by a demand to graduate an increasing number of students, who are expected to reach graduation more quickly as the budgets of public universities are ever more imperiled (Pratt 2013; Berrett 2014). This policy agenda is being legitimated by both conservative and liberal media, from columnists such as David Brooks, to politicians such as Congressman Paul Ryan, and at the other end of the political spectrum, by official statements of the Obama administration and editorials in the *New York Times*. There is a broad, mainstream consensus that tuition needs to be curbed and graduation rates increased. Regressive tax policies codifying debt, cutting public services, and enforcing austerity are accepted by both media and policy makers as necessary if not essential to achieving these goals.

The Curricula of Austerity

Across the nation, policy makers and administrators are increasingly emphasizing a realignment of public higher education curricula to meet the new demands of austerity policy making. A primary and laudable objective is to expedite a seamless transfer of students from community colleges to senior colleges to promote efficiencies such as accelerated time to degree (Strategy Labs 2013; City University of New York 2014a). Policy makers and legislators have articulated concerns about the excess credits accumulated by community college students intending to transfer to senior colleges. Those excess credits are described as being a drag on increasingly scarce dollars available for state investment and rapid progress toward attaining a degree. Seamless transfer by integrating senior and community colleges' curricula and paving new pathways to graduation is seen as a remedy to these inefficiencies. To the extent that students can graduate at higher rates and reduce time to completion without compromising the quality and rigor of their college experience, such policy making is both rational and laudable.

One of the Lumina Foundation's core proposals to achieve higher graduation rates is to increase the percentage of Americans holding "high quality degrees" and credentials to 60 percent by 2025 from 38.3 percent in 2010 (Kelderman 2013). It is on this basis that the foundation is advocating legislation to promote seamless transfer (Lumina 2014). We are left wondering, however, how this goal can be achieved through policies of disinvestment and privatization. Both the logic and the evidence suggest that more rapid movement to graduation accompanied by policies of disinvestment can only be achieved over the long- and short-term through cut-rate forms of curricula and devalued degrees.

An especially compelling example of how this dynamic is diluting curricula occurred at CUNY. The CUNY central administration developed a program in 2011 called "Pathways" to expedite undergraduate transfer within its extensive, twenty-four-campus system of community and senior colleges. This initiative required a reconfiguration of CUNY's general education curriculum. The problem as articulated by administrators was that "of CUNY's 240,000 undergraduates, more than 10,000 transfer from one college to another each fall." A high-level CUNY administrator noted that "for more than 40 years, students' difficulty in transferring their credits was a recognized difficulty that sometimes delayed and even derailed their graduation, a common problem in American higher education" (Logue 2015). Alexandra Logue, executive vice chancellor for academic affairs and one of the architects of Pathways, indicated that CUNY required a centralized, systemwide solution to fix this problem. Management therefore proposed that a uniform general education curriculum be instituted across the whole CUNY system. Only in this way, she asserted, could lost credits and, consequently, greater time to degree be corrected (Logue). Management argued that the magnitude of lost transfer credits justified a dramatic reconfiguration of the general education curriculum. Their logic was challenged by faculty. To quickly achieve this goal, the CUNY administration decided to bypass established faculty governance structures in both developing and implementing Pathways. This unilateral decision, legitimated by faculty committees hand-picked by CUNY management, resulted in a groundswell of faculty resistance on a number of campuses, described in greater detail in chapter 7 (Vitale 2014, 39). Faculty governance structures on five CUNY campuses refused to approve Pathways courses. It was within this context that dozens of faculty resolutions rejecting the process of Pathways' implementation and the content of the courses passed. Finally, a vote of no confidence in the Pathways curriculum, sponsored by the faculty union, the Professional Staff Congress (PSC) in the spring of 2013, produced a dramatic outcome. Of the seventy-two hundred full-time faculty at CUNY, more than forty-three hundred voted, and 92 percent voted no confidence.

Why did such staunch faculty resistance emerge in response to management's articulated and seemingly benign intention to solve systemic transfer problems for CUNY undergraduates transitioning from community to senior colleges? To begin with, faculty objected strenuously to the decision to bypass existing governance structures. They argued that it was indicative of management overreach and a violation of a basic precept of university governance embraced widely over the last century that faculty expertise is the linchpin for curricular development and revision. Once that pin is loosened, curricula can be unilaterally changed on the basis of managerial fiat or centralized *diktats* emphasizing matters of efficiency rather than the historic push-pull between the administrative drive for efficiency and the faculty's commitment to quality in course structure and content. CUNY faculty also argued that the Pathways curriculum cheapened the general education of CUNY undergraduates (Vitale 2014, 39; Cooper 2013).

It is necessary to cite a few facts about Pathways that link it to the discussion above about the metrics of graduation rates aligning with cheapened forms of curricula during an era of austerity. CUNY management's claims regarding Pathways are belied by the following facts:

- Management never quantified the extent of the transfer problem between CUNY colleges or across the university. This is especially curious given the sweeping changes proposed by Pathways in the name of seamless transfer (Sailor 2014).
- The impressionistic data cited in relationship to the excess credit problem in the primary management document (the "Wrigley" report) emphasized the lack of availability of course offerings to fulfill graduation and/or major requirements. When combined with a need to take a full load of courses to remain eligible for student grants and loans, the incentives to take additional courses are clear (Wrigley 2010, 1–3).[3] The latter point was consistently

stressed in the Wrigley report as the primary reason for students' accumulation of excess credits.

- Quick and incomplete studies conducted by CUNY faculty on credit transfer issues indicate that the problem is modest when compared to other public universities. The data still do not support the assertion by CUNY management that Pathways is a solution to the problem of transfer (Martell 2012; Sailor 2014).

If Pathways does not solve the problem of transfer, then why was it introduced at all? The answer to that question is, unsurprisingly, embedded in the mushrooming demands of an intensifying regimen of austerity education.

In New York City, 70 percent of public high school graduates attending college enroll at CUNY. The conjunction between this fact and issues of the college readiness of this substantial cohort of public school graduates has had powerful consequences, particularly for CUNY community colleges. The *New York Times* reported in 2011 (about the time Pathways was being conceived) that the number of "remedial students has now swelled so large that the university's six community colleges—like other two-year schools across the country—are having to rethink what and how they teach, even as they reel from steep cuts in state and local aid" (Foderaro 2011, A-21). According to one estimate, eight of every ten New York City public high school graduates who enter CUNY require remediation in English or mathematics (Gonen 2013). To move students more quickly to graduation requires a specific strategy. On the one hand, government can invest more money to promote academic development and encourage faster progress to graduation. This has been done to a limited extent for community college students at CUNY through its Accelerated Study in Associate Programs (ASAP). This enriched remedial program, although expensive, significantly lifted community college graduation rates and reduced time to the associate's degree for participants (Kirp 2014). ASAP, although very successful, has not been scaled up through enlarged investment, with fewer than seven thousand students admitted since its inception in 2007 (City University of New York 2014b). Rather, it languishes at the margins of the educational experience for the vast majority of students attending CUNY's community colleges. In an era of intensifying austerity, the probability of such a major investment in the short term is highly unlikely. This point is further illustrated by recent policy decisions in Florida and Texas to further disinvest in remedial education (Mangan 2013, A-4).

If investment is not an option for most students requiring remedial education, what policy alternatives exist to reduce time to degree and increase graduation rates? The answer to that question for policy leaders is the same as it was for K–12: narrow and cheapen curricula to create a better fit between reduced funding and the need to demonstrate increased productivity. In K–12 the metric of choice is high-stakes testing. In higher education it is time to degree and graduation rates.

As we have seen with Pathways, we are also left to wonder how virtual learning can transform the very meaning of a college degree. How does online learning harmonize with the project of offering a complex and challenging college education? If a college education is entirely or largely structured, for example, through online MOOC-type courses, we can be reasonably certain that per unit costs will sharply decline because of the potential number of students who can be included in a single class along with a declining need for both faculty and students to be in physical classrooms. In turn, the decline in per unit costs and the MOOC form that produces it increases both the profit margins for private companies and expected revenue streams for starved public universities. Alternatives such as blended learning, which use online instruction to complement embodied classroom experiences, may not be as attractive because of their greater costs and diminished or entirely absent profit margins.

Pathways and various forms of online learning, although dramatically different in structure and articulated objectives, have a common thread. They are implemented by administrators as the public university is asked to do much more with much less. It is within this context that Pathways was born, and the use of online learning will likely continue to grow. The incentives to use such programming and technology to generate increased private revenue, improve graduation rates, and assure institutional survival in an era of austerity are substantial. Such a dynamic in turn tends to dilute curricula for students who deserve and require better strategies for improving higher education (Bowen 2012).

Technology as the Tool of Austerity Managers

Matthew Goldstein, former chancellor of CUNY, in a recent speech entitled "The Future of Higher Education" indicated that "despite competitive forces driving pricing policies, as educational offerings and delivery channels (embodied, blended or online) become more challenging universities need to listen to the cues from potential students" (Goldstein 2013). Goldstein's reasoning has less to do with quality than it does with his faith in a business model of education: "Successful businesses and industries," he goes on to note, "watch consumer trends carefully and provide services and products that improve customers' opportunities for the future." As a result, profitability is enhanced, sound investments are made, and quality can be maintained in a business climate that promotes innovation. Goldstein bemoans the fact, however, that faculty governance and "entrenched interests" (read "unions") slow innovation and "promote calcification." And so he concludes that "the threat to the power of new ideas to lower costs and boost quality is the power of entrenched interests to protect their habits." Goldstein's logic and rhetoric are increasingly popular among higher education managers caught in the crosscurrent of austerity policy and sharp restrictions on tuition increases. Innovation and technology are seen as offering a competitive edge in expanding the student census and side-stepping other forms of revenue decline or restriction. Equally important, faculty governance and union structures are perceived as impeding innovation. Higher education managers' need to consolidate their authority over faculty, however, has much less to do with innovation than it does with the need to properly determine "best fit" between academic quality, faculty power, the economics of austerity, and fiscal survival. Faculty have historically had some measure of control over the rhythm and content of their work. This relative autonomy is yet another factor that academic managers must consider as they implement a vision and structure for higher education that aligns with austerity financing. Faculty autonomy and/or control over their work is being destabilized, however, by the rapid adjunctification of the workforce. This dynamic is largely explained by the greater vulnerability of this part of the workforce to managerial exploitation and control as increasing use of contingent teachers erodes the full-time faculty.

In a moment of unstable public financing, slowing rates of increase in student enrollment, volatility of the faculty labor force, and intensified competition among institutions of higher education, academic managers increasingly see the technology of online learning as a way to save public higher education during an era of austerity and rapid change. Technology is uncritically offered up by university managers such as Matthew

Goldstein as the solution to the present crisis, and faculty members' collective sources of power such as unions and governance structures are described as primary impediments to the "innovation" necessary if public higher education is to survive.

Technology, particularly hybrid forms of online learning, represents an important new frontier for higher education that has the potential to both enhance and transform learning.[4] We are not arguing for a knee-jerk rejection of technology uses in higher education; we clearly recognize the value and momentum of current innovations. We are not naïve about either the potential value or specific contexts that define uses of emergent technologies. Technology implementation is not value neutral in highly charged and unstable political and economic environments like colleges and universities.

The present political agenda of disinvestment and reassembly of basic educational services into increasingly mechanized, discrete, uniform, and cheaper forms of educational intervention aligns with some of the proposed advantages of online learning, as we discuss in greater detail in chapter 6. In an environment of heightened attention to the bottom line and monetization of public services, the conjunction between online technology and reform will emphasize a political agenda of diluted curricula, reduced labor costs, maximized profit, and/or diminished per capita investment in instruction. As costs are reduced, the quality of what is offered will continue to suffer. The political-economic forces driving the rapid dissemination of new forms of technology, disinvestment, and profit making will shape and reshape these technologies to meet the demands of an intensifying austerity policy agenda. The content of what is offered online, presently in its infancy, will be structured to align with these dynamics. It is within this context that the very meaning of higher education as a public good is being dramatically changed.

When Matthew Goldstein suggests that higher education can have its cake and eat it too, he is engaged to some extent in weaving a romanticized fantasy that this new technology is a neutral force that managers can harness to transcend present challenges and constraints. We argue in chapter 6, however, that unrestrained implementation of MOOCs, for example, as a panacea for what ails the university will only exacerbate present fiscal tensions while simultaneously degrading the elemental relationship between instructors and students that is an essential precondition to complex, rich learning.

Perhaps most important to this discussion, university managers by and large comply with austerity and profit-making constraints to survive professionally and perhaps even rise in administrative hierarchies (Carlson 2014, A3–A4; Lewin 2014, A11; Erwin and Wood 2014, 3). To be sure, there have been some instances of resistance. For example, the president of the University of Virginia, Teresa Sullivan, was dismissed in 2012 by the school's board of visitors because of her unwillingness to bypass faculty governance bodies in remaking curricula through online learning partnerships, despite intense pressure from the board. Sullivan was subsequently reinstated after an outpouring of faculty and student support in opposition to the board's unilateral actions. The *New York Times* reported that the turmoil leading to her dismissal "opened a window onto the pressures public universities face nationwide, as they grapple with shrinking state support, rising tuition and the pressure to shift resources from liberal art programs to education in business and technology" (Pérez-Peña 2012). Sullivan's challenge to the board's fundamentalist managerial orthodoxy of excluding faculty from critical curricular decision making and reflexively embracing rapid technological changes is the exception, however, not the rule for university administrators. In the absence of university managers who are willing to resist the joining of technology to austerity and profit making, the present trends in public higher education are unlikely to be altered. In 2014 the president of the University of Texas (UT) faced the same kind of power struggle over the future of his school. It pitted UT board members embracing a view that "fundamental change is needed to turn universities into engines of economic development for their states and reduce their roles as centers of scholarship" with a president continuing to be committed to building a more academically and politically autonomous university (Fernandez and Pérez-Peña 2014, A-14). Similar to the University of Virginia, the backdrop for this struggle at UT "was years of declining state subsidies, unpopular program cuts, and tuition increases, and fear of rising competition from online courses" (A-14).

The reengineering of technology to align with goals other than profit making and austerity or, ideally, with an enriched education, will likely emerge out of broad dissatisfaction with degraded working and learning conditions. The addiction to technology, like any other addiction, produces distortions that too often result in a spiral of poor choices. One choice in this instance is to turn over more of the learning environment to vendors of technology that claim to have the tools to reform education, but not the incentives to enhance learning or improve working conditions. Whether this watershed moment produces a bitter or enriched fruit for higher education will be determined by the outcome of battles presently being waged. These conflicts contest the nesting of technology in profit-making and austerity politics as contrasted to using technology as a tool to meet complex learning needs. Clearly, these goals are not complementary.

College Readiness, Low Graduation Rates, and Fiscal Starvation

As noted earlier, graduates of K–12 public schools increasingly lack the basic skills or knowledge necessary to successfully complete higher education. Many high school graduates are simply not college ready (Gonen 2013). Tests indicate that only "23 percent of students in New York City graduated ready for college or careers in 2009. . . . That is well under half the current graduation rate of 64 percent, a number often promoted by Mayor Michael R. Bloomberg as evidence that his education policies are working" (Otterman 2011). Similar numbers regarding college readiness are being registered across the country, particularly in the poorest communities of color in large urban areas. Sean Reardon, a sociology professor at Stanford, has recently completed a study on the impact of race and income on academic readiness. Reardon argues,

> While race once predicted scores more than class, the opposite holds now. By eighth grade, white students surpass blacks by an average of three grade levels, while upper income students are four grade levels ahead of low income counterparts. . . . The racial gaps are quite big but income gaps are bigger. . . . The gap in scores of high and low income students has grown by 40 percent (during the past twenty-five years) even as the difference between blacks and whites has narrowed. (DeParle 2012, A1)

The preparatory academic work of K–12 public education increasingly leaves the poorest students of color severely underprepared to succeed in college. There are many reasons for this, including, but not limited to, the following: underinvestment in K–12 schools in poor communities when compared to their more affluent counterparts; the turnover of teachers and consequent losses of classroom expertise and continuity;

student estrangement from an increasingly mechanized, cheapened, and test-driven curriculum; and, finally, less out-of-classroom learning enrichment than that enjoyed by more affluent peers. Intensifying underinvestment in the academic potential of very poor students, in and out of school, creates substantial barriers to college admission and completion. A large part of this inequality can be traced to austerity policies.

The difficulties poor students face in successfully completing college are not entirely explained by academic challenges. The *New York Times* and other media have, for example, reported that the crushing pressures of accumulating debt and the growing need to work while attending college have disproportionately affected poor and working-class students, stalling and "dead-ending" movement toward degree completion by even the most gifted students. These economic stresses, when combined with academic challenges, have produced a seismic shift in the proportion of poor students earning college degrees. Martha Bailey and Susan Dynarski, economists at the University of Michigan, have reported that "thirty years ago there was a 31% difference between the share of prosperous and poor Americans who earned bachelor's degrees . . . Now the gap is 45%" (DeParle 2012, A-1). Greg Duncan, an economist at the University of California, Irvine, notes that "on virtually every measure we have the gaps between high- and low-income kids . . . widening" (A-1). These data also contain a critical subtext. As the gap in academic achievement between poor and affluent students grows by race and class, it is accompanied by ever-widening income and gender disparities, especially of young males of color. For example, black women undergraduate students at CUNY's senior and community colleges, according to a 2005 *Inside Higher Education* report, "outnumbered [black] men 2 to 1 (a ratio that is quite common nationwide)" (Jaschik 2005). As college entry and completion become more difficult for the poorest students, female and male, their job market prospects are invariably narrowed to taking low-wage work. So, the unequal financing of public education mirrors and reproduces the class, racial, and gender dynamics in the larger political economy as it contributes to a swelling concentration of wealth and income at the top and increasingly meager subsistence wages for an expanding part of the population at the base of the income pyramid.

The stripping away of resources needed to adequately educate very poor students represents a triple betrayal. Present austerity policy making is a betrayal of every student's birthright to a K–12 education that provides the foundational knowledge and skills necessary for entry to college, and more specifically, the capacity to read, write, and solve complex problems necessary to successfully complete college. A second betrayal occurs when public universities are less and less able to meet poor students' academic challenges as they enter college. Investments in necessary remedial support to assure student success, programs that have always been historically deficient, are now diminishing at increasingly rapid rates. Students are more often left to swim in the very fast current of academic expectations without the necessary support or time to upgrade their academic capacities or potential given the financial demands on many of them to hold jobs while attending college. Instead, they incur debt, invest time, and all too often do not graduate, thus failing to realize either their academic potential or develop marketable skills (Carnevale 2012; Eaton et al. 2014). These experiences lead to the third and perhaps most fundamental betrayal: the evisceration of the prospects of a college degree and, in turn, the dimming hope of entrée to the American Dream. As *New York Times* reporter Jason DeParle notes, "there is a growing role that education plays in preserving class divisions. . . . With school success and earning prospects ever more entwined, the consequences carry far: education, a force meant to erode class barriers, is fortifying them" (DeParle 2012). Stanford's Sean Reardon adds: "It's becoming increasingly unlikely that a low-income student, no matter how intrinsically bright, moves-up the socioeconomic ladder. . . . What we're talking about is a threat to the American Dream" (DeParle 2012).

Resetting Course: Investing in Disposable Citizens

The second era of neoliberal reform has created the basis for globalizing, monetizing, and virtualizing the business of higher education. The architecture of electronic technology provides a large part of the basis for shifting the locus to online learning and profit making in higher education across the nation and the globe. It also increasingly intensifies competition for scarce public resources among nonelite universities, threatening their very survival. These changes in higher education are remaking the very meaning of the college experience and the college degree.

It is especially important to remember that the transformative power of the present moment is not class neutral. To the contrary, this second era of neoliberal reform will have especially undermining consequences for the poorest students of color as the first has. As curricula move online and faculty are more likely to be bifurcated into the roles of invisible part-time laborers or prominent academic superstars, the latter helping to draw thousands of students on the basis of name recognition to the world of virtualized education, the experiences of undergraduates will be increasingly determined in the spaces of virtual access. This outcome, unless it is corrected through substantial investment in hybridized online learning and individual mentoring, leaves poor students at a marked disadvantage. The particular learning needs of academically challenged students entering college require enriched forms of face-to-face instruction. Such enrichment is predicated, to a large extent, on the capacity of faculty members to invest the time necessary to build relationships with students as well as those students' actual academic capacities. This kind of pedagogy is best created not exclusively in virtual space with hundreds and even thousands of largely anonymous and physically distant students, but in place-based classrooms. Sadly, in an era of unfettered austerity policy, such investment is unlikely to occur. If this trend persists, then higher education will continue to aid and abet the widening gaps in income and opportunity that are increasingly reorganizing the larger society.

This second-stage moment of neoliberal reorganization creates an increasingly profound threat to public higher education, the public commons, wealth, and, most important, the very fiber of collective responsibility with which strong democratic ideas are woven. The trend toward disinvestment puts an ever-greater strain on a historically fragile but nonetheless continuing commitment to a common democracy and to the future. Present policy ever more expansively emphasizes individual gain at the expense of collective health. And the social and economic cost of this policy is compromising the quality of life for society at large. This is of course occurring within issues as diverse as climate change, rates of incarceration, the loss of civil liberties, and the dimming hope of bettering one's life. As these costs grow, escaping to gated sanctuaries will no longer provide the imagined relief. The forms of fallout—whether illness and pandemic, children living on the street, lawlessness, or dramatic climate change—will penetrate psychological and physical fortresses imagined impregnable.

We believe this darkening future can be relit through strategic forms of public investment that promote fierce engagement with the critical issues of the day. What better place to make such investment than in public higher education, a site that has historically helped provide answers to some of the most vexing questions of democracy, human behavior, environmental threat, and disease? The university has long played a role in transporting the past into the present and future. It has been the repository for our signifiers of civilization, and it continues to be an incubator for reimagining that civilization. Most pertinent to this discussion, the public university, as we indicated in chapters 2 and 3, has served as an instrument for reducing social and economic inequality. It is important not to romanticize the impact of public universities in narrowing racial, class, and gender divides or promoting democracy. And yet it is important to acknowledge that the recent history of public higher education has offered a near universal access to a quality higher education for a growing cohort of citizens. At the moment, however, the public university is not only less able to play such a moderating role, but also increasingly reinforces and reproduces trends of inequality that are growing throughout American society. Policies of austerity and disinvestment largely account for the diminishment of quality of public higher education. How present public higher education practices reproduce inequality is discussed in the next chapter.

[5]

The Public University as
an Engine of Inequality

The crisis facing public and private universities is rapidly intensifying. The combination of deep public budget cuts, unsustainable tuition increases, and greater policy emphasis on rewarding or punishing universities on the basis of "metrics of success" is destabilizing public higher education. This fiscal decay is disproportionately affecting the least elite institutions, which serve the most academically challenged and economically needy students. This unequal impact was described by the credit reporting agency Moody's in 2013 as "assign[ing] a negative outlook for the sector in 2009, but upgrading the most elite ones to stable in 2011–2012" (Martin 2013).

Elite universities are buffered by substantial endowments and predictable alumni support in ways that nonelite public colleges lack. Despite this insulation the same forces battering the public sphere, and more specifically the most accessible schools, are also affecting even the most elite private schools. As Moody's explains, "even the best colleges and universities faced diminished prospects for revenue growth, given mounting pressures to keep tuition down, a weak economy and the prospect that a penny-pinching Congress could cut financing for research grants and student aid" (Martin 2013). Moody's analytical framework is derived from a business model of education. The model advances an agenda to "reduce costs and increase operational efficiency," doing more with less to balance university budgets (ibid.). Moreover, the report describes the increasingly competitive higher education market causing many universities to upgrade their branding and ranking by expanding their number of buildings and increasing student services. These choices are made with increasing frequency at the expense of investment in classroom instruction. Equally important, reduction of costs associated with this business model is linked to an expansion of online learning because it "could also provide new ways to make money and provide schools with broader audiences" (ibid.).

The Moody's report concisely describes the application of business principles to higher education as a public good. Predictably, the application of this framework to public higher education is having both anticipated and unanticipated effects. For example, such an approach assumes that the public university of the present and future cannot depend on government subsidies to sustain, no less expand, its operations. Rather, the university must increasingly rely on tuition, private-sector borrowing, private donations, cost cutting, and technology to survive. These sources of revenue or savings must be judiciously allocated, systematically nurtured, and strategically grown into an ever-larger share of university operations and culture. The interplay between this fiscal restructuring and the redefinition of the meaning of public higher education has received scant attention in the general public. Equally important, the differential impact of these policies by institution, student income, and race remains relatively invisible. The conjunction of fiscal austerity, imposition of a neoliberal business model, and consequent institutional restructuring has resulted in public higher education becoming an active agent in the growth rather than reduction of social inequality. This is perhaps the most important back story of the current radical restructuring of higher education.

Presently there is little political will to increase investment in public higher education as a corrective to the market forces creating ever-greater poverty and inequality. More disturbing, however, is that present higher education policy making is leading public universities to abet and even directly develop practices that produce chronic, growing inequality in the larger social order. Thomas Piketty in *Capital in the Twenty-First Century* suggests we need to "consider first the mechanisms pushing toward convergence, that is, toward reduction and compression of inequalities. The main forces for convergence are the diffusion of knowledge and investment in training and skills. . . . It is fundamentally a process of the diffusion and sharing of knowledge—the public good par excellence—rather than a market mechanism." Alternatively, the unequal diminishment of public higher education as a force for social opportunity, mobility, and increased citizenship participation is exacerbating larger trends regarding inequality (Piketty 2014, 21).

The increasingly powerful role the market is playing in restructuring higher education is expressed through an array of changes affecting every facet of higher education from the wholesale importing of business practices, to the expansion of for-profit colleges, to the capitalization of online instruction, and the conjunction between student debt and capital accumulation. The market, however, is organized to evolve private rather than public goods. More to the point, the imperative of the market is to grow capital or profit, and its inclination to incentivize disparity or inequality in the allocation of expansive wealth and income has implications for how the public good of higher education is presently being reconfigured.

As noted in chapter 2, public goods were historically created in part to redistribute accumulating market wealth and to promote greater opportunity for those at the bottom and middle of the social order. Although redistributive policies have been relatively modest in the United States, this policy intention has characteristically distinguished public goods from private commodities. Policy makers and politicians alike saw public higher education as a means of reallocating or redistributing opportunity. Public education has been described by Georgetown University's Anthony Carnevale and Jeff Strohl, for example, as "a uniquely American third way between the high risk that comes with doctrinaire market fundamentalism and the dependency that comes with an expanded welfare state" (Carnevale and Strohl 2010, 83). Carnevale and Strohl conclude that access to education, particularly "high quality post-secondary education has borne more and more of the weight that comes with the nation's founding commitment to equal opportunity and upward mobility" (ibid.). However, as much as we may disagree with this interpretation of "the nation's founding commitment," it is clear that part of the mythology is the US commitment to broadened opportunity for its citizens and promotion of a more robust democracy. No matter how remote, unstable, and differentially applied, this enduring myth has existed at least in part as a source of social legitimacy for much of US history. As public higher education is increasingly allocated unequally, paralleling the growing monopolization of marketplace wealth, the very legitimating discourse of the American experiment steeped in leveling advantage and creating opportunity is less powerful. This is an especially important contradiction.

British economist Alfred Marshall described public education more than 140 years ago as a basis for "steadily accept[ing] the private and public duties of citizenship." As a public rather than private good it would be "a universal common experience rather than a sorting device." Marshall believed an equality of citizenship could only be assured through access to education and social services. This social contract's premise was that access to education made everyone more equal as citizens and better able "to live the life of a civilized being according to the standards prevailing in the society" (Carnevale and Strohl 2010, 81). Differences in access to a quality education, however, were not mentioned. Carnevale and Strohl indicate that Alfred Marshall's concern regarding "ambiguity on the subject of education as a democratizing force is still germane and is amplified by the increasing stratification of the education system" (ibid.).

The stratification of public education by race and class is a growing problem in both the United States and Great Britain. As noted by Marshall, Americans "rely on education as an economic arbiter more than do other modern nations." Europeans have relied more on policies that invest in a direct redistributive role for the welfare state to reconcile citizenship and markets. "Americans have always preferred education over the welfare state as a means for balancing the equality implicit in citizenship with the inequality implicit in markets" (Carnevale and Strohl 2010, 83). This reliance on education contrasted with a mature welfare state to promote redistributive policies is especially salient in this moment when access to quality higher education is less and less available to the poorest students.

That public education is the most effective path toward middle-class status is both generally accepted and empirically validated. Equally important, it is a fact that quality education has been differentially allocated on the basis of social class and race since the founding of the Republic. Something, however, has changed in the past thirty-five years. Following the rapid restructuring of the economy from manufacturing to service based in the 1980s, the relationship between a college degree and income as well as wealth has grown. Unionized, blue-collar jobs, which had earlier assured a middle-class lifestyle to many Americans, were simultaneously either being shipped away to other parts of the world or replaced by new forms of technology. The shift from an industrial to a knowledge-based service economy pressured job applicants in the re-structured marketplace to get college and postgraduate degrees. This transformation emphasized a college degree as the best bet for securing a well-paying job in an economy where such jobs were becoming increasingly scarce, ever more competitive, and difficult to secure. These trends have been accompanied by policies further disadvantaging the already disadvantaged in an especially volatile political moment. Although the wealthy have always had an "edge" in their own and their children's access to quality higher education, it is presently being widened by public policies that diminish access to a quality postsecondary experience (Goldin and Katz 2007).

Disinvestment in public higher education, dilution of the quality of instruction evidenced in part by the expansion of part-time faculty, and debt financing have been unequally distributed. The next sections of this chapter will more specifically examine fundamental inequalities associated with contemporary policies that are actively restructuring public higher education. There has been a much greater impact on poor students, especially those of color, in recent policy shifts that have reduced public subsidies historically supporting universities and increased the reliance on tuition for institutional revenue. These trends have had especially harsh consequences for community colleges, as well as middle-tier comprehensive colleges and universities. It is important to keep in mind, however, that the inequality seeping ever deeper into the soil of public higher education is not restricted to students. It can also be found in the increasing segmentation of the teaching workforce, especially the reliance on underpaid, part-time instructors. Also, the escalation in the numbers of college administrators, many with outsized salaries relative to those of the instructional workforce, is another marker of growing inequality (Erwin and Wood 2014, 1). In the California State University system, for example, while the number of faculty positions between 1975 and 2008 remained essentially flat at approximately twelve thousand, the total number of administrators more than tripled from thirty-eight hundred to more than twelve thousand in the same years (Campos 2015). What happens inside and outside of public higher education is not preordained or natural; rather, it is, as Piketty reminds us about the general history of inequality, "shaped by the way economic, social and political actors view what is just and what is not, as well as by the relative power of those actors and the collective choices that result. It is the joint product of all relevant actors combined. . . . Furthermore, there is no natural, spontaneous process to prevent destabilizing, inegalitarian forces from prevailing permanently" (Piketty 2014, 20–21).

Unequal Investments in Public Higher Education

Any discussion of inequality regarding access, completion, and readiness for higher education must explore predicate K–12 experiences of poor students. The differential access to a quality education by race and class long entrenched in the K–12 school system is systematically reproduced within higher education (Carnevale and Strohl 2010, 1). The difficulties of catching up and becoming college ready are described by Monica Vendituoli in a 2014 article in the *Chronicle of Higher Education*. The data in that article indicate that low-income, Hispanic, black, special education students, and those for whom English is a second language are "far off track" (Vendituoli 2014). Summarizing the ACT study, completed by Chrys Dougherty, Vendituoli continues: "Students were deemed 'far off-track' by scoring more than a full standard deviation below the 'on track' target of ACT test scores for their respective grades in school" (Vendituoli 2014; Dougherty 2014, 2). The variable of social class was especially powerful in projecting college readiness: "Fourth and eighth graders who qualified for free and reduced-price lunches were less likely to meet ACT standards in all three categories [reading, math, and science] four years later than were students in both grades who did not qualify for the lunch programs" (Vendituoli 2014). Perhaps more important, "low-income fourth graders who lagged behind were much more likely than low-income eighth graders to meet standards four years later" (ibid.). This trend suggests that issues of basic academic capacity and college readiness not only persist but in fact deepen as students approach transitional ages for college entrance.

While the conditions within K–12 public education systematically underprepare poor students for both college and the job market, their ability to attend and graduate from college is further diminished by the reallocation of resources away from need-based financial aid. Although financial aid has always favored full-time, four-year college students, it is increasingly being restructured to meet the needs of relatively affluent and academically prepared students (Cauthen 2009). More to the point, the "purchasing power" of Pell Grants, the nation's largest source of need-based financial aid, has declined precipitously: "When the program was established in the 1970s, grants covered three-quarters of the cost of attending a public four-year college or university. By 2007, the maximum grant covered only a third of such costs" (ibid.). Compounding the decline in Pell Grant funding is the vestigial course credit ceiling for receiving financial aid. The twelve-credit requirement is an artifact of an earlier era when a flat fee bundled with twelve credits per term covered what students needed to graduate on the proscribed schedule (Baum, Conklin, and Johnson 2013). Today, however,

> students in community college and other nonselective schools, unlike many of their counterparts at private colleges and top state schools, have to pay as much as 25 percent more if they want to enroll in 15 hours' worth of classes. Since Pell students get no additional federal support, the 12-hour floor essentially becomes a ceiling. Few can pay without help so they stick with what the program allows, which essentially makes it impossible for them to graduate on time. (Ibid.)

As the federal role in providing grant-based financial aid has declined, colleges are shifting from need to merit-based grants. The pressure of competing for rankings and the importance of enrolling relatively affluent students in an ever more austere public financing environment largely accounts for this change. Jeffrey Selingo, a reporter for the *Chronicle of Higher Education*, remarks that "as the cost of college continued to rise over the past decade—making it difficult for more and more families to pay the full tuition bill, or even close to it—the merit-aid game took another turn. As more and more colleges use aid to play the rankings game, the strategy isn't proving as effective. Now some colleges needed 'merit' aid to discount their prices to affluent students further up the income scale just to fill their classes and balance their budgets" (Selingo 2014, A-30). This point is supported by recently published data. ProPublica, a policy think tank, noted in a recent report that "from 1996 through 2012 public colleges and universities gave a declining portion of grants—as measured by both the number of grants and dollar amounts—to students in the lowest quartile of family income. That trend continued even though the recession hit those in the lowest income brackets the hardest" (Wong 2013, A-16). ProPublica concludes that "when those institutions raise tuition and don't offer more aid, low-income students are often forced to decide not just which college to attend but whether they can afford to attend college at all" (A-16).

Simultaneously, students are being asked to bear an ever-greater share of the burden of the financing of their college educations. Equally important data indicate that the share of tuition increases "retained by public research universities after financial aid expenses were deducted went up by 50 percent during the 2000s—to reach $9,067 per student" (Eaton and Habinek 2013, 2). More to the point, the rate of tuition increase lagged behind growth in funding for student aid. This cost-benefit calculus has had a particularly telling impact on poor and working-class students. In general, the shifting of costs away from financial aid and toward increased tuition is part of the continuing drift toward disinvestment in public higher education.

Suzanne Mettler, a professor at Cornell University, elaborates on this theme of increasingly inequitable access to quality public higher education for three-quarters of American college students. She indicates that public colleges offer the

> best bargain around, yet even there, tuition increases have bred inequality. For those from the richest fifth, the annual cost of attending a public four-year college has inched up from 6 percent of family income in 1971 to 9 percent in 2011. For everyone else, the change is formidable. For those in the poorest fifth however, costs at State U have sky-rocketed from 42 percent of family income to 114 percent. (Mettler 2014, 8)

To fill the gap between college costs and diminished grant aid, an increasing proportion of low- and moderate-income students must work while attending school. Equally important, the number of hours students allocate to work in order to remain in college has grown. The proportion of full-time students who are employed has increased from 34 percent in 1970 to 50 percent in 2000 (Cauthen 2009). As important, in 1970 only about 15 percent of students worked more than twenty hours per week, the standard definition of part-time employment. More than thirty years later that percentage has doubled (ibid.). The conjunction of employment and college attendance is especially consequential for poor and moderate-income students. The more students work, the less likely it is they will either graduate on time or at all. Equally important, obligations outside the classroom affect students' ability to remain engaged with academics inside and outside of the classroom. Nancy Cauthen summarizes the data powerfully when she states, "Research is very clear about the impact of work on student outcomes: Working more than 15 hours per week interferes with students' ability to complete their degrees" (ibid.).

A number of studies have indicated that there is also a growing class and racial gap regarding college completion:

> Matthew Chingos of the Brookings Institution found that low income students finish college less often than affluent peers even when they outscore them on skills tests. Only 26 percent of eighth graders with below-average incomes but above-average scores go on to earn bachelor's degrees, compared with 30 percent of students with subpar performances but more money. . . . These are students who have already overcome significant obstacles to score above average on this test. . . . To see how few earn college degrees is really disturbing. (DeParle 2012, A-30)

Martha Bailey and Susan Dynarski of the University of Michigan, as reported by Jason DeParle, describe the growth in this chasm: "Thirty years ago, there was a 31 percentage point difference between the share of prosperous and poor Americans who earned bachelor's degrees. . . . Now the gap is 45 points" (A-30). Sean Reardon, a social scientist at Stanford, correctly states that income has always shaped academic success but its importance is growing (A-30). We would add that the ever-narrower portal to college access and graduation for poor citizens is not an accident but rather a product of systematic disinvestment in public higher education, reallocation of financial grants from need to merit, and the consequent growing requirement that poor and moderate-income students assume the role of part-time and even full-time workers while attending college.

These trends of restricted access and declining probability of completion for poor students, especially those of color, are occurring at a time when there is almost universal agreement that entrée to better paying jobs is increasingly dependent on earning a college degree. Simultaneously, greater reliance on debt financing to support college attendance disproportionately affects the future earnings of poor students. This point is underscored by a Pew Research Center report that recently summarized Federal Reserve data indicating that the bottom 25 percent of the population on the basis of net worth (less than $8,500) accumulated

TABLE 5.1

National Student Loan Debt Owed as Share of Household Annual Income & Wealth, 2010

	Share of student loan debt owed (%)
Household annual income:	
Lowest fifth (<$21,044)	24
Second fifth ($21,044–$36,723)	10
Third fifth ($36,724–$59,623)	12
Fourth fifth ($59,624–$97,585)	7
80%–89.9% ($97,586–$146,791)	7
Richest 10% ($146,792+)	2
Household wealth:	
Lowest fourth (<$8,562)	58
Second fourth ($8,562–$79,739)	17
Third fourth ($79,740–$311,222)	15
75%–89.9% ($311,223–$982,565)	6
Wealthiest 10% ($982,566+)	3

Source: Fry 2012. Data adapted from Pew Research Center report.

58 percent of the total amount of student debt. Alternatively, the top 25 percent (net worth of $311,000 to $983,000) accumulated only 6 percent of the total debt, while the top 10 percent with a net worth of more than $983,000 held 3 percent of the debt (Severns 2013, 6). Poor students are apparently counting on the fact that they will be able to outrun debt repayments over time on the basis of the anticipated enlarged income yielded by possessing a college degree.

This bet may seem reasonable and rational, but it is also rife with risk. The lack of an economic margin for poor and moderate-income students and their families means that there is little to no cushion to pay off the debt. Also, the share of future income that debt repayment claims is likely to be greater for poor and moderate-income students attending less prestigious universities, which, more to the point, convey less cultural capital than elite institutions attended by relatively affluent students. This lack of cultural capital is in turn more likely to yield interviews for jobs that offer modest salaries. The persistence of racism in the job market also restricts poor and moderate-income students' access to the best-paying jobs. When you add to this circumstance the proportion of poor students who do not complete college, the economic outcomes are both clear and dire.

Claims on future earnings are increasingly destabilizing the economic circumstances of low- and moderate-income students by contributing to defaults on loans and/or diminished opportunities to gain entrée to middle-class status. Recent data indicate that student loans are more likely to be delinquent than any other type of debt. The Federal Reserve Bank of New York suggests that if you exclude borrowers who have deferred their loan payments, the share of delinquent borrowers is more than 20 percent (Severns 2013, 6). The significant role played by for-profit colleges in both expanding the level of debt among poor students, especially those of color, and spiking up their default rates is described by Andy Thomason, a *Chronicle of Higher Education* writer: "Borrowers who attended for-profit colleges represented about 32 percent of all borrowers entering repayment in the 2011 fiscal year, up from 28 percent in the 2009 year, and for-profit-college students accounted for 43 percent of the defaults" (Thomason 2013, A-6). The University of Phoenix, the largest for-profit university in the country, "had the most outstanding federal student loan debt, with 1.1 million borrowers collectively owing $35.5 billion in 2014," according to a fall 2015 *Inside Higher Education* article (Stratford 2015). Moreover, a recent federal report on student loan debt noted that among the 2009 cohort of University of Phoenix student borrowers "about 47 percent had defaulted [on their loans] within five years" (ibid.). We will return to the particular role for-profit colleges and universities have played in the reallocation of federal higher education financing, diminishment of college graduation rates, and heightened economic and educational vulnerability of poor students (especially those of color) later in the chapter.

Cheapening Public Higher Education

Poor and working-class students' tenuous relationship with the job market is further weakened by intensifying pressures to increase enrollment and graduation at public universities. The policy intention to move more students through college more quickly leads to a lowering of academic standards. Without increased financing, and facing an expanding pool of academically underprepared students, public universities face daunting challenges. When these factors are then combined with policies of state-level disinvestment, the content of higher education curriculum suffers.

The policy-level tension in public higher education between quality of experience, time to degree, and austerity has surfaced in Colorado, Texas, New York, California, and Wisconsin (Berrett 2014, A-19; Nocera 2013, A-14). Carol Geary Schneider, president of the Association of American Colleges and Universities, which advocates for quality in undergraduate liberal arts education, recently remarked: "It seems to me that the completion engine has hurtled down the track with a lot of states putting in financial rewards and penalties for speeding up completion and cracking down on excess credits. Then there's the quality engine, still struggling to get out of the shed" (Berrett 2014, A-19). The penalties of a diluted curriculum are especially burdensome for poor students who are most likely to attend especially underfinanced public institutions, including community colleges and midlevel state colleges and universities.

Any discussion of higher education as an incubator of inequality by policy design must connect the otherwise disconnected phenomena of individual debt, expansive efforts to finance college tuition through loans, relatively low rates of college completion, and the slotting of poor students into the most underfunded institutions of higher education. This linkage is essential to understanding how public policies intensify both individual struggles to attend and complete college and institutional struggles to adequately invest in classroom instruction. These trends combine to create a postsecondary system of education that is an active agent in driving growing inequalities by race and class. It is to this part of the story that we now turn.

Jason DeParle reported in the *New York Times* in December 2012 that education plays a growing role in preserving class distinctions. Poor students have long trailed affluent peers in school performance, but from grade-school tests to college completion, the gaps are growing. With school success and earning prospects ever more entwined, the consequences carry far: education, a force meant to erode class barriers, appears to be fortifying them (DeParle 2012, A-1).

All colleges are not created equal, and the hierarchy within higher education is extremely stratified on the basis of investment per student, institutional resources to assure a quality education, and postgraduation employment opportunities. The most underfinanced institutions of higher education also have the highest concentrations of poor students of color.

According to Carol Hoxby, a professor at Stanford University, institutions of higher education are ordered into the following categories: most selective, selective, and least selective (Carnevale and Strohl 2010, 112). Hoxby has suggested that the ever-greater differential investment of resources across these institutional types is in large part a consequence of "growth in a national admissions testing regime, the nationwide reach of communications and information technologies and lower transportation costs" (112). She suggests that the growing investment disparity by institutional type is linked to a postsecondary system with increased vertical stratification: "In 1967 the least selective colleges spent in (2007 dollars) about $3,900 per student and the most selective schools about $17,400, with other colleges fanning out in between—a difference of $13,500. By 2006, the low-selectivity colleges had resources of about $12,000 per student and the most selective colleges had about $92,000 per student, a difference of $80,000" (112). Community colleges, which disproportionately serve the poorest and least prepared students, suffered the greatest financial hardships. The Delta Cost Project, a nonpartisan agency investigating university financing, reported that "historic enrollment increases combined with sharp losses in per-student revenues from state appropriations and meager increases in net tuition revenue, resulted in significant cuts to academic spending per full-time equivalent (FTE) student. Community colleges concluded the decade spending less per student than they had ten years earlier" (Desrochers and Kirshstein 2012, 1). Nationally, across all types of public higher education institutions, data indicate that "while state spending on higher education increased by $10.5 billion in absolute terms from 1990 to 2010, in relative terms state funding of higher education declined. Real funding per public FTE dropped by 26.1 percent from 1990–1991 to 2009–2010" (Quinterno 2012, 3). Equally important, "states collectively invested $6.12 per $1,000 in personal income in 2010–2011, down from $8.75 in 1990–1991, despite the fact that personal income increased by 66.2 percent over the same period" (3).

The current population of young adults is "much larger in size, much more racially and economically diverse and more apt to enroll in college" (Quinterno 2012, 3). Thus, policies of disinvestment have been especially harmful to the expansive educational aspirations of poor students of color. Intensifying disinvestment has occurred as the cohort of whites within the college-age adult population (eighteen to twenty-four) declined between 1990 and 2010 from 71.7 percent to 57.2 percent (3). There is a clear relationship between declining per capita investment in public higher education and the shifting racial composition of colleges.

Policies of disinvestment have been especially acute in California and New York State. In New York State, for example, funding for both SUNY and CUNY fell from $5.43 billion in 2007 to $4.72 billion in 2011, a 13 percent decline (Hiltonsmith 2013, 1). Funding per full-time student (FTE) has declined by 17 percent since 2007 (1). At Berkeley, the University of California's (UC) flagship campus, a 32 percent increase in tuition and corresponding public cuts were enacted in 2010 (Gardner 2013, A-20). The California State University system (CSU) also experienced repeated funding cuts, which were described in a memo from Benjamin Quillian, the chief financial officer of CSU. This memo "requires administrators to report their plans for significant reductions in the faculty and staff workforce as well as drastic cuts in student enrollment" (California Faculty Association 2010, 1). In California, the higher education state budget per FTE declined between FY 2007–08 and 2011–12 by 28.2 percent. Moreover, the higher education system in California "was now in the middle of the worst financial crisis since the Great Depression. In the last year, the state has cut $750 million from the system's budget. This year, for the first time, the system receives more from tuition than from state aid" (Medina 2012, A-14).

Obviously, state disinvestment from public higher education has had deleterious impacts on the quality of higher education. This is a result of increased class sizes, higher course loads, reduced time for teacher-student interactions, and the narrowing of educational content. An especially telling statistic is that between 2003 and 2012, state-level investments nationally in higher education declined by "12 percent overall while median tuition rose 55 percent across all public colleges" (US Government Accountability Office 2014). California offers a representative example of state disinvestment in public higher education. Most important to this discussion, California data underscore the relationship between budget cutting endemic to austerity policy, the differential impact on poor students, especially those of color, and consequent diminished access to and quality of public higher education.

California's public higher education system encompasses more than 140 separate campuses divided across its three-tiered structure. The economic precarity of the state's students as measured by the percentage of the student body receiving Pell Grants is greatest in community colleges

(53 percent), less acute in the California State system (39 percent), and relatively modest in the UC system (20 percent) (Johnson 2014). This conjunction between increased rates of relatively poor students and the status of each of three tiers of the California system is not an accident. It is the result, rather, of conscious decisions by policy makers more than six decades ago when the vaunted Master Plan was approved. In general the poorest students attend those schools that are the most underfunded. These trends have been exacerbated by recent dramatic cuts in state funding in the last five years, significantly affecting every part of the system.

The entry level for higher education in California is the Community Colleges system, which educates more than two million students annually within its 112 separate campuses. In addition, the CSU system has 23 separate campuses and a student body of more than 450,000. Finally, the UC system, focused on research institutions, has 10 campuses and a student populace of nearly 240,000.

In general, the community colleges serve a larger number of students of color and individuals from lower-income backgrounds, while Latinos and African Americans tend to be underrepresented in the UC and CSU systems. For the fall 2014 semester the undergraduate student body in the UC system was 25 percent white, 22 percent Latino, 36 percent Asian, and 3.7 percent black, out of a total of 194,812 students (University of California 2015). The composition of the CSU system undergraduate enrollments in fall 2014 was 26.5 percent white, 29 percent Latino, and less than 4.4 percent black (California State University 2014). Within the California Community Colleges system, however, Latinos made up 42.7 percent of enrollments, blacks comprised 6.6 percent of the student population, and whites 28.1 percent (California Community Colleges, Chancellor's Office 2015). In recent years, the community college system has seen a dramatic reduction in its black student body, especially black males. One study found a 17 percent decrease in black student enrollment in the community colleges between 2008 and 2012 (Bohn, Reyes, and Johnson 2013). These findings are summarized by Hans Johnson of the Public Policy Institute of California: "At both UC and CSU, and among transfer students from the community colleges, Asians and whites are overrepresented (relative to their share of all high school graduates), and Latinos and African Americans are underrepresented" (11). Johnson (2012) notes, "Overall, the evidence suggests that . . . the university enrollment rates of recent high school graduates have declined for each of California's four largest ethnic groups (Latinos, whites, Asians, and African Americans). Declines are sharpest among African Americans and are the lowest among Latinos" (12).

In his 2012 study on the defunding of higher education in California, Hans Johnson noted that "despite large increases in the demand for higher education, state general fund spending in this area has declined notably over the past ten years. California spends more on corrections than public universities" (Johnson 2012, 1). The California State legislature in a draft 2014 bill on higher education funding pointed out that in "the 1970s, the State General Fund provided $12 for every dollar that students paid in fees. By 2009, this figure had fallen to $1.40 for every dollar in student fees" (California Legislative Information 2014).

Johnson (2012) has pointed toward a number of strategies that the public higher education system has employed to manage decreases in funding: "cutting courses, programs, and student services, as well as making administrative cuts," limiting enrollments, and shifting costs onto students (2). Each of these austerity measures has had a dramatic impact on educational access and quality. As suggested earlier, these shifts have affected all three tiers of the California system of public higher education. For example, the community colleges have focused intensely on expanding online courses (Johnson, Mejia, and Cook 2015). For many working-class students and families, particularly families of color, the net impact has been to divert access to education and saddle individuals with increasing amounts of student debt, which disproportionately affects them (Huelsman 2015). While community colleges have faced cuts and reduced access that disproportionately affect students of color, the UC and CSU systems have also had to respond to budget cuts in ways that disproportionately affect low-income and working-class students of color.

The UC system slashed staffing to save money. According to one UC budget document (University of California 2012), "more than 4,200 staff have been laid off and more than 9,500 positions have been eliminated or remain unfilled since the most recent fiscal crisis began." This report also indicated, "Over 180 programs have been eliminated and others consolidated for an estimated savings of over $116 million" (S-17). Tuition was increased substantially, doubling between 2004 and 2014 (Tatum 2014). Subsequently, students took on increasing indebtedness, with more than half of UC students incurring debt to underwrite their education in 2012 at higher amounts than they had to in the past (ibid.).

The UC system, which is legally obligated to offer an enrollment option to all eligible students, has also decreased its enrollment targets and limited access to its most prestigious institutions, especially UC Berkeley and UCLA. Balancing the promise of the public's free access to higher education while restricting access to the most elite campuses has been managed by referring students who are eligible for UC admission to other campuses, which serves in many instances to divert students from attending a UC program at all (Johnson 2012). Johnson concluded, "Many students and their families might be willing to pay tuition of $13,000 per year at [the more prestigious] Berkeley or UCLA but not at [the less prestigious] Merced" (8). Unlike the UC system, the CSU system is not obligated to enroll eligible students. Accordingly, CSU denial rates have skyrocketed over the past decade—"from fewer than 4,000 applicants . . . in fall 2008 to almost 15,000 applicants . . . in fall 2011" (8).

Perhaps most telling in regard to inequitable student funding, particularly as it has interacted with the economic crisis, was the watershed 2011 state audit of CSU financing (California State Auditor 2011).[1] While noting that the budgeting process for allocation of state general funds was extremely difficult to decipher and upon inquiry was explained by administrators in generalizations that they did not quantify, the state-auditing agency also pointed out the stark differentiations in per-student expenditures by race. The state auditor said, "Although we found no evidence that the Office of the President considered the racial or ethnic makeup of the campuses' enrollments as part of its budget process, the process resulted in lower-than-average per-student base budgets for the four campuses that have a higher proportion of students from underrepresented racial or ethnic groups" (37).

Since the publication of this audit, the CSU system has initiated "rebenching" to make its funding allocation process more equitable (Kiley 2013). However, the results of rebenching have not yet been fully evaluated, and concerns have been raised by advocates and legislators because of the increasing proportion of out-of-state students migrating to the CSU system, who pay higher rates of tuition. Legislators have called for a state audit of the process, with the chair of the state's Legislative Audit Committee stating, "We cannot wait years to determine whether our

TABLE 5.2

Share of California Student Financial Aid by Institution and Source, 2011–12

	Pell Grant (%)	Other federal grants (%)	State grants (%)	Local grants (%)	Private scholarships (%)	Institutional grants (%)	Total, all sources (%)	Total amt. of aid[a] (millions of $)	No. students (FTE)	Aid[b] per FTE[c] ($)
CSU	39	1	53	0	1	6	100	1,929	353,900	5,450
UC[d]	20	8	7	0	8	57	100	1,723	236,707	7,278
Private nonprofit, 4-year	8	3	6	0	19	64	100	2,557	282,332	9,057
Private for-profit, 4 year	52	27	11	0	0	10	100	617	133,676	4,616
Community college (see note)	53	5	35	2	2	4	100	3,104	790,216	3,928
Private for-profit, 2-year	84	6	10	0	0	0	100	485	111,669	4,347
Private for-profit, <2 year	96	2	2	0	0	0	100	197	62,251	3,612

Source: H. Johnson, Public Policy Institute of California, 2014. Estimates based on IPEDS Data Center (NCES) and California Board of Governors waivers reported by California Legislative Analyst Office.

[a] Distributions are based on total dollar value.

[b] Aid amounts vary by institution type.

[c] FTE (full-time enrollment) includes all students.

[d] "UC" excludes UCSF Medical School and Hastings Law School.

policies are effective, and when students are facing tuition increases, it is our responsibility to ensure that their sacrifice is not wasted. . . . That is why I am requesting this new audit to assess the Universities' initiatives that impact per-student funding, the methods for determining resident and nonresident enrollment targets, and to examine the compensation for UC top executives" (Gipson 2015).

As noted throughout this section, a key statistic in understanding the relative impact of recent budget cutting in California is the differential investment in students by race as well as a college's position in the hierarchy of the three tiers of higher education. Specifically, where poor Latino (36.7 percent) and black (7.2 percent) students were most concentrated during 2011, community colleges, the aid per FTE was $3,928. For undergraduates in the CSU system, which has the next greatest concentration of Latino (30.7 percent) and black (5.1 percent) students, the level of aid per FTE during the same time period jumps to $5,450. Finally in the UC system, where the share of black (3.7 percent) and Latino (19.3 percent) students is lowest, the aid per FTE spikes to $7,278. Clearly, many factors affect these differential allocations of student aid. However, what cannot be disputed is that as students are slotted into more elite public colleges the proportion of black and Latino students declines and the FTE aid increases. This in turn likely produces greater difficulty for poor black and Latino students in managing the expenses of college and gaining access to more elite and presumably more qualitatively enriched experiences of higher education. Each of these points is illustrated in table 5.2.

Qualitative Shifts in the Experience of Public Higher Education

Expansive disinvestment and inequality in higher education are also affecting the quality of classroom instruction. For example, the *New York Times* reported that the UC system does not offer the same quality of education as even a decade ago (Medina 2012, A-14). This situation is particularly acute for CSU and the community colleges, the middle and bottom tier of the state's tripartite higher education system. These unevenly distributed cuts have had profound national implications for higher education curricula.

According to the Delta Cost Project, these budget-cutting trends have been exacerbated by the massive recession that began in 2008. The Delta authors note that nationally, in 2010, "community colleges suffered the greatest financial hardships" and "the deepest cuts in state and local appropriations per student"; "all types of institutions spent less on the academic mission"; and "public funding per student for higher education reached a decade-long low." "Sharp increases in net tuition revenues were not enough to offset these losses, and for the first time, public research and master's institutions generated more revenue from net tuition than from state and local appropriations" (Desrochers and Kirshstein 2012, 1, 3).

Private and public investment per college student has grown in direct relation to selectivity and student test scores (Carnevale and Strohl 2010, 94). Stated more simply, the more selective the institution, the greater the per capita investment in students. Even more concretely, "per student, per year investment at two-year public colleges has declined, and spending at four-year public colleges has remained flat, but spending per student at private colleges has increased by 8 percent at schools giving only a baccalaureate" (97). Stacy Berg Dale and Alan Krueger found that college selectivity produces robust postgraduation earnings that result from the greater resources available to students who attend selective colleges (115). Because poor students of color are most likely to attend either community colleges or less selective four-year public colleges, they are therefore least likely to attend flagship or elite public or private universities (115).

There is a growing understanding within policy-making and business circles that the highest per capita student investments should be made in those individuals most likely to maximize personal opportunities from receiving a quality or elite education. Students not defined as "elite or gifted" are expected to bear the costs of diminished investment in higher education. Current policies of unequal investment in postsecondary education as measured by per capita student expenditures across college type further benefit the already advantaged while disadvantaging poor and moderate-income students who require greater academic and social supports to succeed. Clearly the logic and outcomes coursing through the larger social order producing expanding inequality are penetrating and redefining higher education as well. In higher education, however, these processes, practices, and outcomes have been produced as a matter of conscious policy design.

The unequal impacts of public disinvestment are compounded by the need of fiscally stressed colleges to borrow in order to survive. Public universities are "less able," Kevin Kiley has argued in an *Inside Higher Ed* article, than "their private university competitors to fund capital improvements with philanthropic gifts [. . .] public universities have and will continue to turn to the debt market to fund capital projects, driving debt for public universities higher for the foreseeable future, and prolonging a long-term trend established over the past decade" (Kiley 2012). In part, this borrowing Kiley suggests is accounted for by ongoing public disinvestment that has produced "aging campuses, several years of backlogged maintenance projects, increased competition for students (and the tuition that comes with them) and little hope that states are going to fund the construction they need" (ibid.). It is anticipated that these costs will in turn be passed on to students, a risky long-term assumption at best because those attending public institutions are disproportionately the most economically disadvantaged. Equally important, nonflagship or less elite public universities' access to cheap debt is constrained by statutory regulation. Highlighting the issue of growing institutional inequality is the fact that "for institutions where growth is stagnant, particularly comprehensive public institutions in states with a shrinking number of college-aged students, the financing change represents a real problem" (ibid.). Ultimately, these social forces are going to have a powerful and unequal impact on public higher education. Over time we are seeing "all of these forces coming into alignment. [. . .] You've got aging campuses, less capital, more borrowing, colleges are running up against debt limits, backlogs [of need] are going up to a point of critical concern, where problems are going to be very, very noticeable soon" (ibid.).

Increasingly, public colleges, particularly those that are least selective and especially underfinanced (community and four-year state college systems) have fewer and fewer options and face a growing number of fiscal dilemmas. For example, do they decide to hold off on renovations and maintenance while incurring debt in the short term only to produce more expensive renovations and the need for greater borrowing in the long term? Another dilemma involves trading off faculty or student services essential to a quality education to invest in capital projects that address fundamental issues of expanded instructional spaces and facility decay. In the end, such choices affect both the quality of the higher education experience and the competitiveness of the school in the market for new students. As these trends affecting resource-starved institutions grow, "the institutional hierarchies that result seem frozen in place, with few opportunities for transitions between the upper tier of selective four-year colleges and the lower tier of non-selective four-year institutions and community colleges" (Carnevale and Strohl 2010, 160). The growth of inequality can be traced in part to this ever-larger stream of debt financing intended to stave off the worst effects of consistent disinvestment. It is important to keep in mind that the very same dynamic of relative deprivation and debt financing for already marginalized segments of the citizenry led to growing fiscal instability in the housing market and larger economy in 2008.

It is within this context that the Georgetown Public Policy Institute has gone as far as to argue that the "postsecondary system is more and more complicit as a passive agent in the systematic reproduction of white racial privilege across generations" (Carnevale and Strohl 2013, 1). The Institute's report indicated that "African-American and Hispanic students who are prepared for college are disproportionately tracked into crowded and underfunded two-year colleges and open-access four-year colleges" (8). The "slotting" into relatively underresourced colleges results in students of color receiving less per capita public investment in their educations. In this way, "the postsecondary system leaves a substantial number of qualified minorities on educational pathways that don't allow them to fulfill their educational and career potential" (8). The authors of this report also note that "between 1995 and 2009, more than eight in ten . . . new white students have gone to the 468 most selective colleges and more than seven in 10 of . . . new African-American and Hispanic students have gone to the 3,250 open-access, two- and four-year colleges" (8). The authors continue, "More than 111,000 African-Americans and Hispanics who graduate from high school each year in the top half of their class do not achieve a two- or four-year degree within eight years. If these students had attended one of the top 468 colleges and graduated at similar rates, 73 percent would have graduated" (11).

The association between differential investment, institutional type, and student outcome is clear. "The completion rate for the 468 most selective four-year colleges is 82 percent, compared with 49 percent for open-access, two- and four-year colleges." The Georgetown authors conclude, "Virtually all of the increase in drop-out rates and the slowdown in completions are concentrated in open-access colleges in substantial part because they are too overcrowded and underfunded" (11).

The relationship between per capita investment in students and quality of education provided by a college is also explained by the makeup of instructional staff. Those public colleges suffering the greatest disinvestment are increasingly reliant on relatively cheap, part-time instructors. Part-time faculty as a proportion of the total instructional workforce has exploded over the past thirty years. Between 1975–76 and 2011 the rate of growth for part-time instructors was 221.7 percent as contrasted with an increase of only 23.4 percent in full-time faculty during that same period (Curtis 2014, 21). And, not surprisingly, the proportion of part-time faculty varies dramatically in relation to institutional type. The number of part-time instructors increases significantly when tracked from the most to the least selective institutions in terms of admissions. For example, in the fall of 2011 the proportion of part-time faculty was 72.3 percent in for-profit institutions, 70.3 percent in community colleges, 50.3 percent in master's-level programs, and 19.9 percent in doctoral and research programs (21).

For part-time faculty members cobbling together a living as adjunct faculty within the academy, there is far less time to meet with students outside of the classroom. Contingent full-time instructors need to move from class to class, often at multiple institutions, to sustain a minimal income to survive, while their lack of benefits or job security undermines their capacity to effectively support and instruct students. We will revisit the phenomenon of part-time or contingent labor later in this chapter. For the purposes of this part of the discussion, however, it is important to note the trend lines that indicate a strong association between targeted disinvestment, increased utilization of part-time faculty, and the hierarchical status of a college. It is within this context that poor students are systematically undermined in their pursuit of a college degree. Their greater personal indebtedness is buying a public good or postsecondary education in an accelerated state of decay.

Ironically, as President Obama and major foundations advance a policy agenda of "double-digit increases in [college] completion rates a cross section of states are rolling back remedial programs" that are essential for preparing academically underprepared students for higher education (Mangan 2013, A-8). From Texas to Florida to Connecticut, state legislatures are restricting access to remedial support services and programs. In Connecticut, these services are limited to one semester. Texas lawmakers are simply looking to dramatically reduce remediation costs "and put more students directly into college classes, bumping many of its least prepared students from remedial education to adult basic education" (A-8).

Public disinvestment and new measures of institutional accountability, such as reduced rates of tuition increases, are cohering into a financing crisis for public higher education. Tuition freezes will result in an expansion of student access. What remains unanswered is what greater access will yield for poor students. These tuition freezes will be accompanied by policies that continue to degrade public higher education programs by disinvesting in students with the greatest academic challenges. The immediate realities of remedial education cutbacks, heightened demand for metrics incentivizing reduced tuition, and a fiscally parched landscape promoting disinvestment in public goods can best be understood in the context of historically inequitable investments by race and class in K–12 schools. Only through this more complex analytical lens can we more fully see why the record of time to degree completion and rates of graduation are especially disappointing in the lowest tiers of higher education. Current federal and state policies of disinvestment in public higher education unequally undermine the academic progress of poor students, especially those of color, who require greater support to successfully transition from high schools to college and progress to graduation.

Social policies designed to incentivize reductions in time to degree and increased rates of completion through "metrics of accountability" are troubling precisely because they mask the role of disinvestment in degrading both the outcomes and experiences of public higher education. These standards must be accompanied by a sense of public responsibility for greater investment especially in the lowest-tier schools if they are to be regarded as anything more than a cynical policy-making exercise. Equally important, as Carnevale and Strohl (2010) note, "there is very little excess capacity in much of the public system, where all the new students are crowding in and there are already quality deficits. In the public institutions, especially the community colleges, overcrowding, capacity shortages, and increases in enrollment in combination with declining per-student investments have resulted in declining quality" (91). They go on to point out that "absent specific goals for including minorities and low-income students, the combined effects of affordability and accountability goals can lead to a self-reinforcing spiral of inequality" (91). We would further suggest that this kind of policy making is also prompting colleges to rewrite curricula and dilute course requirements to meet new federal requirements of higher completion or graduation rates.

The Ascent of For-Profit Colleges

The steady descent of public higher education has been accompanied by the rapid ascent of for-profit colleges. This phenomenon has contributed to a further intensification of unequal access to quality postsecondary college experiences by poor and frequently academically underprepared students. The rapid growth of for-profit colleges is underscored by data on "For-Profit Higher Education" collected by the US Senate Committee on Health, Education, Labor, and Pensions. In their 2012 report the committee noted that "Pell grants flowing to for-profit colleges increased at twice the rate of the program as a whole, increasing from $1.1 billion in the 2000–1 school year to $7.5 billion in the 2009–10 school year" (US Senate 2012, 2). Equally important, "the share of revenues received from Department of Education Federal student aid programs increased more than 10 percent, from 68.7 in 2006 to 79.2 in 2010." The growing conjunction between for-profit expansion and public revenue financing is perhaps most powerfully illustrated by the fact that "the 15 publicly traded for-profit education companies received 86 percent of revenues from taxpayers" (2). In fact, the proportion of financing for for-profit colleges is about 86 percent greater than for most public colleges.

This explosion in public financing of for-profit colleges joined a rapid increase in the number of degrees awarded by these institutions. By 2010, for-profit colleges granted 77 percent more associate degrees and 136 percent more bachelor's degrees than they had in 2004 (US Senate 2012, 2). Of the nearly six hundred thousand students who enrolled in for-profit colleges in 2008–09, "54 percent left without a degree or certificate by mid-2010." The US Senate report went on to note that among those seeking two-year associate degrees enrolled in for-profits, "63 percent departed without a degree" (4–5).

Especially germane to the larger discussion in this chapter, the yield of graduates relative to public dollars invested is far worse in for-profit colleges than in public postsecondary institutions, and yet tax levy dollars continue to pour into for-profit schools. In 2009–10, according to a study conducted by Democrats in the US Senate, the for-profit "sector received $32 billion, 25 percent of the total Department of Education student aid program funds" (US Senate 2012, 2). For-profit colleges are much more expensive to attend than community colleges, which draw their student bodies from comparable demographic groups, and for-profit graduates are much more likely to incur much higher indebtedness and to end up unemployed, according to a fall 2015 Brookings Institution report (Looney and Yannelis 2015). Yet for-profit schools continue to eat up inordinate amounts of federal student loan dollars. The reasons for this counterintuitive trend, especially in an era of ever-greater calls for accountability, are not without irony. For-profit colleges offer the least efficient yield of graduates to public investment, and yet recent public policies emphasizing private sector principles to increase the productivity of public colleges are not equally applied to their private-sector counterparts. We will return to this contradiction later in the section.

Ninety-six percent of students enrolled in for-profit colleges take out loans as compared to 13 percent of those attending public community colleges and 48 percent of students at public senior or four-year colleges (US Senate 2012, 7). Equally important, for-profit college students borrow much more to finance their degrees; 57 percent of the students graduating from for-profit colleges owed, on average, $30,000. In contrast, 12 percent of students graduating from public sector schools assumed a comparable debt load (7). Student default rates in fiscal year 2011 were also significantly higher in the for-profit sector. Borrowers from "for-profit colleges represented about 32 percent of all borrowers entering repayment in the 2011 fiscal year, up from 28 percent in the 2009 year, and for-profit-college students accounted for 43 percent of the defaults" (Thomason 2013, A-6). A single for-profit company, Education Management Corporation, partly owned by Goldman Sachs, collected $11 billion in student tuition fees between 2003 and 2011, 90 percent of it in federal student aid (Saul 2015, A17). Even after federal regulatory tightening in 2012, 100 for-profit schools with student loan default rates that exceeded 30 percent still received $116 million in student aid from the US Department of Education in 2014 (Cohen 2015). Successful efforts to steer an expansive pool of low-income and minority students to for-profit colleges are in large part carried out by a substantial cohort of for-profit staff recruiters. Investors' demands for profit growth put significant pressure on recruiters to enroll "a steady stream of new student enrollees or 'starts'" (US Senate 2012, 3). Profit margins are sustained by increasing growth in the student census and imposing relatively high tuition rates. Especially salient is that the tuition cost of a degree is 20 percent higher in for-profit colleges than in flagship public universities, and the cost of associate degree programs averaged four times the cost of degree programs at comparable community colleges (3).

Relatively low investments in faculty instruction also bolster the bottom line of for-profit colleges. A sample of for-profit companies showed they dedicated 22.7 percent of all of their revenue to marketing and recruiting; the profit margin of this subgroup of was 19.7 percent. Alternatively, only 17.2 percent of all revenue was spent on instruction. Particularly significant for this discussion, for-profit colleges spent less on instruction than on either marketing or recruiting (Kirkham 2012).

To sustain a steady stream of students willing to pay relatively high tuition, the US Senate Committee report noted that "recruiting materials indicate that at some for-profit colleges, admission representatives were trained to locate and push on the pain in students' lives" (US Senate 2012, 4). Further, as the Senate report notes, "they were also trained to 'overcome objections' of prospective students in order to secure enrollments." The report continues, "Companies trained recruiters to create a false sense of urgency to enroll and inflate the prestige of the college" (4). The performance of every employee of the college from the recruiting team to the admission staff was rated on the number of new students they enrolled.

Instructional costs in for-profit schools are relatively low because of a great reliance on part-time faculty. The US Senate report pointed out that "in 2010, 80 percent of the faculty employed [in for-profit colleges] was part-time. Ten companies had more than 80 percent part-time faculty and five companies had more than 90 percent part-time faculty" (US Senate 2012, 5). Arnold Mitchem, president of the Council for Opportunity in Education, testifying before the Senate, noted that "first of all we have to understand that there's a radical difference in educating and graduating a low-income first-generation student than there is a middle class student." He continued, "In the for-profit sector they address the financial barriers, but they have not adequately addressed the supportive services barriers" (4).

We would argue that the financial barriers for students attending for-profit institutions are little different than for their counterparts attending traditional colleges, public or private. Students can gain access, but only at the exorbitant cost of high tuition, increased personal debt, and the high probability of not graduating or finding adequate employment postgraduation. That is a rather ruinous transaction of cost versus yield for already vulnerable students.

We believe that it is fair to argue that, on the basis of substantial public revenue streams subsidizing for-profit colleges and private wealth accumulation, there should be clear standards of accountability. Recent history, however, suggests otherwise. Accountability demands have effectively been fended off by well-financed for-profit lobbying campaigns. And while lobbying protects for-profit higher education from accountability, it also serves to systematically redistribute public dollars away from public institutions. In this way it widens the gulf between poor youths, especially those of color, and the rest of the population in securing access to a quality postsecondary education.

What differentiates for-profit colleges from public institutions is their primary purpose: to earn dividends for investors and stockholders. This goal consciously and systematically functions as an engine for inequalities of debt, declining quality of education, dropout rates, and predatory practice. As more and more public resources are rededicated to for-profit colleges, we can expect spikes in the challenges faced by the very poor, including economic crises, inadequate job skills, and, if they are even able to finish their programs, degraded degrees and certifications. Poor people of color are left with stark choices as they move down the pyramid of colleges. Every step down creates greater economic burdens and a misfit between learning needs and the college curriculum that is supposed to meet those needs. Why, then, do for-profit colleges continue to have legitimacy in a moment when their record is so poor?

The for-profit college sector is an especially powerful opponent of the Obama administration's efforts to regulate and sanction postsecondary institutions with unsatisfactory student dropout, default, and indebtedness rates. The lobbying comes in many forms. For example, Donald Graham, past chairman and chief executive of the *Washington Post*, which at the time generated most of its revenue from Kaplan Education, visited Senator Tom Harkin, chair of the US Senate committee investigating for-profit colleges in 2010 as his committee was holding hearings on the for-profit industry. John Sperling, founder of the University of Phoenix, the largest for-profit institution in the country with more than 425,000 students, emailed every member of Congress "seeking help opposing the regulations" (Lewin 2010, A-16). Relatively faceless for-profit colleges elevated employee profiles in their lobbying campaigns to resist the regulation of the institutions they managed or owned. For example, as *New York Times* reporter Tamar Lewin pointed out, "the Education Management Corporation, the second-largest for-profit company, hired DCI Group, a public relations firm, to contact its employees for information that would be used to create a personalized letter" to be sent to legislators (A-16). In addition, as Eric and Joel Best reported in the *Chronicle of Higher Education*, "the ferocity with which the [Association of Private Sector Colleges and Universities] lobbies against the most modest gainful-employment and default rules is telling. While those institutions correctly point out that they often cater to unconventional and at-risk students, those are reasons to encourage more regulation in the sector, not an excuse to relax standards" (Best and Best 2014, A-33). They conclude by noting that "operating an educational institution is a privilege and a great responsibility, and those that are not willing to put students first should be gradually wound down with little public concern beyond the cost of eliminating those institutions" (A-16).

The power of the Association of Private Sector Colleges and Universities (APSCU) has been widely reported, particularly related to its opposing regulation. Chris Kirkham, reporting in the *Huffington Post*, noted the association's "mount[ing] federal court challenges to nearly every new regulation the Obama administration has proposed regarding the industry." Further, "since the Department of Education began crafting stricter regulations for the industry in 2009, [APSCU] has significantly increased its lobbying efforts, spending more than \$4 million on lobbyists since President Obama took office, according to disclosure forms" (Kirkham 2012). Arguing against such strong-arm tactics, student advocacy groups have consistently asserted that for-profit colleges' dependence on public money demands that the government both regulate and monitor their spending (ibid.).

Some politicians have noted, however, that the lack of public oversight of for-profit colleges has contributed to their destabilization. For example, the closing down of American Career Institute, Corinthian Colleges, and American Enterprises got "the attention of [Maryland] senators, who wrote to the US Department of Education to ask why oversight agencies missed the problems that led to the colleges' closures and how the 'triad' of state and federal regulators and accrediting agencies could be improved to prevent future closures" (Field 2013, A3). These shutdowns have exacerbated the difficulties faced by students in for-profit colleges as they have had to wait for refunds on loans, find alternate colleges, halt their progress toward a degree, and transfer credits. This level of instability, creating friction between profit-making ambitions and the provision of a quality education, is even affecting the giant of for-profit colleges, the University of Phoenix. *Inside Higher Education* reported in 2013 that the "accreditation woes are more serious than the for-profit giant had been told to expect, with a site team from its regional accreditor recommending . . . that the university be placed on probation because of concerns about a lack of autonomy from its holding company, the Apollo Group" (Fain 2013a).

Yet another indicator of growing inequality within postsecondary education is the expansive income gap between contingent and full-time faculty. Equally important, the role, influence, and incomes of university administrators have dramatically expanded, frequently at the expense of faculty. Each of these issues will be examined in the remainder of the chapter.

Accountability in an Era of Austerity

As noted in the earlier section, President Obama and a range of foundations have called for greater accountability for colleges receiving federal funds to assure higher rates of graduation, accelerated movement to graduation, lower accumulated debt, and improved postgraduation employment. What remained unaddressed, however, was the need for a systematic "unpacking" of the impact of federal rating systems on the distress levels of public colleges. It is important to note at the outset that although these federal goals are independently laudable and especially salient in an era of high student debt, relatively low graduation rates, and shrinkage in the number of well-paid jobs, they must be viewed within the larger framework of austerity and disinvestment politics. These goals should be applied with special rigor to for-profit colleges because of the low level of investment these institutions make in instruction and student support services. The disparity between public revenue directed to students inside and outside of the classroom and resources channeled to recruitment and profit making must be investigated and properly regulated.

These issues, however specific to for-profit institutions, must be separated from the circumstances of public colleges and universities.

The proportion of revenue directed to classroom instruction in public universities remains quite high in comparison to for-profit institutions. The vexing issue for public universities is the intensification of public disinvestment. We have already addressed the phenomenon of disinvestment in public postsecondary education. The question that must be addressed here is how federal and state accountability systems presently under consideration will likely exacerbate diminishing opportunities for poor youths of color to either attend public colleges or, once there, to receive a quality postsecondary education.

On a road trip undertaken in late 2013, President Obama traveled across the country to "shame universities into easing costs." He noted that it was time for the federal government to "stop subsidizing schools that are not producing good results" (Shear and Lewin 2013, A-18). The president said he would urge Congress to pass legislation to link student aid to a new rating system that would emphasize relative cost, graduation rates, and speed to graduation. In response, Jane Wellman, the executive director of the National Association of System Heads, noted, "The federal government has never been in higher education policy before—it has just administered financial aid—and I'm not sure that you can just take that role and stretch it like a rubber band" (Shear and Lewin 2013, A-18). Caroline Hoxby, a Stanford University professor, went further, indicating that the effort would simply fail. She said, "I do not believe the federal government currently has the capacity to generate a ratings system that would even be neutral. . . . I think it's more likely it will be harmful to students." She went on to note, "Let's say you looked at Harvard, Yale and Stanford. . . . You'd say they have all of these great outcomes. But that doesn't necessarily mean that's the value added by those colleges because their students were terrific to begin with" (Kaminer 2013, A-1).

Representatives of public colleges have pointed out that withholding aid from poorer performing institutions is especially unfair to low-income students, because they more frequently choose schools based on geography and are not likely to cross state or county borders to attend another school (Thompson 2013). Bradley Bateman, president of Randolph College—a private school focused on the liberal arts—concurs that the new ratings system will have an especially severe impact on public institutions that have been historically underfunded and serve the most academically underprepared students. He notes that these "colleges are also relatively poor themselves, and do not have the ability to work with at-risk students in the same robust way as wealthier schools" (Bateman 2013). The American Enterprise Institute, a politically conservative think tank, suggested that "basing incentives for colleges on student success could end up rewarding institutions for whom they admit rather than for how well they educate their students" (Blumenstyk 2014, A-9).

An especially compelling critique of this emergent federal policy argues that incentives are being created that will increase the probability of colleges turning away the least prepared students (Mangan 2013, A-16). Kevin Carey, director of the Education Policy Program at the New America Foundation, a nonprofit, nonpartisan research organization based in Washington, indicates there are few "incentives to enroll students who face the greatest financial and preparatory challenges. . . . That . . . is a powerful, powerful headwind to change" (Stripling 2013, A-4). Gary Rhoades, a professor of higher education at the University of Arizona has discerned a relationship between the embrace of metrics, the completion agenda, and quality of education. In critiquing a report by Complete College America (CCA), funded by the Bill and Melinda Gates Foundation (which echoes President Obama's reform proposals), Rhoades noted that it places "the production of graduates and degrees— over academic quality" (Fain 2013b). Although the CCA report acknowledged that a lack of attention to quality is a serious concern and should be addressed through analog metrics, Rhoades remains unconvinced that such a project would have any significant yield. "The fixation on narrow, reductionist measures of (undergraduate) completion underemphasizes professional and graduate education, knowledge creation, and the preparation of citizens for a democratic knowledge-based society" (ibid.).

The linkage of "student performance" metrics and state funding is likely to disproportionately affect open access community college and state systems already systematically underfunded. In turn, they are ever more likely to cut instructional corners for the neediest students because of the evaporation of funding. To stay afloat, these institutions that are already heavily reliant on part-time faculty will most likely expand use of both online technology and cheaper labor costs via hiring of more contingent teachers to balance their budgets. The ever-greater reliance on contingent faculty is likely to further exacerbate trends toward inequality.

Cheap Part-Time Labor as an Austerity Fix

Earlier in the chapter, we discussed the nexus between part-time faculty and diminished access of poor students to a quality education in public, postsecondary institutions. The story of growing inequality within the academy, however, cannot and should not be entirely seen through the experiences of students. To the contrary, the rapid growth of contingent academic labor is also a significant factor in the inequitable restructuring of higher education and must be independently examined. At the same time, the particular experience of part-time faculty earning all or most of their livelihoods within the academy offers a wider lens for viewing the relationship between the conditions of student learning and instruction. Between 1975 and 2003, full-time, tenured college faculty positions declined from 37 percent to 24 percent of all faculty positions (Curtis 2014, 6). The vast majority of the replacement faculty positions filled in the last quarter century were contingent, and these numbers have swelled since the 2008 recession. Part-time faculty constitute over half of the professoriate. The 2014 congressional report "The Just in Time Professor" notes that "more than one million people are now working as contingent faculty and instructors at US institutions of higher education, providing a cheap labor source even while students' tuition has skyrocketed" (House Committee on Education and the Workforce Democratic Staff 2014, 1). The conjunction of increased student tuition and indebtedness with increased reliance on part-time faculty is not accidental. As state funding has been withdrawn, public universities have relied on cheap academic labor and rising tuition to keep afloat financially. Public university managers are tacitly complicit because they have failed to point out the link between student debt, soaring tuition, and the intensified exploitation of a cheap labor force. Instead, university managers have silently adapted to this circumstance by shifting the fiscal burden onto students and contingent faculty to sustain the university.

The low wages of part-time faculty are well documented. The Coalition on the Academic Workforce recently estimated that "the median pay for a standard three-credit course is $2,700" (House Committee on Education, 5). The House report found that "a large number of respondents [to the congressional survey on contingent faculty] reported making between $15,000 and $20,000 per year, at or mostly below the federal poverty line for a family of three" (5). The report continues, "In contrast, the median salary for a full-time faculty member is $47,500" (6). To achieve a comparable wage, a part-time faculty member must teach seventeen courses per year. Alternatively, a full-time faculty member's workload ranges between four and eight courses per year (6). Part-time faculty also have little access to health care benefits and little to no job security. The inequality in wages, benefits, and job security between part-time and full-time faculty and the resulting need of contingent instructors to cobble together a living in an increasingly harsh academic and economic environment produce other consequences, heightening inequalities of instruction.

Both the Campaign for the Future of Higher Education (CFHE) report "Who Is Professor 'Staff' And How Can This Person Teach So Many Classes?" and the congressional report "The Just in Time Professor" describe the strong association between part-time faculty status and quality of instruction (Street et al. 2012, 1). The CFHE report persuasively argues that part-time faculty working conditions undermine learning conditions for students inside and outside of the classroom (1). Surveys conducted by both CFHE and the congressional oversight committee indicate part-time faculty are often contacted about their availability to teach just before a class is to begin. This practice in turn erodes instructors' abilities to properly prepare their courses. The narrow window between contracting for a course and teaching it is linked to a lack of support, financial or otherwise, to invest in developing a syllabus or course notes. It requires that contingent labor prepare classes "just in case" they get a last minute contract to teach them (6). This structural dynamic erodes the quality of instruction.

In addition, quality of instruction is undermined by part-time faculties' inadequate access to essential materials such as "syllabi, curriculum guides, libraries, office spaces," and technology (Street et al. 2012, 5; *New York Times* Editorial Board 2014, A-22). Impediments to securing such key teaching resources also undermine the provision of a quality educational experience for students. Equally important, the lack of compensation for holding office hours for students and the low-priced piecework of contingent labor also affect the quality of instruction. Although contingent workers often carve some time out of the classroom for student meetings, they are hard-pressed to sustain such contact because of their especially difficult schedule of courses, a result of the necessary connection for many adjuncts between basic economic survival and the large number of classes they must teach. The work demands of traveling between classes, campuses, and university systems to meet basic material needs in combination with inadequate or nonexistent office space result in diminished out-of-classroom instructional encounters between part-time faculty and their students.

A recent editorial in the *New York Times* reinforced these points by noting that a report based on seventy-one thousand teachers "found that part-timers faced many challenges." The report, released by an institute at the University of Texas, found that "because they are treated almost like transient workers, they are given little reason to make an investment in the institution." The report went on to note, as the *Times* editorial board pointed out, that instead these workers are implicitly told, "Just show up every Thursday at 5 o'clock and deliver a lecture to your class. Give a midterm and a final exam and then turn in a grade and the college will pay you a notably small amount of money." The editorial board goes on to note—in a decidedly understated manner—that the situation is "especially undermining for students from disadvantaged backgrounds" (*New York Times* Editorial Board 2014, A-22).

As noted earlier, part-time faculty are concentrated in the middle and bottom tiers of public colleges and nonprofit universities. It is important to reiterate that this dynamic in turn has implications for the quality of instruction afforded to the most academically challenged students. The interplay between disinvestment, disproportionate withdrawal of public funds from the most underfunded colleges stimulating greater reliance on cheap labor, and diminishment of educational investment in students by race and class is the result of policies implicitly or explicitly designed to grow inequality.

Managing Public Universities in a Time of Inverted Priorities

The decline in the number of full-time faculty and the concomitant growth in part-time instructors have been accompanied by a growing trend of rapid increases in the number of high-level administrators. According to Rudy Fichtenbaum, between 1991 and 2011 the number of high-level academic administrators increased by 35.9 percent and the number of other full-time noninstructional professionals grew by 110.5 percent in public two-year colleges (Fichtenbaum 2014, 3). Fichtenbaum contrasts this to the number of full-time faculty, which grew by only 18.5 percent during the same period (3). This reallocation of resources to upper administration took place as student enrollment increased by 31 percent over those two decades. The disjuncture between expanded enrollments and reduced investment in classroom instructors is striking. Equally important, the choice to make disproportionate investments in noninstructional full-time administrators and/or staff is at the very least curious and at worst a poor allocation of resources (3). The data for four-year public universities are similar to these trends in community colleges.

An expanding dual labor force is emerging within the public university. On one track are relatively well-paid infrastructural and managerial jobs, a growing institutional priority. On the other is a corporate model of education that increasingly relies on a cheap and part-time classroom instructional workforce to wrest greater "efficiencies" out of public university budgets. This investment in noninstructional support and managerial staff can be explained in many ways, including, but not limited to the following:

1. the corporatization of public universities and the creation of more elaborate command and control structures centralizing information, monitoring the workforce, and extending the authority of managers;
2. austerity politics, which drives demand for increased centralization ostensibly to "wring inefficiencies" out of public systems;
3. an increased number of university administrators with nonteaching and nonacademic backgrounds defining resource allocation, undervaluing investment in classroom instruction, and overvaluing investment in administrative and support services, including technology; and
4. increased demands of regulatory reporting to federal and state entities.

The growing inclination of top-level university management to invest in out-of-classroom administrative staff is underscored by a recent report by the Delta Cost Project. It indicated, according to a *Chronicle of Higher Education* article by Scott Carlson, that "the number of full-time faculty and staff members per professional or managerial administrator has declined by 40 percent" between 2000 and 2012, or to a ratio of about 2.5 to 1 (Carlson 2014). More specifically, there were declines nationally, in some cases sharp ones, in the ratio of full-time faculty members to administrators between 1990 and 2012 in various types of public and private colleges and universities, a key measure, along with the explosion in adjunct hiring, of the rapidly changing nature of the higher education workforce. Public research universities, for example, experienced a 37 percent drop in the full-time faculty-to-administrator ratio in this twenty-two-year period, while in public bachelor's colleges the ratio declined 42 percent. Community colleges had the most modest shift, a drop of about 18 percent. The changing ratios of full-time faculty positions to administrative staff positions between 1990 and 2012 by university type are illustrated in table 5.3.

Considering these hiring trends in higher education over the past two decades, Howard J. Bunsis, a professor at Eastern Michigan University and a member of the AAUP's Collective Bargaining Congress, wasn't surprised by the conclusions of the Delta study. "You see it on every campus," he told Scott Carlson, "an increase in administration and a decrease in full-time faculty, and an increase in the use of part-time faculty." Bunsis concludes that "what's broken in higher ed is the priorities, and it's been broken for a long time" (ibid.; Campaign for the Future of Higher Education 2015, 6–7).

The pay disparity between faculty and administrators is yet another indicator of growing inequality within the academy. This chasm is most vividly illustrated through the salaries of presidents relative to faculty. Full-time faculty salaries nationally "were essentially flat," in the words of the Delta report, between 2000 and 2012 (Carlson 2014). The typical

TABLE 5.3
Ratio of National Faculty and Staff Positions to Administrator Positions, by University Type, 1990–2012

University type	Faculty and staff positions per administrator positions, by year		
	1990	2000	2012
Public research universities	3.5	2.7	2.2
Public master's institutions	4.5	3.4	2.5
Public bachelor's colleges	4.3	3.3	2.5
Public community colleges	5.5	5.6	4.5
Private research universities	3.2	2.5	1.9
Private master's institutions	3.2	2.6	2.0
Private bachelor's colleges	3.3	2.5	1.8

Source: Carlson 2014. Data adapted from Delta Cost Project report (Desrochers and Kirshstein 2014).

public college president earned three times more than a full professor in 2010–11. Increasing numbers of college presidents, however, stray very far from the mean presidential salary of $421,395. For example, E. Gordon Gee, former president of Ohio State University (now president of the University of West Virginia), earned close to $2 million annually, as did the president of the Texas A&M University system, Michael McKinney (Stripling and Fuller 2011, A-1). Ten public university presidents (including McKinney and Gee) earned between $750,000 and $2 million in 2009–10 (Stripling and Fuller 2012, A-4).

The ascent of very highly paid public university presidents was recently reported in "The One Percent at State U: How University Presidents Profit from Rising Student Debt and Low Wage Faculty Labor" from the Institute for Policy Studies. In an interview with the *New York Times*, the report's co-author, Marjorie Wood, noted that "universities that have top-heavy executive spending also have more adjuncts, more tuition increases and more administrative spending" (Lewin 2014, A-11). Wood and Erwin, the IPS report's authors, reported that as students went "deeper in debt administrative spending outstripped scholarship spending by more than 2 to 1 at state schools with the highest-paid presidents." They went on to indicate that "average executive pay at the top 25 [public universities] rose to nearly $1 million by 2012—increasing more than twice as fast as the national average at public research universities" (Erwin and Wood 2014, 3).

The issue of debt within the academy is not restricted, however, to students and tuition. As public funding has plummeted for higher education, university borrowing has escalated. Like their students, public universities have developed a debt problem. As Charles Eaton and Jacob Habinek, doctoral students at UC Berkeley, have noted, "the rising burden on the students is partly driven by the indebtedness universities have taken on" (Eaton and Habinek 2013, 1). This debt is largely traced to the cost of capital construction projects increasingly financed through the private market rather than government. More to the point, between 2002 and 2010, "the total debt liabilities of public research universities increased by more than 50% or $26,615 per student—and debt service payments went up by more than 86%." These increased borrowing costs are largely passed on to students through increased tuition (1).

Within the politics of public disinvestment and austerity, specific managerial goals emerge. There is an intensified focus on diminishing labor costs, "rationally raising tuition," and "judiciously" enlarging university debt to keep public universities afloat. The elite administrator is rewarded or punished on the basis of how well or how poorly these goals are met. In essence, these goals represent a zero-sum game of university fiscal survival at the expense of faculty and students. These dynamics are not surprising and are illustrative of the elite managerial embrace of an inequitable public higher education reform agenda, in turn producing rising inequality within the academy.

Every segment of higher education must adapt to both social inequality and being an active participant in driving increasing levels of inequality. The shift in public higher education is particularly advanced and acute. From accelerated degradation of the quality of education for poor students of color caught in the web of inequitable policies of investment and outcome; to the growing use of part-time faculty stripped of job security, subsistence wages, and benefits; to the evolution of an expanding managerial elite wedded to protecting their status and implementing harsher policies to assure institutional survival in a more hostile, austere political environment, the ingredients for the academy's increasing role as an agent of social inequality are cohering.

As austerity policies restructure the purposes, educational experience, and culture of public higher education, the very meaning of the institution is radically altered. Politicians, policy makers, and public university administrators are increasingly employing a set of "objective" metrics to assess the value of public higher education—including time to graduation, reduced expenses or "efficiencies," completion rates, postgraduation employment rates and income to justify ever-deeper cuts in public subsidies. The economic aspects of this equation increasingly define the policy agenda, determining winners and losers on the basis of the simplest indicators of completion and alumni incomes. Although these are important indices of success, they are highly incomplete and secondary to the most critical work of making a robust postsecondary educational experience available to every citizen. A quality education is best assured through public investment in smaller class sizes, increased out-of-classroom time for instructors to meet with students, a much larger full-time faculty, regard for the professional expertise and autonomy of faculty members, expanded student and employee support services, universal access to college assured by needs-based support, and university managers who understand and actually support the mission of a public university. The shift away from this larger conception of higher education as a public good has been accompanied and made possible by the ascent of cheapened, privatized forms of higher education, especially for poor and working-class students.

Christopher Newfield, a faculty member at UC Santa Barbara, remarks that the "regulative ideal was that even if you couldn't get into the most selective universities—Harvard, Oxford, et al.—you could receive an education of quality similar to what you received there" in a public university. He continues, "Massive public funding enabled this rough equalization, this evolving democratization, of academic quality." Newfield concludes that "active learning is a *public good*, of great benefit to society and of little negative benefit to the organization that conducts it." If the investment in a quality higher education is cheapened at precisely the moment that specific skills are ever more precious in an increasingly volatile, mobile, and competitive global economy, where does that leave graduates of the most underfinanced public colleges providing increasingly standardized and cheapened forms of education? We would suggest that it leaves them largely unprepared for the best, albeit increasingly scarce, high-paying jobs. "What is the loss?," Newfield asks. His answer: poor and working-class students receiving the cheapest forms of education will in turn "receive lower wages, cost society less money, [and] learn to make fewer demands" (Newfield 2013, 4–6).

As the American economy faces increasing challenges in response to broader global competition, there is downward pressure on wages while there is a growing need for a workforce with highly evolved skill sets. At the same time, the relationship between a college education and achieving a middle-class lifestyle is less and less likely. As a matter of policy, investment in public higher education is seen as a losing proposition, especially for the poor and working classes in a declining economy. The defeatism of such policies joins college access to a cheapened public good that offers less and less possibility for lifting economic and intellectual fortunes postgraduation. In this way, the propagation of inequality within the public university is joined to the growth of inequality in the larger social order. The achievement of a college degree historically offered a legitimating marker of historic success in gaining entrée to the middle class. It also stabilized social relations in the short run by hewing closely to the basic tenets of meritocratic belief in rewarding individual initiative and personal worth. Over time, however, as cheapened degrees lead to intensified relative deprivation, the legitimation of such relationships will be washed away. To apply Newfield's insight about Great Britain's policies to the United States, "at the heart of the government's higher education plan: there is and shall be no collective betterment and thus no need for collective investment" (Newfield 2013, 6).

The "brave new world" of austerity public higher education and its active role in enforcing as well as expanding inequality is increasingly joined with and encouraged by the introduction of new forms of online learning. We begin with the assumption that the technology of online learning is value neutral. This technology is capable of making extraordinary contributions toward increasing access and quality. At the same time we should not be naïve. The use and value of online learning will be influenced by the context shaping and deploying it. It will be affected by the growing inequality presently reorganizing the experience of public higher education; the degree to which agents external to the university are defining the development, application, and intentions of technologies; and the extent to which participatory democratic processes led by faculty and students produce instructional innovation. It is to this vital aspect of the present and near future of public higher education we turn in the next chapter.

[6]

Technology as a "Magic Bullet" in an Era of Austerity

The history of early industrial capitalism teaches us that the implementation of new technologies in workplaces to improve efficiency and productivity is hardly a value-neutral proposition or process. Who controls the implementation and pace of technological change, and the stated rationales for and impact of its introduction, is vital. Labor historian Herbert Gutman aptly noted, "Technological change never occurred in the abstract. . . . Technology altered power relationships inside the factory, but power relationships always affected the introduction of technology and its consequences" (Gutman 1987, 251). These relationships often determined who benefited from and who was exploited by such technology-based transformations of work and work relations. Applying that fundamental insight about technological change to contemporary universities and colleges is essential to understanding the motivations of many academic administrators with respect to instructional technology. This is especially the case in this moment of austerity budgeting in higher education. Given that labor costs constitute upwards of 75 to 80 percent of all university budgets, they are the obvious place to target if one's goal as an administrator is to contain or reduce operating expenses in an era of austerity. As Karl Marx noted about nineteenth-century industrial capitalists, contemporary academic administrators have two choices to realize labor savings: they can draw on the massive reserve army of the unemployed, in this instance replacing full-time faculty with part-time, poorly paid, and exploited adjuncts; or they can introduce various forms of mechanization of instruction and basic administrative functions to increase academic and administrative productivity. Twenty-first-century academic administrators have at their disposal the same tools and techniques textile manufacturers in England during the 1860s utilized: sweated labor and technological innovation. But unlike early capitalists, who felt little need to justify their use of new technologies beyond their desire to increase their profit margins, university leaders are prone to making arguments for the digital transformation of their institutions via grand appeals to justice or the broadening of democratic access to higher education.

This chapter explores the historical background of contemporary public and private university administrators' embrace of computer-based technology as a "magic bullet" to solve a range of issues facing their institutions. This enthusiasm has occurred, not coincidentally, at the same time as tuition costs at public and private universities have skyrocketed, tax support for public university systems has sharply declined, and private for-profit colleges such as the University of Phoenix have fundamentally challenged public universities' historic role as providers of higher education for large numbers of poor and working-class students. For-profit institutions met this challenge by ensuring easy access to higher education through aggressive recruitment and enrollment of tens of thousands of underprepared students, especially students of color, and by rapidly deploying a variety of fully online programs and services. Traditional public- and private-sector higher education institutions—spurred in part by the dramatic early successes in the 1990s of the private, for-profit universities, which were further enabled by a student loan industry and venture capitalists committed to generating profits from distance education—soon initiated a series of their own online-learning experiments. In general, these efforts by traditional universities used digital technologies to decouple or at least decenter existing faculty and pools of new students from physical classrooms. This experimentation with distance learning outreach by major private and public universities first emerged in the midst of the "dot-com" bubble, an economic distortion that dramatically and temporarily inflated the US economy in the final years of the twentieth century. These early digital initiatives were designed to quickly launch traditional universities into online/distance learning that was expected to yield enhanced reputations and higher revenues. While these early online university ventures ultimately would fail, continuing fiscal and enrollment pressures on public and private, nonprofit universities in the dozen years since the dot-com bust led to continued attraction to and embrace of digital technologies.

These post-2000 digital efforts by college and university administrators took two basic forms, nonprofit (e.g., the free and open posting of digital syllabi, course materials, and videotaped lectures online for a broad public and international audience seeking access to educational materials) and profit generating, both using online formats to generate new students and (in the case of profit-generating programs) new revenue streams. MOOCs took center stage beginning in 2012 in debates about universities' digital futures, straddling both nonprofit and profit identities. Academic administrators, supported and often forcefully led by their boards of trustees, expressed growing enthusiasm for MOOCs and related online course delivery systems. Public and private, nonprofit universities had three principal, often overlapping aims in embracing MOOCs: to allow fast entry of their schools into the online technology to help contain rising operating costs; to bolster institutional reputations by building university "brands"; and (hopefully) to generate revenue in an era of increased fiscal austerity.

Digital technologies, including (or perhaps especially) MOOCs, have often been seen and prescribed as a panacea for the welter of problems and concerns facing contemporary higher education, both public and private, a universal solution that assumes all classrooms are homogeneous spaces where everyone learns the same way and where knowledge can simply be downloaded. MOOCs are but the latest illustration of the imagined power of such technological interventions to fix the growing problems of higher education, especially the viselike grip of austerity in the form of reduced public financing that increasingly defines much of the contemporary public higher education landscape nationally. Yet, with astonishing consistency, while they rush to embrace the newest technologies, most contemporary college leaders suffer from a kind of collective historical amnesia in understanding what various educational technologies in the distant and immediate past promised and proved unable to deliver to their institutions and higher education more generally.

Expanding beyond Classroom Instruction

Tracing the historical origins and evolution of instructional technologies allows us to better understand the logic and genesis of administrators' enthusiasm for these technologies in our own time. The point of origin of the instructional technology revolution on college campuses was the correspondence course. It was conceived in the final decade of the nineteenth century and made possible by the "cheap postage stamp," as one of its early proponents aptly described it. Correspondence "instruction" by mail was implemented by two very different forces: entrepreneurs capitalizing on increased public interest in vocational training and university leaders hoping both to protect academia from private-sector competition and to generate new sources of revenue (Bittner and Mallory 1933, 3; Ferster 2014, 19–24; Noffsinger 1926, 99–120; Noble 2001, 5).

International Correspondence Schools (ICS), the nation's largest and most successful proprietary correspondence school, launched the entrepreneurial movement in 1892. Over its first quarter century, the company offered more than three hundred instruction-by-mail courses on a range of vocational subjects that several hundred thousand students studied. By the mid-1920s total student enrollment nationally in correspondence schools was four times that of US colleges and universities combined (Noffsinger 1926, 12–13, 16; Noble 2001, 6). Correspondence schools emphasized the notion of self-paced instruction, just as online education does today, in which the typical correspondence student according to one advertisement, "works at his own tempo set by himself. . . . He can begin when he likes, study at any hours convenient to him, and finish as soon as he is able" (quoted in Noble 2001, 7).

Public and private nonprofit colleges and universities felt compelled to compete with the for-profit correspondence schools by mimicking their mail-order delivery methods. The University of Chicago began the first university-based correspondence program, its "Home Study Department," in the same year that ICS was founded. The University of Chicago offered credit courses to students unable to attend classes on its campus. These courses were taught, according to technology critic David Noble (2001), by "an assortment of instructors, readers, associate readers, fellows, lecturers, associate lecturers, and assistants . . . paid on a piece rate basis—roughly thirty cents per lesson. . . . In order to make out, the Home Study instructors were compelled to take on a large volume of work that quickly devolved into uninspired drudgery" (11). This description of academic labor evokes a social reality similar to that of contemporary adjunct instructors in our own digital era. This should come as no surprise since the intention in both historical epochs has been to drive down instructional costs.

Many public universities soon followed Chicago's lead. The University of Wisconsin–Madison launched its Correspondence Teaching Department in 1906, and the public universities of Oregon, Kansas, Minnesota, and California quickly followed (Noble 2001, 15; Bittner and Mallory 1933, 19–20, 25). By 1919, seventy-three public and private universities were offering correspondence courses, and all placed a heavy public relations emphasis on the democratization of education as the rationale for their programs. They also focused their attention on tapping into "the lucrative market exploited by their commercial rivals" (Noble 2001, 9).

The correspondence course market, which expanded dramatically in the 1920s, was indeed lucrative, generating $70 million annually (almost $1 billion in today's dollars) in tuition fees. This revenue figure was one and a half times greater than the combined tuition fees received by all the colleges and universities in the country (Noffsinger 1926, 69). The financial success of these correspondence courses was in large part a consequence of the aggressive recruitment tactics of a bevy of high-pressure salesmen, anticipating by almost a century similar efforts by online, for-profit colleges in our own time. The correspondence schools devoted as much as one-third of their mail-order revenue in the 1920s to extensive publicity, including illustrated advertisements in popular magazines (the mass media of their day), which one critic aptly described as "frauds" designed to snare "gullible and inexperienced youth," practices roundly condemned by business groups and governmental agencies alike (Bittner and Mallory 1933, 27; Noffsinger 1926, 38). The same critic estimated that the course completion rate in a representative sample of private correspondence schools was 6 percent, strikingly parallel to the student completion rates in many of today's MOOCs (Noffsinger 1926, 54, 66). Many of the college and university correspondence programs, while understandably intent on separating themselves from the taint of the 1920s proprietary correspondence school scandal, continued, nonetheless, to use their own correspondence programs several decades longer to maintain their universities' "pecuniary gains" (Bittner and Mallory 1933, 1).

Traditional forms of higher education instruction were further expanded by the invention of audio-visual media in the early twentieth century. Thomas Edison was so enthused about the prospects of the educational uses of early films, for example, that he claimed in a New York newspaper in July 1913, "Books will soon be obsolete in the schools. Scholars will soon be instructed through the eye. It is possible to teach every branch of human knowledge with the motion picture. Our school system will be completely changed in ten years" (quoted in Saettler 2004, 98).[1] Like the predictions of almost all techno-enthusiasts, Edison's was wildly off the mark. However, his optimism was understandable, given the unprecedented surge in the creation and widespread dissemination of various audio and visual communications technologies in the four decades that followed. Beginning with silent films and then sound films and broadcast radio, business leaders, philanthropists, and educators formed marriages of convenience to try to incorporate each of these new technologies into classroom instruction, largely at the K–12 level, but also in colleges and universities. Their efforts were driven by several, often conflicting purposes including the urge to democratize education, to make classroom instruction more efficient and thus more cost effective, and, for many, to generate profits. But the embrace of each of these technologies ended in failure. While some colleges and universities latched onto film as a teaching medium in the first half of the twentieth century, use of film never developed a secure foothold in university instruction or public outreach efforts. The biggest producer of educational films turned out to be the federal government, which used them as a means of public information, education, and propaganda, especially after US entry into World War II (Saettler 2004, 106–9).

Radio, the dominant mass communications medium for entertainment and news after its commercial launch in 1920, seemed to hold greater possibilities for classroom use. Several public colleges and universities, including the University of Kansas, Oregon State College and the universities of Wisconsin and Michigan, created educational stations—"schools of the air"—in the 1920s, which broadcast history lectures, foreign language lessons, music programs, and selected faculty lectures to the general public (Davidson 2006, 115). Although some university administrators in the 1920s and 1930s thought that radio broadcasts of recorded lectures might spur college enrollments or generate positive publicity for their colleges, no one quite figured out how to make money from the idea. This led prominent college leaders such as Columbia's Nicholas Murray Butler to dismiss radio with "indifference and condescension" (Saettler 2004, 197–98, 202).

By the 1940s, however, several of the national radio broadcast networks succeeded in forging working relationships with various colleges and universities by offering credit-bearing courses on the air. NBC, for example, created *The NBC University of the Air,* linking its Chicago-based *World's Great Novels* radio series to the universities of Louisville and Tulsa and Washington State University, which offered college credit to listeners who enrolled in "radio-assisted correspondence courses in literature," an interesting combination of forms (Dunning 1998, 728). But *The NBC University of the Air* proved to be an exception. Most college and university leaders' interest in radio took the form of outreach efforts to the general public via free cultural programming rather than specific instructional, for-credit, and tuition-bearing courses via radio broadcast. As Paul Saettler concludes, before the 1940s college educators were "generally apathetic toward educational radio broadcasting," as they had been toward educational film (Saettler 2004, 204).

Television proved to be an entirely different story. With its rapid and all-encompassing spread as a mass communication medium in the early 1950s, broadcast television embodied the aspirations and possibilities of postwar American society, not only as the primary vehicle for the commercialism and consumerism that shaped and even defined the country in these decades, but also as a means of making democratic education widely available. American political and business leaders made a very large bet on expanding higher educational opportunities in the United States for millions of returning World War II veterans, along with their children, who were born in the postwar years. Despite an enormous building boom in colleges and universities in the quarter century after the war's end, especially in public systems, there were still not enough seats and, more importantly, not enough qualified teachers to meet the seemingly insatiable demand for expanded higher education opportunities (Ford Foundation 1961, 1; Saettler 2004, 401, 468). Broadcast television, similar to the way the Internet has been more recently heralded, was thought to be an ideal vehicle to solve the educational conundrum posed by broad access to quality higher education. By 1952, the Federal Communications Commission (FCC) agreed to set aside almost 250 broadcast channels for educational use. This action spurred local and state politicians as well as many national foundations to support what would become a new era in educational television (Saettler 2004, 361–62).

No charitable philanthropy played a larger role in promoting educational television than the Ford Foundation. Ford provided seed funding for educational television in the 1950s and 1960s, awarding a total of $70 million over these two decades ($550 million in 2015 dollars) in support of local efforts to establish educational television stations as instructional media for both K–12 and higher education. Ford Foundation president Henry Heald (who had recently finished serving as chair of Governor Nelson Rockefeller's New York State higher education commission) remained disappointed by the end of the decade in the slow expansion of educational television usage. Ford consequently commissioned a major national study that appeared in 1961 under the simple title *Teaching by Television*. The report described the high point in the national effort to employ broadcast television as a direct college classroom teaching technology.

The Ford report, in terms strikingly similar to the current enthusiasm for online course delivery, asserted that "television's unique advantages as a medium of instruction are: first, it can vastly extend the reach of the nation's 'master' teachers; and second, it can bring to students educational experiences that are quite beyond the potential of conventional means of instruction" (Ford Foundation 1961, 2, 4). Noting that fifty million American homes owned television sets in 1960, the report discussed the way this huge installed base could be used for direct instruction, specifically televised college courses. In 1958, the Ford Foundation had already collaborated with NBC to develop and broadcast *Continental Classroom*, which offered credit-bearing televised classes to more than four hundred thousand regular viewers.[2]

The primary focus of Ford's *Teaching by Television* report was the use of television as an instructional medium in college classrooms. The foundation's Fund for the Advancement of Education had awarded a grant in 1954 to Pennsylvania State University (PSU) to answer a series of research questions about the utility of television as a college-level teaching tool. That grant launched "the most extensive program in the use and evaluation of televised instruction in American higher education" (19). By 1958 more than one in four PSU undergrads was registered in one or more of thirteen large (150–200 students) lecture courses taught over the university's closed-circuit television system, perhaps the largest experiment in the use of electronic media in a single major academic institution ever undertaken. In the experiment, PSU faculty members lectured alone in empty classrooms while looking into a single camera; students viewed these lectures live ("synchronously" in today's parlance) on televisions installed in small classrooms across the campus. The report noted that the only other "personnel" needed besides the instructors were classroom proctors, usually "responsible graduate assistants" available to answer any student questions about the lecture material (since the faculty lecturers were considered unavailable). The report concluded by noting wryly, "Of course, not all teachers were sorry to see questions eliminated" (Ford Foundation 1961, 20; Saettler 2004, 425).

A number of other public universities—including the universities of Florida, Missouri, and Texas, Miami University (Ohio), Oregon State, and Wayne State—soon followed PSU's lead in offering television courses for credit, supported by $2 million in Ford Foundation grants to thirty-six institutions (largely used to buy released time for faculty to prepare television lectures for use in their courses) (Ford Foundation 1961, 28). The *Teaching by Television* report noted that "the most common use of television at the college level has been to combine it with traditional techniques—to mix televised lecture-demonstrations with face-to-face sessions in smaller groups for discussion, problem solving, recitation, or laboratory work." The report's call for a mixed pedagogical approach of face-to-face and televised instruction is precisely what many experts are calling for in today's ed-tech environment, a hybrid model that embraces the advantages of both approaches. But the hybrid model demands a significantly greater investment in instructional costs to produce increased quality of education. That investment, however, is at odds with the overarching intention of many, then and now, who implement the technology to reduce labor costs or to produce profit, all in the service of better alignment with austerity policies. Educational television in 1960, much like computer-supported instruction in our own time, offered "endless variations" on how best to utilize technology within traditional classrooms. An experiment at NYU, for example "showed that three times as much material could be covered in a televised lecture as in a conventional one, because of the better preparation of the instructors and the absence of interruptions by the students" (22).

Teaching by Television also reported the results of a formal evaluation conducted during the fall 1956–57 semester, comparing a traditional two hundred–student PSU psychology lecture course with a closed-circuit television psychology course of comparable size. The evaluation concluded that there was "no difference in achievement between the classes taught by the two methods" (Saettler 2004, 425). Ford also reported "no differences in achievement" in a comparison of televised and conventional lecture courses in science, law, humanities, and social science at PSU, humanities courses taught at NYU, and humanities and social science courses offered at San Francisco State College, hardly an endorsement of televised learning's greater efficacy (Ford Foundation 1961, 25).

According to the report, many PSU faculty members "viewed the innovation with disfavor," because "they did not have contact with the students; they could not give the students individual attention, gauge the students' responses to the presentation, or have the students ask them questions." These responses accord with what one might expect in a poll of faculty today regarding the limitations of computer-assisted instruction (Ford Foundation 1961, 26–27; Saettler 2004, 403). Student opinions about the uses of televised lectures were similar to those of the faculty. PSU, Miami University, and San Francisco State students indicated they preferred "a conventional class, and usually think they learn more in such a class" (Ford Foundation 1961, 27–28). The report also analyzed the financial feasibility of developing televised lecture courses. The key to "breaking even" on costs of televised classes versus conventional lecture courses required that two hundred or more students be taught simultaneously in a televised course. This proved possible at a large state university like PSU (as it would be at UC Berkeley in the early 1960s), because more than a thousand students enrolled each semester in its freshman and sophomore introductory courses (Ford Foundation 1961, 29). This calculus of cost, class size, and support staff remains remarkably consistent across educational technologies a half century later.

The *Teaching by Television* report concluded that "televised teaching can be expected to grow as an effective new asset in the task of maintaining the quality of instruction in American higher education" (Ford Foundation 1961, 28). There is, however, little evidence to have justified the report's optimism. While televised lectures continued to be used in a number of US colleges in the next few decades, successful college teaching by television failed to realize the cost saving this revolutionizing technology, as well as the Ford Foundation, had promised (Saettler 2004, 425). Like so many other foundations, Ford would soon switch its grant-making focus to yet another vision of educational television: the creation of public television, the "fourth network."

The Carnegie Commission on Educational Television had issued a historic report in 1967 calling for the transformation of "educational television" into "public television." President Johnson quickly signed the Public Broadcasting Act in November of that year, which included

$38 million in federal funding for the creation of the Corporation for Public Broadcasting (CPB) in 1968 and, in turn, then created Public Broadcasting Service and National Public Radio (Saettler 2004, 378). While early public television produced a number of admirable programs in the 1960s that had serious intellectual purpose and pedagogical possibilities, its presence in college classrooms after 1970 was essentially incidental, serving only as an occasional video supplement to traditional classroom instruction (403). The transformative power of broadcast television to remake higher education—envisioned by the Ford Foundation in the 1950s, argued for in the 1960 *Teaching by Television* report, and reiterated in the 1968 founding of CPB—would remain an elusive and unrealized dream.

The Emergence of Digital Technology

Digital technologies made possible by the postwar mainframe computer revolution opened up new avenues for educators and their supporters interested in incorporating technology into teaching. It was anticipated that the computing power of mainframes could help improve students' learning outcomes. Early computer-assisted instruction (CAI) consisted largely of onscreen drill-and-practice exercises. It was within this context that the University of Illinois, Urbana–Champaign, launched the Programmed Logic for Automated Teaching Operations (PLATO) system, which had two ambitious goals: "First, to investigate the potential role of the computer in the instructional process; second, to design an economically and educationally viable system incorporating the most valuable approaches to teaching and learning" (quoted in Saettler 2004, 309). The brainchild of several engineering faculty members, PLATO went through four iterations in the dozen years following its 1960 launch, receiving substantial NSF funding in 1968 and 1972. During its fourth iteration, PLATO employed a basic programming language (TUTOR) to develop computer-based drill-and-practice materials for students enrolled primarily in science and mathematics courses at the university. PLATO IV also pioneered several innovative computer design features including touch-screen, plasma display panels. These features allowed what appeared to be an "interactive and conversational relationship" to develop between the computer and the student. Much like the Turing test, however, PLATO was a highly controlled behaviorist experiment designed to guide students to structured learning outcomes. Despite the program's innovative features, NSF's evaluation of PLATO IV in 1978 concluded that it "had no significant impact on student achievement," a result that mirrored many previous and subsequent evaluations of ed-tech experiments (Saettler 2004, 309–11, 318; Ferster 2014, 94–97, 101). According to educational technology historian Bill Ferster, PLATO also failed because it was unable to lower instructional costs per student, which was one of the NSF's key criteria in evaluating CAI success. The early iterations of PLATO were simply too expensive to justify wide adoption. Ultimately, the University of Illinois sold PLATO in the mid-1970s to Control Data Corporation (CDC), which invested $900 million to deploy it in the K–12 market. Despite their expectation of it making billions of dollars, CDC ultimately had to sell PLATO at a substantial financial loss (Ferster 2014, 101–2; Saettler 2004, 404).

Educational technology researchers in the 1960s and 1970s seemed unwilling to apply lessons learned from earlier assessments of the limited effects of analog technologies on improving learning outcomes and lowering teaching costs. Saettler describes a "no-significant difference" finding across the range of analog and digital educational technologies applied to classroom instruction during this thirty-year period (Saettler 2004, 411). Early digital technologists incorrectly assumed that the newest technology would automatically improve classroom instruction and thus lead to better student learning outcomes, regardless of the underlying form of its presentation, the actual operating costs involved, or the negligible effect it had on the development of interpersonal relationships within the classroom that are so often critical to student engagement. Ed-tech proponents seemed unable to grasp the basic fact that the process of student learning had less to do with the platform on which it was delivered and much more to do with the quality and nature of how it facilitated student engagement in the learning process, which in turn promoted critical thinking, discussion, and writing about the subject matter being studied (439–40, 453, 459). The variability of academic achievement and students' academic readiness for digital or any nontraditional form of learning are two essential factors that need to be considered when trying to find the best fit between the particular technological choice of learning tool and the level of student engagement with the content or substance of what they are expected to learn. This more nuanced approach to the application of learning technology was rarely considered during this early era of digital experimentation. It has similarly been largely ignored in the current rush to expand online learning. Entrepreneurs inside and outside of universities, in their headlong pursuit of cost savings and profits, often blunt efforts to identify the most pedagogically effective approaches to improve teaching and learning in college-level classrooms, both physical and virtual.

The Rise of DigitalU

Capitalism and the entrepreneurs who drive the market are unstintingly restless in creating new products and markets. The dot-com boom beginning in the final decade of the twentieth century was a signal illustration of this process. And like a great deal of the history of industrial capitalism, financial and infrastructural support by the federal government—whether in the form of land grants for public university construction and the transcontinental railroads' right-of-way during the nineteenth century, or creation and funding of the underlying infrastructure of the Internet in the 1960s—proved essential in launching the digital platform allowing "self-made" entrepreneurs to greatly profit from foundational public investments. University faculty, staff, and graduate students, many of them working at public institutions such as the University of California, the University of Utah, and CUNY while supported by federal research dollars, also made essential contributions to the Internet's initial development and the establishment of its key operating protocols and open standards in the 1960s, 1970s, and 1980s. By the mid-1980s the Internet had begun to be privatized following the NSF ceding control over the system's infrastructure to commercial interests (Rosenzweig 1998, 1545–50). Suddenly, "e-things" began surfacing all over the Internet. These "virtual" offerings were easily accessible to a broad public, thanks to the development of the first global web browser, Mosaic, developed in 1992 by the National Center for Supercomputing Applications at the University of Illinois, Urbana–Champaign. Mosaic made the Internet graphically interesting and easily accessible. The next generation browsers that quickly replaced it (first Netscape Navigator, then Internet Explorer and Safari) made possible the vast expansion of the World Wide Web with tens of millions of new users coming online each year (by 2000 there were already nearly four hundred million Internet users worldwide).

Escalating stock prices and huge amounts of available venture capital in the 1990s led eager investors to seek out and underwrite a series of online ideas and start-up high-tech companies. Higher education was quickly identified by tech gurus and venture capitalists as a growth market in which to introduce "disruptive technology," the management catch phrase that Harvard business professor Clayton Christensen coined in 1995 and has served as the mantra to tech entrepreneurs, venture capitalists, and many educational technologists alike.[3] By the end of the decade Merrill Lynch estimated that investment in the e-learning market in higher education exceeded $1.2 billion. At the same time, a number of university administrators at private and public institutions across the country quickly entered into formal agreements with private companies and digital entrepreneurs to market their existing courses and, where possible, to develop new, specially designed web-based offerings to be marketed to the general public. A nagging fear existed throughout higher education that institutions not engaged in a rapid makeover necessary to become digital universities would be left behind.

Several examples of those early university/digital start-up partnerships—involving UCLA and Columbia University—illustrate the larger trend of university officials' increasing infatuation with distance education. We could have chosen other digital higher education partnerships—including NYU, Temple University, the universities of Maryland, Massachusetts and Pennsylvania—but the early UCLA and Columbia instances have been sufficiently analyzed and in fact are emblematic of the feeding frenzy that would soon grip many public and private university leaders in this moment of the digitalization of higher education.

UCLA administrators got into e-learning quite early. In 1993 they began extensive legal negotiations with the Home Education Network (THEN), a newly formed start-up whose leaders were interested in securing the electronic rights to the large number of UCLA Extension (UNEX) program's courses. UNEX was advertised as the nation's largest single-campus continuing higher education provider, with forty-two hundred courses and more than one hundred thousand enrollments annually. THEN's initial CEO was Alan Arkatov, who had served as a senior media consultant on Bill Clinton's successful 1992 presidential campaign. The company's founding goal in 1993 was to become "the leading global supplier of branded distance learning for the continuing higher education market" (Noble 2001, 40–41; Woo 1997; *Business Wire* 1997).

In 1994, the UC regents agreed to grant THEN exclusive rights for ten years to develop videotaped and later online continuing education courses. THEN was awarded the exclusive use of UCLA's name and UNEX's courses. Corporate managers boasted that they would launch a groundbreaking distance-learning program. The ever more explicit conjunction of corporate and public university interests and staffing was further solidified when John Kobara, who had been UCLA's vice chancellor of university relations, left UCLA in early 1997 to take over the daily operation of THEN as its president and CEO while Arkatov remained chairman. In exchange for granting THEN exclusive online rights to its courses, UNEX agreed to forward all the tuition fees it collected from the electronic courses directly to the company. In return, THEN would send UCLA a percentage of the gross receipts, escalating from 6 to almost 9 percent over the ten-year term of the contract, plus reimbursement for expenses incurred in developing the electronic versions of its courses. THEN's income projections from the UNEX contract were expected to reach $3 million to $4 million within two years (circa 1996–97). That sum was anticipated to "grow exponentially" to an estimated $31 million by year four of the original contract (circa 1998–99). By the time THEN began renegotiating its contract with UCLA in 1996 (THEN had failed to include Internet rights in the original contract), the five-year profit projection of UCLA's share had dropped precipitously to $400,000. Despite this financial setback, Kobara, according to a report in *Business Wire*, immediately began in 1997 "to oversee the aggressive expansion of THEN's online continuing higher education program. This effort was enabled by a multimillion-dollar infusion of capital from Sylvan Learning Systems," described as "the largest private-sector education service firm in North America." THEN and its descendant, Online-Learning.net (OLN), formed several years after the original UCLA agreement, did not meet even the most modest of its early projections. By 1999 OLN had limited enrollment and lost $2 million in its first year of operation and "according to insiders" continued to lose $60,000 a month thereafter (DistanceEducator.com 2001; Confessore 1999, 26–28; Noble 2001, 57, 65).

David Noble, via an open records request, brought the THEN-OLN/UNEX legal arrangements to light in a series of widely read and widely discussed articles and a subsequent book.[4] These arrangements included the failure of UCLA administrators to secure the intellectual property rights to the UNEX courses it granted THEN-OLN. Those same administrators also failed to inform the UCLA Faculty Senate about the legal negotiations with THEN-OLN. Their final failure was to provide copies of the contracts for faculty review and comment despite having already established the Academic Information Technology Board (AITB), a joint administration-faculty committee to oversee UCLA's technology issues and questions. As these issues surfaced, the AITB publicly clarified in late 1999 the faculty role in signing off on such agreements. The board confirmed that faculty members, whether professors or part-time instructors, indeed controlled the intellectual property rights to their courses, which remains a continuing and nettlesome problem for academic administrators across the country. This "clarification" by UCLA administrators was a modest victory for faculty and shared governance. The limited income generated by the OLN's relationship with UNEX never came close to justifying the original claims made by the UCLA administrators or Arkatov's company, whose original intention was to develop "the most comprehensive continuing distance learning program of its kind in the United States" (UCLA ITPB 2001; Noble 2001, 40).[5]

A second early entrant in the "e-learning" market was UNext, an online educational start-up company. It was conceived and headed by Andrew Rosenfield, who served as its CEO and chairman. He was also a senior lecturer at the University of Chicago Law School and a member of the university's board of trustees. Founded in 1996, UNext was underwritten initially with several hundred million dollars of venture capital provided by Michael Milken, of junk bond infamy, and Larry Ellison, the CEO of Oracle Software. In 1998, Rosenfield and UNext partnered with a series of prestigious private entities, including the University of Chicago, Columbia University, the London School of Economics, Stanford, and Carnegie Mellon University, to develop a series of online courses and degrees targeted at a general and relatively affluent audience. To create a more robust public profile and burnish UNext's brand, Rosenfield appointed three University of Chicago economists to the company's board of directors (including Nobel Prize–winner Gary Becker) (Blumenstyk 1999; Blustain and Goldstein 2004, 8–9, 15–16).

Columbia enthusiastically signed on with UNext, the first university to do so. The dean of its graduate business school, Meyer Feldberg, described his reasoning for signing up his school: "We knew distance learning was like a freight train. We knew we could get run down, get onboard, or get out of the way." Feldberg's logic regarding emergent online technology was widely shared by university administrators across time and space. A key contemporary and historical assumption in higher education has been that universities must either adapt to new forms of technology such as online learning, or else wither and die. Private universities, by the nature of how they are funded and their continuing need to bolster their endowments, tend to be more willing, at least initially, to embrace risky, profit-making schemes floated by organizations like UNext. And public university administrators have then been willing to jump on those digital bandwagons, once their private university counterparts get them rolling.

UNext opened for business in the summer of 2000 as Cardean University, a "start-up e-university," spending a reported $80 million on the launch. Cardean was offering eighty courses and an MBA degree program by the fall. Columbia quickly agreed to let UNext/Cardean use the school's logo and to assign its top faculty to create Cardean's online courses, which would be offered for credit. The contractual agreement granted Columbia shares of stock in UNext and the right to partner with other online education companies to develop its own web-based classes (an important clause in the agreement, as we will see). To burnish the company's brand and reputation, Rosenfield claimed that UNext's pedagogy was built on the latest insights of cognitive scientists and learning theorists who had helped the company develop a "world-class system of pedagogy that used the Internet differently, imaginatively and productively to create educational experiences *that don't resemble in the slightest* the way in which education is delivered in a facilities-based environment." Rosenfield also projected that key university partners would earn $20 million in royalties within five years, a number that doubtlessly attracted other university administrators, private and public. These projected profits and the business model and underlying fiscal logic advancing them could only be imagined in the midst of the ever-expanding dot-com bubble (Bok 2004, 79–80; Gajilan 2000; Blustain and Goldstein 2004, 10, 15; Noble 2001, 21–22; Steinberg and Wyatt 2000; Pizzo 2001).

Predictably, in 2001 when the dot-com bubble burst, Rosenfield and UNext/Cardean were unable to deliver the promised royalties to their university partners. UNext quickly and dramatically downsized. UNext's president lamented the amount of venture capital that his company had burned through: "This is a very expensive undertaking. And the whole business model depends on making a huge up-front investment rather than a business-to-consumer model of selling individual courses. I don't know that anyone will ever do it again, and they certainly won't do it the way that we did it" (Blustain and Goldstein 2004, 3, 10, 24). UNext/Cardean left behind little more than a series of dead webpages, charges that it was in fact a diploma mill, and contentious lawsuits brought by university partners (Cardean University Home Page 2015; Career Overview 2015; Columbia Interactive e-Courses, n.d.; Blustain and Goldstein 2004, 4; Stripling 2008).

Columbia had begun to develop an independent online Columbia University brand even before UNext/Cardean crashed. Michael Crow was the driving force behind Columbia University's immersion in a series of digital technology start-ups that would put the school's courses and intellectual property on the web for mass consumption. Crow, who had been appointed Columbia's executive vice-provost in 1993, was put in charge of Columbia's Strategic Initiatives Fund, financed out of the university's substantial patent proceeds (said to total $143 million in 2000 alone). Columbia used its patent income to provide seed money for innovative projects and initiatives (Blumenstyk 2001; Arenson 2000).

Early in 1999, Crow founded Morningside Ventures, which was followed by the launch of the Fathom Learning Network in 2000. Describing Columbia's new Morningside Ventures in April 1999, *New York Times* education writer Karen Arenson suggested, "Joining the race to the Internet and its riches, Columbia University has formed a company and hopes to make a profit by providing courses, research and other university material on line." Crow told Arenson that Columbia "felt the need for a company that could compete with the wealthy companies that are now flocking to higher education" (Arenson 1999). Crow enthusiastically embraced an entrepreneurial vision for higher education. "We use the word 'academic entrepreneurs,'" he told *Chronicle of Higher Education* writer Goldie Blumenstyk. "We are expanding what it means to be a knowledge enterprise" (Blumenstyk 2001).

One of Crow's first Morningside Ventures hires was Ann Kirschner (Carlson 2000). Kirschner told the *New York Times*'s Karen Arenson in

1999 that Morningside Ventures' "aim was to do for learning what Amazon.com has done for books. 'Amazon.com creates a community of readers and a thirst for books, and then, by George, a way to buy those books,' she said. 'We want to create a community of learners'" (Arenson 1999).

The following year Kirschner launched Fathom (Kirschner, n.d.). She was given three years and $25 million from Columbia's Strategic Investment Fund to undertake the new online endeavor. Columbia's provost, Jonathan Cole, explained the university's willingness to make a substantial commitment to Fathom by amplifying upon Crow's and Kirschner's earlier public statements: "Our motivation is to be entrepreneurial. We've been giving it [presumably meaning Columbia's intellectual content] away for generations. Now we want to get a fair return, always so we can reinvest it" (quoted in Walsh 2011, 29). Education researcher Taylor Walsh[6] quotes Kirschner as asserting that Fathom was "a marketing vehicle to put all the intellectual property together in an attractive format, and develop a large audience for it" and as a "knowledge mall" and "wholesaler" of content. Crow, Kirschner's boss, according to Walsh, "referred to the site's intended audience—educated lifelong learners with the means and inclination to pay for general enrichment courses—as a 'niche market,' and said that at Columbia, 'we use knowledge as a form of venture capital'" (29).

Fathom spent a good deal of Columbia's patent money fashioning a series of online courses. And to expand its capacity to penetrate its targeted market of affluent adult learners, Columbia decided to partner with ten other "elite" universities, libraries, museums, and cultural institutions, including the London School of Economics, the University of Chicago (a now-familiar entrepreneurial partner, as we have seen), the American Museum of Natural History, and the New York Public Library (Walsh 2011, 30). In the end, Fathom's market strategy quickly failed, despite charging relatively modest prices and adding corporate training to its portfolio (Arnone 2002a). By 2002, all of the key players involved confirmed, according to Walsh, "that Fathom never attracted a sufficient number of paying customers and, consequently, revenues did not come close to matching the program's costs." One estimate indicated that the revenue generated by Fathom before it finally closed was only $700,000 (33–34). In that same year, Columbia's University Senate, speaking for many faculty members whose intellectual content Fathom promised to monetize, issued a report critical of the operation (39; Arnone 2002b). Columbia's new president, Lee Bollinger, finally decided to terminate Fathom early in 2003 (Carlson 2003). Michael Crow's future employment prospects were hardly dampened by Fathom's demise, however. In June 2002, the same month that Bollinger assumed the Columbia presidency, Crow was appointed president of Arizona State University. Today he oversees perhaps the most aggressive online public university effort in the country. It promises that "a combination of classroom instruction and online technologies . . . accelerates learning while lowering costs" (Warner 2015a; Crow and Dabars 2015, 274).[7]

The Open Educational Resources Movement

For every UCLA, University of Chicago, and Columbia pursuing venture capital funding to underwrite e-learning ventures, there have been other universities both elite and public institutions, taking a different path. Charles Vest, long-serving president of MIT (1990–2004), drew an important lesson from the very public controversy over Columbia's Fathom project and the failure of its market model: He concluded that college-level e-learning should not be based on a proprietary model. On April 1, 2001, Vest announced that MIT, through its new OpenCourse-Ware (OCW) initiative, was committed to giving away nearly all of MIT's eighteen hundred courses on the Internet for noncredit, noncommercial purposes. OCW placed faculty syllabi, reading lists, and lecture notes (and, in a few instances, accompanying video and other multimedia material) online. Before he made the announcement Vest reached out to the MIT faculty to make certain they agreed with the basic tenets of the project, a step that somehow had eluded UCLA officials a few years earlier. MIT faculty voted in fact to support the initiative two months before OCW's official launch, their enthusiasm no doubt heightened when they learned faculty members who participated would receive several thousand dollars for their work. Vest made it clear a few days later that the OCW initiative was "not providing an MIT education on the web. We are providing our core materials that are the infrastructure that undergirds an MIT education. Real education requires interaction—the interaction that is part of American teaching" (MIT 2001). Vest was explicit that MIT was offering its course materials, not its actual courses. This was both a sound pedagogical choice and a smart business decision because MIT did not want to appear to be giving away an education for which it was then charging upwards of $20,000 in annual undergraduate tuition (Walsh 2011, 57–77; MIT 2001). The public response to Vest's announcement and MIT's "altruism" was rapid and enthusiastic. Vest's initial press release received front-page coverage in the *New York Times*, under the uninspired headline "Auditing Classes at M.I.T., on the Web and Free" (Goldberg 2001).

The positive reception of MIT's OCW initiative helped launch a larger open educational resources (OER) movement that consciously distanced itself from the headlong pursuit of profit driving other university online venture-capital-supported efforts of the prior decade and encouraged other smaller and less famous academic institutions, including public ones, to begin to consider developing their own online resources. The movement officially embraced the OER name with the William and Flora Hewlett Foundation's financing in 2005 of the OER Commons, an open-source course repository for college instructors, which, interestingly, took its title ("Commons") from a favored open-source political and organizational ideal (Guess 2007b). The Hewlett Foundation essentially underwrote the expansion of the OER after 2001 (as the Ford Foundation had done for educational television half a century earlier), spending nearly $110 million over the next nine years on OER projects at a range of colleges and universities, most of them elite private institutions. By 2010 MIT's OCW course site was garnering substantial web traffic, ranging between 700,000 and 950,000 visits worldwide each month, approaching 10 million unique visitors annually with almost 100 million page views of more than 2,300 MIT courses, by far the greatest impact of any Hewlett-supported OER project (Walsh 2011, 219–20; Watters 2011). While many of these visitors were individuals interested in perusing course materials, a sizeable number were college faculty members across the globe at smaller, less prestigious public and private institutions looking to update or initially conceive their own syllabi and reading lists. Funding of OER projects by Hewlett and other foundations (including the Alfred P. Sloan Foundation) ended in 2009 (the foundations decided it was time to move on to support other educational reform ideas), leading several OER schools (though not the well-endowed MIT) to shut down their online initiatives (Walsh 2011, 86–87; Parry 2009a, 2009b; Hafner 2010).

The OER movement also had a public university identity as well, supported by more modest, alternative forms of financing besides Hewlett's funding. One of the most interesting alternative open educational models was developed at UC Berkeley (UCB), where a faculty member, Lawrence A. Rowe, embraced the concept of open educational resources half a dozen years before Charles Vest decided to launch MIT's OCW initiative. In 1995 Rowe began webcasting his own computer science lecture course over what he called the Berkeley Internet Broadcast System (BIBS) to allow his students to review lecture content as a study aid. Rowe also made the fateful decision to offer his webcasts for free on the open web for anyone around the world to see and use. His reasoning was wholly democratic and egalitarian: "I had this fundamental belief that this is a public university funded by public money, and creating content and education is our mission, and so it seemed like publishing this worldwide on the internet was the right way to work towards that mission" (quoted in Walsh 2011, 152). The webcasting of Rowe's lectures proved so successful that his students apparently encouraged him to expand the project beyond computer science, which he was willing and able to do. Other UCB faculty members also agreed to have their lecture courses webcast. It was on this basis that the number of BIBS courses grew to twenty-six by 2000.

When Rowe retired in 2001, UCB staff in the Educational Technology Service (ETS) office took over Rowe's BIBS, renamed it "webcast .berkeley," and expanded the number of available webcast courses beyond science to include humanities and social sciences classes (webcast.berke ley 2015; Edmonds 2008, 76). The webcast.berkeley initiative took another important step in 2006–2007 when it decided to post its video and audio materials on Google Video and Apple's iTunesU and to set up its own YouTube channel to expand public access to its online lecture courses (Read 2006; Guess 2007a). The project, which was financed internally, cost UCB a modest $700,000 a year. Individual videotaped courses, which numbered more than five hundred, cost approximately $5,000 to put online (as compared to the $40,000 Yale spent on each of its OER online courses) (Walsh 2011, 155–57). Public usage of webcast. berkeley materials soared from half a million downloads annually in 2002 to more than two million by 2007, with more than eighty million people worldwide downloading webcast.berkeley video and audio courses by 2010 (Edmonds, 76–77; Opencast website 2015; Walsh 2011, 168).

What is striking is how uninvolved, until the last few years, senior UCB administrators had been in the daily operation of the webcast. berkeley project. The development of the project was left largely to UCB faculty and ETS staff members (Walsh 2011, 155–57, 170–71). UCB's top administrators were content to reap the positive press and reputational benefits that accrued to the campus from the webcast.berkeley operation. This benign attitude began to change after 2008 in the painful aftermath of the Great Recession. All three California public university systems faced severe budgetary cuts, which led the UC schools to consider enrollment caps and the UC regents to institute a "Declaration of Extreme Financial Emergency" in 2009, imposing 20 percent budget cuts on all UC campuses (Bady 2009; Stripling 2009; Walsh 2011, 173). Those austerity measures put webcast.berkeley and, more importantly, the larger UC system in jeopardy, with UCB administrators struggling to meet the targets of their gigantic budget cuts. The University of California Online Education Initiative (UCOE), an ongoing project of the upper administration, was created and funded in 2009 to evaluate the feasibility of developing an eleventh "virtual university," offering fully online courses that "could be offered for credit either to enrolled UC students or, eventually, as part of full online undergraduate degrees" (Walsh 2011, 175–76; Bowen and Tobin 2015, 121–24). After almost five years of planning and failed pilot projects, UCOE finally came to a quiet and warranted end in 2014 (Bowen and Tobin 2015, 125–26).

Walsh concludes her chapter on webcast.berkeley by noting that in 2009, then UCB provost George Breslauer seemed "intrigued" by the revenue-generating possibilities of online courses. He thought, much the way that UCLA administrators had in the 1990s, that UCB's extension programs could become "a cash cow for the campus," telling Walsh, "There's a huge upside potential for leveraging the university extension" (quoted in Bowen and Tobin 2015, 125–26). That attitude is sadly emblematic of the ways in which a democratizing belief in making academic work available online to a broad public audience, as Rowe and his UCB colleagues had done since 1995, could be "repurposed" to meet the needs of austerity-era budgeting. Without adequate support, webcast.berkeley, like UCOE, limped along for the next five years. Early in 2015, UCB administrators announced that because of cost considerations the school would no longer make new videotaped lectures available online to the general public beginning in fall 2015, reserving webcast.berkeley exclusively as a study aid for enrolled UCB students, a sad diminution of UCB's public education mission (webcast.berkeley website, 2015).

The Khan Academy

Simultaneously with the OER, the rise of the Khan Academy (KA), a non-university-based online initiative, had far-reaching implications for the evolution of the university-based educational technology movement. Salman Khan, an MIT-trained computer scientist and former hedge fund analyst, developed a series of clever one-on-one video tutorials on basic mathematics for his family members that he posted on YouTube. The Khan videos went viral. As a result of this early success he officially launched the Khan Academy site in 2006, establishing it as a nonprofit corporation, hiring staff, and quickly expanding its operations. Initial financial support was provided by Bill Gates and the Gates Foundation, followed soon after by a number of major international foundations and corporations. Khan's online high school mathematics videos quickly expanded to include more advanced college-appropriate tutorials and exercises in other disciplines including art history, finance, history, the theoretical sciences, music, and economics. The Khan Academy demonstrated that a significant market existed for freely available educational content delivered via the web and geared to self-directed individual learners. There are currently more than six thousand Khan Academy video tutorials. They were designed to be self-paced to meet individual learners' needs and skill levels (and to dispense with the need for personal engagement with face-to-face teachers). The videos, which increasingly incorporated sophisticated graphic techniques, proved to be invaluable study aids for many, whether high school or college students attempting to bone up on core subject matter before an exam or professionals interested in reviewing key concepts and processes in their own or related fields. By 2012, the Khan Academy's video tutorials had been viewed two hundred million times online. The pedagogy of the Khan videos was not above reproach, however. For example, some teachers critiqued Khan's math content and teaching methodology. And the videos on other subject matter such as US history can too often sound like a disembodied voice speed-reading a list of "the facts" about complicated historical processes and issues far more nuanced and complex than the videos suggest. Critics have questioned the Khan Academy's employment practices. The nonprofit has recently advertised a series of one-year "Content Creation and Curation Fellowships" at the company's California headquarters, in lieu of offering full-time paid positions, to generate new content in various academic subject areas, a tack taken by many contemporary corporations, nonprofits, and elite universities to reduce labor costs (Khan Academy 2015a; Khan Academy 2015b; Thompson 2011; Noer 2012; Strauss 2012; Talbert 2012).

Khan, like the general OER movement, decided not to monetize his creation beyond seeking foundation and corporate contributions. KA's undeniable online presence and pedagogical design would soon inspire more entrepreneurially remunerative ways to monetize the web. This in turn would have a direct impact on the ways both public and private higher education institutions responded to austerity pressures that define and shape the current economic and political moment for colleges and universities.

MOOCs and the Reshaping of Public Higher Education

MOOCs, as they catapulted into public consciousness, are essentially videotaped lectures on specific academic subjects, often (though not exclusively) delivered by big-name academic "stars" and made available as courses of individual study via the Internet. MOOCs assumed several organizational forms when they initially appeared in 2012: private, for-profit companies such as Coursera and Udacity that were underwritten by venture capitalists creating proprietary Web delivery platforms; and nonprofit consortia of universities and cultural organizations such as edX (co-founded by MIT and Harvard in 2012 and building on MIT's OpenCourseWare work described earlier) financed through start-up investments by their two founders (estimated at $60 million) and distributed as online courses through free, open-source software (Kolowich 2012). When these two forms of mainstream MOOCs began, those who enrolled "distantly" over the Internet did so without receiving college credit or formal certification. Nonetheless, the online courses generated enormous buzz in the mainstream and education press, far beyond the kind of public notice (not to mention acclaim) that the OER movement or webcast.berkeley generated. Pundits such as Thomas Friedman and

David Brooks were convinced, just as Thomas Edison had been about silent films a century earlier or the Ford Foundation about educational television half a century ago, that MOOCs were the disruptive technology poised to totally remake higher education (Friedman 2012; Brooks 2012). The *New York Times* quickly declared 2012 "The Year of the MOOC" and, according to one estimate, more than $100 million in venture capital was invested in developing proprietary MOOCs within the first nine months of 2012 (Pappano 2012; Siemens 2012). Three years later the word "MOOC" yields more than 11.5 million results in a standard Google search.

The online courses were initially pitched as part of a broad democratic-access or justice agenda for higher education, reaching millions of self-motivated students globally who could learn for free from the great master teachers. Anant Agarwal, the president of edX, called it a "true, planet-scale democratization of education" (quoted in Bolkan 2013a). And while there were well-advertised cases of hard-working, poor students in the underdeveloped world studying and learning from MOOCs (Mooney 2015), the justice imagery rapidly dissolved as completion rates in MOOCs barely edged above the single digits and the number of MOOC enrollees from nondeveloped countries remained relatively small. Conversely, relatively affluent consumers and those already college educated were the ones most attracted to them (Ho et al. 2014, 2–3; Selingo 2014). Even when certifications of course completion were made available to MOOC registrants, as HarvardX and MITX did in their first year of operation (2012–13), only 5 percent actually received certificates across the sixteen MOOCs offered initially under the edX banner (Ho et al. 2014, 14). And in the case of profit-seeking MOOCs, the substantial capital and institutional investments ultimately (and sometimes rapidly) needed to be recouped. Proprietary providers, including Udacity and Coursera, therefore began seeking income from the following sources: participation fees from colleges and universities; charging individual students for course completion certifications and/or course credit; and even charging fees to match MOOC completers with potential employers, as Udacity and Coursera proposed doing early on, functioning as sort of online job agencies (Kolowich 2012; Bernhard 2015).

But MOOC history does not begin in 2012 with the separate launches of Coursera, Udacity, and edX. The idea and the very term/acronym itself had its origins four years earlier in Canada, in a progressive educational experiment that emerged in parallel to the open educational resources movement. Two Canadian educational researchers, Stephen Downes and George Siemens, taught a University of Manitoba continuing-education course entitled Connectivism and Connective Knowledge in 2008 that was based on a model of open learning and distributed content that encouraged, according to Siemens, "creativity, autonomy and social networked learning" (The MOOC Guide 2008; Siemens 2012). The class brought together two-dozen fee-paying university continuing-education students with several thousand wholly online students from across the globe. The online students participated for free in the course through blogs and discussion groups. A third Canadian academic involved in the Connectivism course, David Cormier, is credited with coining the term and acronym MOOC in 2008, which he applied to Siemens and Downes's connectivist course (Kolowich 2012; Lorenzo 2013). Downes preferred the term "cMOOC," or connectivist MOOC, to differentiate his and Siemen's open educational effort from the more commercial variant that would soon follow (he later dubbed these "xMOOCs," perhaps playing off the final letter in edX's name), "cMOOCs focus on knowledge creation and generation," Siemens argued, "whereas xMOOCs focus on knowledge duplication" (Siemens 2012; Crowley 2013; Hilgerch 2014).

The xMOOC "knowledge duplication" business had officially been launched in 2011 by Sebastian Thrun, a Stanford computer science professor clearly more inspired by the Khan Academy's dramatic online outreach and publicity than by Siemens and Downes's Canadian constructivist MOOC or even by webcast.berkeley's demonstrated online video successes. Thrun co-taught a popular Stanford artificial intelligence (AI) course that he decided to open up online for free to any student anywhere in the world. The initial response—160,000 people from 190 countries signed on to the online version of the course—proved irresistible to the entrepreneurial Thrun. He founded Udacity early in 2012 to capitalize on this previously untapped market that quickly became known to the general public as "MOOCs," a dramatic repurposing of Cormier's original meaning (Udacity 2015; Chafkin 2013). Thrun's concept was mimicked by two fellow Stanford computer science professors, Daphne Koller and Andrew Ng, who launched Coursera in the same year with similar intentions and venture capital underwriting as Udacity. The big difference between Udacity and Coursera was that Koller and Ng determined from the outset that they needed a large number of university participants to legitimate their online products. They therefore partnered initially with Stanford, Princeton, and the universities of Michigan and Pennsylvania before formally launching Coursera. This approach parallels that of Columbia's Fathom project in the earlier round of university online mania. Within a year the university co-sponsor list for Coursera had grown to almost three dozen, including a number of top-tier public research universities (Lewin 2015). The early involvement of public universities was an indicator at least in part of the continuing anxieties of public university administrators and their boards of trustees, like their predecessors during earlier waves of technological innovation, that they would be left behind in the explosion of online learning. This fear, when combined with the continuing need to cut per capita instructional costs in the midst of a major recession and the unrelenting policies of austerity imposed on the public by state politicians and boards of trustees, created substantial incentives to rapidly expand MOOCs (Lewin 2012).

Udacity quickly recognized, as Coursera and edX had, that the existing and extremely well-financed higher education market (total spending on higher education in 2012 approached $500 billion) was a key site for moving traditional courses online, especially in undergraduate instruction (NCES 2015; Ho et al. 2014, 4–5). Two separate Udacity and edX experiments in California's massive public university system in 2013 are especially revealing regarding the challenges MOOC providers faced as they sought to both transform public higher education and realize radical cost savings in undergraduate instruction. The MOOCs' promise of cost savings and production of new student revenue streams was amplified by edX's president when he noted that "a single professor and one TA . . . can teach anywhere from 100 to 1,000 times as many students as they would teach in a normal class" (quoted in Bolkan 2013b). In spring 2013 Udacity's proprietary platform was used to launch several online courses. The MOOCs were offered as alternatives to traditional remedial and introductory mathematics courses taught at San Jose State University (SJSU), one of twenty-three campuses in the California State University system. University administrators were, in the words of a *Chronicle of Higher Education* (*CHE*) report "looking for creative ways to reduce education costs at a time of budget stress" (Young 2013). Rather than a "superstar" instructor teaching the online course (as Thrun had done with his first Stanford-Udacity AI MOOC course), the SJSU math courses, according to a *New York Times* report, were a pioneering effort in which professors at a public university collaborated with a major MOOC provider to create "for-credit courses with students watching videos, taking interactive quizzes, and receiving support from online mentors . . . hired and trained by Udacity" (Lewin and Markoff 2013). The online mentors turned out to be Stanford graduate students whom Thrun paid to help assure positive learning outcomes in the SJSU experiment. The participating SJSU undergraduates were charged anywhere from one-third to one-fifth the standard tuition fee for taking a Udacity course, an especially appealing price given rapidly escalating California public university tuition charges. The college, it turned out, received approximately one-quarter of the reduced tuition fees paid by each MOOC student; the remaining revenue was claimed by Udacity (Rivard 2013b).

The SJSU-Udacity experiment was not a success. In the words of a *CHE* report "students in the 'Udacified' versions of the courses performed significantly worse overall than did their [traditional] classroom counterparts," with only a 25 percent pass rate compared to 65 percent in face-to-face math courses (Kolowich 2013b). SJSU faculty ire was directed at the Udacity experiment, with the SJSU Academic Senate seeking to limit the administration's power to unilaterally impose new pedagogical forms and practices and to monetize faculty's intellectual property rights to their course materials without prior consultation with and involvement of faculty in such critical decisions. This response was echoed by other college faculties in response to administrative pressures to "go online" (Kolowich 2013c; Waters 2013a; Kolowich 2013d, 2014; Fredette 2013).

Faculty consultation (or the absence of it) was also central in another 2013 MOOC experiment at San Jose State. In this instance a MOOC version of a videotaped philosophy lecture course by Harvard professor Michael Sandel was made available to students via the edX platform. SJSU philosophy faculty reacted strongly to the idea that an edX course was being substituted for one taught face-to-face by an SJSU professor. Faculty argued in an open letter to Sandel that the edX course would "replace professors, dismantle departments, and provide a diminished education for students in public universities" and that "this model of education has turned [the SJSU professor] into a glorified teaching assistant." Harvard's Sandel quickly responded to the open letter by indicating he did not wish his televised course to replace the work of fellow faculty members at SJSU. Subsequently, the college's administration, led by the president, quickly withdrew the edX philosophy course (SJSU Philosophy Dept. 2013; Kolowich 2013b).

Despite these setbacks, other major players in the ed-tech biz, including Pearson, Desire2Learn, and Blackboard, decided in 2013 to join the frenzy at public universities by expanding their existing online products to accommodate MOOCs (Schaffhauser 2013a). We examine one such effort, MOOC2Degree, a dreadfully named initiative launched early in 2013 by Academic Partnerships (AP), a self-described online "enabler" company that "helps colleges and universities with services associated with online education, such as curriculum development, enrollment management and marketing, and provides the software platform to offer courses online" (Academic Partnerships 2013; Straumsheim 2015a). AP's founder and CEO, Texas education entrepreneur Randy Best, made his first fortune in K–12, founding "one of the most lucrative literacy programs in public schools" in the post-NCLB era, which he ultimately sold for almost $400 million (Michels 2012; Basken 2015). Best pivoted to online college learning, founding Academic Partnerships in 2007. His senior board of directors included disruptive innovation guru Clayton Christensen and former southern governors James B. Hunt (D, NC) and Jeb Bush (R, FL) (Academic Partnerships 2015). In exchange for providing services to a dozen second-tier public universities and programs— including the universities of Arkansas, Cincinnati, and West Florida; Florida International (FIU); Cleveland State; and the UT at Arlington and Ohio University nursing programs—to convert their traditional courses to online ones, these public institutions agreed to share tuition revenue from enrolled MOOC students with the profit-making company (Lewin 2013a). This pooling of tuition revenue was offered as an alternative to paying AP for the one-time, upfront costs associated with online development. AP did very well within the first year of MOOC-2Degree's launch, earning a reported $10 million from its contract with FIU and a robust $18 million from Ohio U's nursing program, according to a 2013 report issued by the Campaign for the Future of Higher Education, a public university faculty, staff, and student advocacy group (Campaign for the Future of Higher Education 2013; Schaffhauser 2013b). The MOOC2Degree twist was that the first MOOC offered to students was "at no charge" in the hope that "the free courses would serve as a tool for recruiting students into [the public universities'] online degree programs" (Jaschik 2013). AP CEO Randy Best later claimed that an astonishing "72 to 84 percent" of the students who took the first MOOC2Degree course for free ended up signing up for a second online course at the participating public colleges. Even better than the online "freebie" for students, Best suggested, is that the free MOOC offered by his company "will potentially attract larger numbers of qualified students into their [the participating universities'] degree programs" and more importantly "give[s] its university clients a risk-free way to try out students before admitting them" as regular students, sort of like an Off-Off-Broadway performance (Kim 2013; Nelson 2013; Michels 2012; Kolowich 2013a; Negrea 2014). In addition to AP's promise of vetting quality students, these public universities were also reaping continuing cost savings in essential labor and space generated by the MOOC-based courses that AP produced. Within two years of its initial launch, MOOC2Degree introduced a third version of its online platform when the first two proved inadequate. This version emphasized "prioritizing interaction" (presumably between students and teachers, a recurring failure of early MOOCs, including AP's), "increasing compatibility with more devices" (presumably students' growing use of hand-held devices), and helping universities expand their global presence (a step that big MOOC players like Coursera were also taking) (Sufrin 2014). Best readily conceded in January 2015 that MOOCs "may have been more faddish than altruistic" (Best 2015). Perhaps more telling, AP also announced in April 2015 a revenue-sharing model with public university faculty who agreed to put their courses up on the MOOC2Degree platform, offering 3 percent of the tuition revenue AP generated from each of its public university partnerships (Straumsheim 2015a).

Best's business model, which focused on public universities, apparently continues to grow, with the announcement in July 2015 of a new deal to help the financially troubled University of Akron put a dozen core courses online to attract new, nontraditional students, using a rapid expansion of the Ohio school's nursing online program as the cash cow, as nursing is especially ripe for digital disruption because of state licensure pressures on nurses and nursing programs to move from two- to four-year degrees (Poster 2013; Jaschik 2015). University of Akron faculty are understandably troubled about losing significant control of the school's core curriculum to an online provider and about what the school's new emphasis on profit making and rapid enrollment growth will mean to the quality of the university's overall academic enterprise (Basken 2015).

The San Jose State University experiments by edX in philosophy and Udacity in mathematics and the MOOC2Degree efforts at various public universities across the country were initially justified as a basis for improving undergraduate educational success. Clearly, they were far more about deploying online education solutions to cut operating costs at public institutions, or, even more troubling, to transfer public dollars to privately managed, profit-making and nonprofit ventures alike. Examples of monetizing public higher education by using MOOCs to expand the size, scope, and purpose of traditional college classrooms led one instructional designer, without a hint of irony or disapproval, to describe online learning and MOOCs as "the Walmart of education" (Grush 2013). This characterization does seem entirely apt, given Walmart's reputation for employing cost-cutting, low wages, and market monopolization practices.

The initial contractual arrangements between public universities such as San Jose State and profit-making MOOC providers such as Udacity and MOOC2Degree, and even the nonprofit edX, largely eluded public exposure in 2012–13. Each of these agreements was a relatively invisible, no-bid deal that did not go through typical state procurement procedures, which require state registration of prospective outside vendors, a competitive bidding process, and public disclosure of all signed state contracts. However, *Inside Higher Ed* reporter Ray Rivard, in a stunning exposé published in July 2013, was able to secure copies of these no-bid contracts via open records requests. These documents, according to Rivard, revealed that

> though MOOCs gained attention as free classes for the masses, the providers each have nascent business models that demand outright payments (the University of Texas System paid $5 million in a no-bid agreement to join edX) or seek to share in tuition revenues (Udacity expects to make $2 million from a three-year partnership with the Georgia Institute of Technology that was also not competitively bid). In contracts with elite institutions, Coursera offers to host courses for free but then requires up to 94 percent of any revenue generated. In contracts with non-elite institutions, the company can generate revenue by asking universities to pick from a menu of different fees depending on how they want to use the courses.

Rivard correctly noted that all of the deals he examined "include contractual language that could be used to divert untold amounts of taxpayer or student tuition money to outside vendors" (Rivard 2013a).

Despite initially substantial investments by public universities in MOOC experiments, they largely failed to realize promised benefits, either financial or, more importantly, educational, as even some of their early proponents have concluded (Bowen and Tobin 2015, 172). For all their supposed innovations, xMOOCs such as Coursera, in the words of CUNY educator Luke Waltzer, are nothing more than learning management systems, a "Blackboard with a hipper style-sheet and a slightly enhanced feature set" (Waltzer 2013). Perceived advantages in terms of reduced cost and providing greater student access to higher education could not overcome the greater propensity of most MOOCs to neglect especially important qualitative aspects of teaching and learning. These relational, complex learning needs are especially salient for poor and underprepared undergraduates, many of them students of color, who typify the undergraduate populations at many state universities and most community colleges across the country.

These state universities and community colleges are the institutions most likely to be pressed by austerity policies and in turn to have administrators who are attracted to the cost reductions promised by online instruction. Pew Research Center data from 2011 indicate that nearly nine of ten public universities have already developed at least some online classes as contrasted to six in ten private four-year colleges (Parker, Lenhart, and Moore 2011). Many public university students, however, need both remedial instruction *and* ongoing active engagement with faculty members, graduate assistants, and their student peers to overcome the lack of proper preparation for college-level learning and thinking that can be traced to inadequate K–12 education. These factors help explain the greater attrition and failure rate of poor and underprepared students when enrolled in fully online courses as compared to the better educational outcomes they achieve in traditional, face-to-face courses (Meisenhelder 2013, 13–14). Political scientist Suzanne Mettler correctly concludes that "as public universities move to online education, graduation rates among students who already face challenges in college completion may continue to fall, unless substantial efforts are made to provide student support" (Mettler 2014, 33).

But required levels of student support are increasingly eroded by austerity budgeting and an overreliance on online instruction. A massive 2013 study of more than forty thousand Washington State community and technical college students taking online courses, for example, revealed that "males, younger students, Black students, and students with lower grade point averages . . . suffered decrements in performance in online courses" (Xu and Jaggars 2013). A 2013 study by the Community College Research Center at Teachers College reached a similar conclusion that "online courses may exacerbate already persistent achievement gaps between student subgroups" (Community College Research Center 2013, 5; Fenton 2015). And a 2015 Canadian study of online learners similarly concluded that less motivated and more challenged learners do not do well in MOOCs because of the absence of interpersonal engagement and encouragement, the kinds of emotional and pedagogical interconnections made possible in effective face-to-face classroom teaching (Veletsianos 2015). Some Coursera MOOCs, for example, were reported to have started with a warning to students not to email the professor (Jacobs 2013). Academically challenged students require especially proximate interpersonal relationships and interactions with instructors to become successful learners (Straumsheim 2014c; Foderaro 2011). Recent research suggests that it is well-educated, self-motivated students who, in effect, already know how to learn who gain the most benefit from online courses such as MOOCs (Wexler 2015). Those students' greater success is measured in terms of completion rates, acquisition of new skills and knowledge, and/or enhancement of previously acquired skills (Ho et al. 2014, 2; Selingo 2014; Meisenhelder 2013, 15).

The lack of positive educational outcomes of the two San Jose MOOC experiments in 2013 did slow the momentum, at least in California, to supplant traditional public higher education courses with MOOCs and other online education forms. In addition, the MOOC providers could not work out an acceptable business model that actually paid them for their enormous development costs. Though Sebastian Thrun indicated that Udacity had been working on an improved MOOC product for use in college and university classrooms, he also acknowledged by the end of 2013 that in reaction to the "embarrassing failure" of his SJSU alliance, his company's MOOCs were "a lousy product," that MOOCs "were not a great thing for the bottom 95 percent," and that he was now going to devote Udacity's energies to fee-paying corporate training instead (Schuman 2013; Selingo 2014; Waters 2013b). Two years later, Udacity had shifted its focus from higher education to the technology skills training and certification market, where it offered online courses in coding, mobile programming, data analysis, and web development (Manjoo 2015). Coursera followed a similar path toward corporate training, increasingly working with global higher education partners, reminiscent of the search for other, more amenable and profitable international markets that Sylvan Learning tapped into and that the Fathom project at Columbia also pursued prior to its 2002 shutdown. And while AP continued to land second-tier public university clients/partners for its MOOC2Degree product, the company's continued success is clearly the result of the lack of alternatives that many desperate public university administrators face in the wake of intensifying right-wing political pressures to impose austerity policies on all public institutions, especially public universities. MOOCs, like many prior educational technologies detailed throughout this chapter, clearly promise more than they can deliver pedagogically and financially, most notably to stressed public colleges and universities. Online learning techniques such as blogging and group discussions or "flipped" classrooms (where class time is used for individual and group work rather than traditional lecture delivery) can be useful supplements to traditional face-to-face instruction in what is known as a "hybrid" course (as we suggest in chapter 7). When such tools are used to enhance interaction and engagement, however, any labor cost savings, an essential requirement in profit-making MOOCs, quickly evaporate. In the end, good instruction and successful learning require more, not less, human labor and human engagement, both of which cost money and time and eat into profit margins (Young 2008; Fox 2010; Mangan 2012).

Though doubts about MOOCs have grown in the past few years (MOOCs had entered a "trough of disillusionment" by 2014, according to author Jeffrey Selingo), those doubts will not halt the present momentum to convert public higher education dollars into private forms of profit and pedagogy (Selingo 2014). That struggle cannot be won simply on the basis of rational policies or empirical findings. Power and political influence, not beneficence or rational decision making, will largely determine outcomes. While full-blown MOOC mania happily seemed to have passed by 2014, we should never underestimate academic administrators' or venture capitalists' (and maybe even politicians') intensifying need, given the politics of austerity, to embrace new technological tools that they think will lower teaching costs, increase revenue, and, where allowed, make profits and open new markets for online products. The University of Florida, for example, pushed by the Republican-controlled state legislature, entered into a profit-making relationship in 2014 with Embanet, "an online-education services provider" owned by Pearson to create "a reduced cost, online-only baccalaureate program" (O'Neil 2014). Udacity's partnership with Georgia Tech and AT&T to develop "the first fully accredited MOOC leading to a low-cost Master of Science in Computer Science" launched in the Spring 2014 semester to glowing press reviews and strong early student enrollments (Waters 2013b; Schaffhauser 2014; Straumsheim 2014a). And Jerry Brown, California's many-termed Democratic governor—bolstered by actions such as the unanimous passage in 2013 by the California State Senate of a bill granting automatic college credits at all three levels of the state's public higher education system to students who complete MOOC courses—continues to search for new ways to deploy instructional technology solutions to lower higher education costs in his state, despite demonstrated MOOC failures at SJSU and elsewhere (Walters 2015; Meyer 2013; Lewin 2013b).

Neoliberal Reformer: Michael Crow and the "New American University"

Michael Crow, erstwhile chief technology enthusiast at Columbia University who fathered the ill-fated Fathom experiment in 2000–2001, has served for more than a dozen years as the president of the former Arizona Territorial Normal School, now known as the four-campus Arizona State University (ASU), the nation's largest single public university (Stripling 2015). In that time Crow has promoted himself, in the best Clayton Christensen tradition, as a disruptive innovator (in fact he doesn't like the "president" title, preferring to call himself a "knowledge enterprise architect"). He believes that universities and colleges, especially those that rely heavily on the public purse, and the people who lead them, are far too short-sighted, slow, and moored to academic traditions to confront the major changes that their institutions need to make to survive and thrive. Like Clark Kerr a half century earlier, Crow thinks big about "The New

American University," fancying himself as someone who understands the current, rapidly changing dynamics of public higher education. He believes that the public university can only fulfill its basic democratic mission of providing broad access by dramatically refiguring its structure and purposes. Crow primarily argues for increasing the numbers and diversity of the student body (Pulley 2005). Those positions are certainly consistent with basic assertions we have made throughout this book. The means Crow intends to employ to achieve this democratic outcome, however, *are* controversial and ones that we do not embrace. For Crow, greater access is not linked to greater public investment, but rather to a series of big steps in the reorganization of the public university to extract significant savings including the following: a major reshaping of traditional academic disciplines and structures (including closing and merging departments); dramatic expansion and redesign of the public universities' basic research mission (made possible by increased outside funding, private as well as public); rapid and extensive technological innovation, especially in the use of online courses to reach growing numbers of undergraduates; revenue-generating business partnerships with corporations and companies; and increased income generated by raising tuition fees for both traditional and online students. Arizona was one of four states that in fact doubled the tuition it charged at its public universities between 2006 and 2011, according to a 2012 College Board Advocacy and Policy Center report (Ma and Baum 2012, 3). In the new ASU, whether you are an administrator or a faculty member, you either buy in to Crow's expansive vision or you move on (Guthrie, Mulhern, and Kurzweil 2015, 6–7).[8] Crow can sound almost like a progressive when he asserts that universities must "find ways to massively innovate" without ending up with a higher education system where "we let rich kids get taught by professors and poor kids get taught by computer" and that ASU defines itself "by who we include, not who we exclude" (quoted in Blumenstyk 2012; Keller 2012).

Crow's Arizona circa 2015 is unlike Kerr's California in the early 1960s, however. While Kerr could count on broad bipartisan political and economic support for California's tripartite public higher education system as a public good, Arizona is run by right-wing Republican legislators and governors who are committed to zeroing out state public higher education spending, including ASU's. The university had already absorbed almost $200 million in cuts, or 40 percent of its state funding, between 2008 and 2012 (Stripling 2010; Guthrie, Mulhern, and Kurzweil 2015, 11). Crow has been unsuccessful in making the political and economic case for increased public support of public universities (as Kerr consistently did), given the reactionary nature of Arizona's politics and its state legislature. Rather, Crow has undertaken a major reorganization of ASU, including, but hardly limited to, dramatically expanding the ASU student body (numbering nearly eighty-five thousand at present) and delivering an increasing number of undergraduate courses online (the number of students enrolled in online courses at ASU increased tenfold between 2009 and 2014). Crow believes that these changes will allow him to expand his student body by another one hundred thousand to offset further public budget cuts and render invisible their impact on the quality of education the school delivers (Masterson 2010; Guthrie, Mulhern, and Kurzweil 2015, 7). He basically believes he can out-innovate at ASU the countervailing twin forces of austerity and inequality that are hollowing out the very core of public higher education.

Given his Columbia experience, it is not surprising that Crow enlisted ASU in a variety of online educational experiments to help realize this end. He founded ASU Online, the name of the university's overall digital technology initiative, in 2006–2007, for which he established a separate administrative structure, including its own dean. In the words of a recent Ithaka S+R report on ASU, ASU Online is "a mechanism for increasing enrollments dramatically while managing costs—especially capital costs." One way to save on costs is to shorten the length of courses to 7.5 weeks, in the apt words of the sympathetic Ithaka analysts, "in response to market forces" (Guthrie, Mulhern, and Kurzweil 2015, 11, 16, 26). One of the high-profile projects that ASU Online undertook, a 2011 restructuring of freshman mathematics courses (which as Udacity would learn at SJSU two years later can be the jagged academic rock on which ed-tech flounders), was based on the adapative-learning approach of a company called "Knewton." The company charged ASU only $150 for each enrolled student in the online freshman math course, substantially less than the full-price tuition that the course would otherwise have cost. The self-paced software, based on principles first developed by Harvard behavioral psychologist B. F. Skinner in the 1950s and perfected by Carnegie Mellon in its Open Learning Initiative mathematics course fifty years later, managed to improve freshman pass rates in basic math for the more than nine thousand students who took the freshman course. The experiment also allowed ASU to cut faculty costs, realizing a savings of more than $1 million (half of the total teaching costs) by eliminating a total of sixteen full-time adjunct math teachers. ASU and Crow's formula of achieving scale through technological innovation while reducing operating expenses (read "cutting faculty labor costs") per student had seemingly paid off in the case of the school's freshman math course (Fischman 2011; Blumenstyk 2012).

ASU Online did not stop with mathematics. It jointly announced with Starbucks a unique deal in summer 2014 to general public acclaim to offer online degrees via ASU Online to thousands of Starbucks employees nationwide, many having already completed some college credits. Starbucks, which already had a well-established tuition support program for its employees, allowing them to enroll at a variety of colleges, signed an exclusive deal with Crow and ASU Online to channel the company's 140,000 baristas entirely into online higher education provided by ASU. We have obviously come a long way from the educational provisions in the GI Bill, which vets could use at any accredited college, public or private. After its first year ASU Online received 4,000 Starbucks applicants (with 1,000 actually enrolling), and the program was renewed and extended to Starbucks employees who had not accumulated any college credits. In Spring 2015 more than 1,800 Starbucks employees enrolled in ASU Online (Straumsheim 2014b; Guthrie, Mulhern, and Kurzweil 2015, 16; Starbucks 2015).

Chronicle of Higher Education reporter Goldie Blumenstyk analyzed what she called "the economics of online education" embodied in the Starbucks-ASU deal. Every Starbucks employee who enrolled via Starbucks would receive a 21 to 42 percent reduction (depending on whether they were lower- or upper-division students) in ASU Online's standard tuition charge of approximately $1,500 per online course. ASU also agreed to devote 17 percent of the "sticker price" income it received in financial aid to tuition for financially needy Starbucks students (Pell Grants, which Starbucks employees would mostly qualify for, were projected to underwrite up to 40 percent of the total tuition costs, with Starbucks and, of course, the students themselves each paying a more modest amount). Despite a reduction of up to 59 percent off its full-price tuition, ASU was still able to make money. According to Michael Crow, the increased revenue was largely the result of cost savings traced to recruitment and, like

ASU's earlier online math experiment, using adaptive-learning features to require "very little in the way of faculty time." Crow indicated that the lion's share of the instructional contact with StarbucksU students would be done by a combination of lecturers, adjuncts, and graduate teaching assistants, who clearly cost a great deal less than regular professors. As we noted at the beginning of this chapter, educational leaders like Crow are best able to realize their disruptive dreams either by imposing technological solutions or reducing labor costs. In the case of the Starbucks-ASU project, Crow had managed to do both (Blumenstyk 2014, 2015; *New York Times* 2015; Sullivan 2014; Straumsheim 2014b; Howard 2015; Lobosco 2015). The impact of these changes on the quality of an ASU education remains, of course, undetermined.

Crow also announced a partnership with edX in April 2015 to develop ASU's first MOOCs, to deliver by the 2016 academic year an entire set of eight freshman-year general-education courses.[9] This curriculum is to be developed by ASU's own faculty. The new partnership was intended, according to Crow, to open "a new low-cost, low-risk path to a college degree for students anywhere in the world." Potential students did not even need to formally apply to sign up for the Global Freshman Academy (GFA) MOOCs. Crow touted the new initiative, embodying ASU's commitment to a justice agenda of "academic inclusion and student success, regardless of a student's family circumstances." Apparently taking a lesson from earlier MOOC efforts by Coursera, Udacity, and Academic Partnerships, GFA students get "to essentially try before they buy, taking a free course and proving to themselves that they can handle it," in the words of *CHE* writer Jeffrey R. Young (Young 2015). If GFA students are able to pass that free course, they would have "the option of paying a fee of no more than $200 per credit hour to get college credit for it." Students who pass all eight GFA freshman-year courses could buy their way out of the first year of college for a discounted cost of $6,000. GFA students would be excluded, however, from receiving any kind of federal financial aid because of federal requirements designed to limit tuition grabbing from online for-profit colleges. How ASU faculty were recompensed and under what intellectual property terms to develop the GFA MOOCs remains unclear. What is clear, however, is that the cost of producing a typical MOOC, according to edX president Anant Agarwal, is $100,000. Also apparent is that ASU's on-campus instructional costs will be reduced as GFA students are entirely educated via MOOCs "at a distance," instructionally supported at best by overworked and underpaid part-time adjuncts. Moreover, the ASU-edX contract includes a particularly troubling clause, which gives ASU the right via "appropriate review and approval," to grant course credit to any student anywhere who completes an edX MOOC, even those who take non-ASU courses. ASU will presumably grant such college credits by charging a substantial fee (the $200 per credit that GFA students have to pay would likely be a bare minimum). Democratic pieties about wider access aside, the business of extracting maximal dollars from students and further privatizing university costs are clearly primary drivers of this recent ASU-edX MOOC initiative (Huckabee 2015; Blumenstyk 2015; Straumsheim 2015b; edX 2015; Warner 2015b; Warner 2015c).

Technological solutions are never value neutral. They reflect the underlying purposes and assumptions of those implementing them. The ways in which instructional technologies have been incorporated into public higher education over the past two decades have largely served to deepen inequality, further separating educational outcomes and processes for students in public universities from those in private, four-year institutions. Inequality has grown in several ways. Poor students of color, including first-generation immigrants, who disproportionately attend publicly supported institutions facing the most pressing austerity problems, have borne the brunt of technological solutions through their higher failure and lower completion rates in online courses they are often required to take. Increasing reliance on online instruction also cuts off academically challenged students from the pedagogical supports and face-to-face interactions that they need to succeed educationally. In addition, online courses and MOOCs rely heavily on part-time instructors, who are poorly paid, overworked, and lack the job security necessary to resist administration-imposed changes. Increasing "adjunctification" (an ugly term coined circa 2002) further exacerbates the growing inequalities within the public university system with respect to salaries, working conditions, and the employment protections that full-time faculty status affords (Jenkins 2014). The cost-reduction, profit-making, and labor-saving drives of distance-learning technologies when linked to austerity and the market further exacerbate the inequalities described in the prior chapters. If not checked, these developments will be a primary and continuing driver of growing inequality across the higher education system, legitimated by the allure of digital technology and market solutions to public problems. Only when technological innovation—including or especially innovation filtered through pedagogically appropriate instructional improvements—is fully embraced and determined by faculty members, rather than by cost-cutting administrators and/or profit-driven entrepreneurs, will it serve its promised function of enhancing the quality of teaching and learning in a range of academic environments. Faculty- and student-led reform efforts, not only in technology but also in reimagining the broader political economy of public higher education, will be more fully discussed in the concluding chapter.

PART III

RESISTANCE EFFORTS AND THE FIGHT FOR EMANCIPATORY EDUCATION

[7]

Fighting for the Soul of Public Higher Education

Restructuring, Abandonment, and Dissolution

The calls by legislators, private entrepreneurs, and foundations to remake public higher education grow daily (*New York Times* 2015; Fichtenbaum 2015; Ross 2015). In the 1990s corporate reformers cast their gaze on health care and, in the first decade of the new millennium, on K–12 education. As corporate reform focuses on higher education, the intention is to shift the cost of public education from the states to individual colleges and students. This policy agenda has in turn produced outcomes fraught with contradictions. These include soaring student debt, accompanied by their diminished capacity to finish college; the explosion of overworked, part-time faculty as the largest part of the instructional labor force, resulting in less time for students; the imposition of centralized managerial "reforms" organized to extract greater efficiencies that tend to dilute curricula; and an expanding regimen of outcomes based on "metrics" that diverts attention away from the declining quality of education. These contradictions are at the heart of both the unraveling of public higher education and the effort to redistribute public resources away from public universities. As poor and working-class students and their families carry more and more of the financial responsibility, the costs of attaining a degree have become prohibitive. These austerity-driven initiatives have become part of a naturalized policy discourse that assumes no other options exist for achieving a quality higher education.

This "new normal" of disinvestment, privatization, and regressive imposition of increasing tuition charges on working-class and poor students produces many redistributive benefits for the affluent. The entry of for-profit companies into the core work of higher education includes heavy reliance on distance-learning technologies, fundamental transformation of key elements of the undergraduate and graduate curriculum, and outsourcing instruction, as well as support services (Myers 2015; Stripling 2015a; Wittner 2013). The policies sustaining this redistributive agenda both contemplated and already in place are bipartisan. Both the Democratic and Republican parties, nationally and at the state level, are committed to austerity policies of regressive taxation on the one hand and diminished financing of public higher education on the other. The reliance on accountability measures such as graduation rates, time to degree, freezing of tuition, and efficiencies achieved by distance learning are part of a policy agenda in which austerity metrics eclipse public investment as the only rational way to restructure public institutions. The actual experiences of starved public institutions and in turn the diminishment of the quality of the education they provide are accepted as forms of collateral damage.

This reform agenda mimics the experience of K–12 public education. As Naomi Klein has indicated in *The Shock Doctrine* (2008), the rededication of public resources for private gain begins with a crisis. Public higher education's crisis is typically described in terms of low graduation rates and soaring tuition costs. The origins of the crisis are linked to unaccountable public agencies, inefficient professionals, and the absence of corporate principles to guide the management of these public institutions. This framework for defining the crisis of public higher education consequently drives austerity-focused policy solutions. Popular discourse reinforces the notion that public higher education's problems can be solved by emphasizing metrics of accountability and performance-based funding, reduced professional autonomy, the outsourcing of functions to the private sector, and greater uses of technology, and/or breaking worker power as evidenced by "adjunctification" to extract labor savings. These policy reforms fail by design to address the larger problem of underfinanced public institutions. At its core, this policy regimen blames professionals who are forced to teach greater numbers of students and with reduced institutional support. Present state and federal policies focus increasingly on cost savings, in turn yielding

- more part-time faculty to achieve greater efficiencies by lowering labor costs in the classroom (thus increasing inequalities in the provision of this public good);

- greater flexibility in paying back student loans with no intention of eliminating the need to borrow; and
- acceleration of the outsourcing of public functions at universities to produce the revenue needed for the institutions to survive (Field 2015b; Singer 2015; Turkel 2006).

Klein (2008) indicates that these policies are neither accidental nor natural, but rather the product of conscious political and economic decision making to redistribute public resources upward and remake public institutions into diminished, quasi-private offerings. In essence, the diminishment and restructuring represent an abandonment of poor and working-class needs and a further reduction in the quality of public higher education. From Senator Lamar Alexander's announced policy priorities of data collection and assessment regarding the 2015 Reauthorization of the Higher Education Act, to President Obama's proposal for a student bill of rights that emphasizes unfunded mandates, to the *New York Times*'s call for economic diversity to be added to the variables largely measuring private college rankings, and to the Gates Foundation's advocacy for college-degree completion as a basis for rewarding and punishing colleges—the present policy beats the drum for a politics and economics of continued austerity (Fain 2015b; Field 2015b; Stratford 2015). None of these proposals challenges the present overarching policy regimen of privatization, public disinvestment, and diminished quality of public higher education. More to the point, not one of the policy proposals challenges the redistribution of resources through the reallocation of public monies from the bottom of the social order to the top. Unfortunately, we cannot expect public officials or policy makers to contest this agenda when the political process has been flooded with money from dominant economic interests and where the social movements necessary to advance a progressive agenda are either dormant or in decline. It is clear that we are in the midst of a class war, partly illustrated by higher education policy making.

Headlines from a cross section of media echo themes of restructuring, abandonment, and dissolution of public higher education.

- "Killing All State Support": "Arizona has a reputation for frugality with regard to state support for higher education. . . . [An agreed upon deal] would completely eliminate state support for the three largest community districts in the state—while also imposing deep cuts on public universities" (Jaschik 2015, 1A).

- "Welcome to Ohio State, Where Everything Is for Sale": ". . . the game-changing deal we signed in 2012 to lease campus parking—all 37,000 spaces!—to an Australian investment firm for 50 years. The deal was worth almost $500 million dollars" (Conn 2015, B2).
- "Why Government Spends More per Pupil at Elite Private Universities than at Public Universities": "Government subsidies to elite private universities take the form of tax deductions for people who make charitable contributions. In economic terms a tax deduction is the same as government spending. . . . A few years back Meg Whitman, now CEO of Hewlett-Packard, contributed $30 million to Princeton. In return she received a tax break estimated to be around $10 million. . . . The annual government subsidy at Princeton University . . . is about $54,000 per student, according to an estimate by economist Richard Vedder. Other elite privates aren't far behind" (Reich 2014).
- "A *Chronicle* Reporter Wrote a Book About the Higher-Ed Crisis. These 5 Things Surprised Her Most": "Despite the fervor over innovations in higher education, there is also the very real risk that some of the same forces that make it hard for lower-income students to complete college . . . may also undermine their ability to take advantage of those innovations. . . . The few studies that have been undertaken on the efficacy of online education and other kinds of courses with less structure or academic support, and fewer opportunities for social connections, found that students tended to become more frustrated and less likely to continue their education" (Blumenstyk 2014b, A12).
- "Imperiled Leaders": "The President of the University of Wisconsin system . . . said last week that he would resign if the state Legislature and Gov. Scott Walker went ahead with plans to cut $300 million from the university's appropriations over two years and to strip guarantees for tenure, shared governance and academic freedom from state law" (Biemiller 2015, A2; *New York Times* Editorial Board 2015).
- "California and N.Y. are thinking big on higher education. Will the feds?": "Now, it seems, it is the states that are expansive [in their thinking about higher education]. Or at least some of them. That's a takeaway from recent interviews with higher ed leaders from the Empire State and Golden State. . . . SUNY wants to

award 150,000 degrees a year by 2020 [up from 93,000]. . . . The UC Board of Regents has approved a contingency plan to raise tuition up to 5 percent in each of the next five years, unless the state provides enough funding to make the increases unnecessary. . . . Timothy P. White, chancellor of CSU . . . [stated] 'California has two droughts. . . . One is a lack of water. The other is a lack of people with college degrees'" (Anderson 2015).

- "The Must-Attend Event for Education Technology Investors": "With more than 2,000 attendees this year, the conference is an indication of the high political stakes involved in education and of the big money businesses hope to reap in the sector. The event also now serves as an important stop for policy makers seeking to broadcast their commitment to industry growth" (Singer 2015, B4).

This sample of recent headlines illustrates the continuing tension in public higher education with regard to enlarging access, technology used as a cost-saving panacea, disinvestment or austerity as the driver of public education policy, and the continuing decline of educational quality. Correcting the current imbalance in the restructuring of higher education fundamentally requires not only technical or bipartisan policy making, but also the power of a political movement to emphasize within popular discourse and policy making the growing racial and class divides in access to quality public higher education.

The new movement's platform for change must enunciate a commitment to redistributive strategic investment (from the top to the bottom of the social and economic order) and an education, in Nancy Fraser's (2013) analysis, that addresses the need for both a road map to economic mobility or workforce skill development and a guide to intellectual emancipation. The intention to join public higher education and intellectual emancipation is particularly salient to our own analysis. As public higher education is increasingly required to emphasize student outcomes such as graduation rates and time to degree within a context of shrinking resources, it is forced to retreat from a number of its basic historical functions. These functions include fostering critical thinking, engaging in relational interpretations of texts, and establishing intellectual and cultural connections to a larger world. In turn, this increasingly constrained education diminishes the capacity of students to become effective citizens within a democratic social order, thus weakening the basic fiber of our politics and culture. The development of an engaged citizenry has been a consistent, albeit secondary, function of public higher education and K–12 education since their origins in the nineteenth century. The balance between citizenship and workforce development has also been a constant source of tension in higher education's evolution over the past 150 years. As we begin to explore possibilities of an alternative public higher education system to the one now being imprinted on public consciousness in legislation, through the media, and by corporate intention, we must pull back for a moment. We must also consider how public higher education has historically been a site of struggle relating to an intention to remake the lives and occupations of the poor and the working class.

Higher education has historically been seen as one of the surest paths to upward mobility, which includes finding a stable job, owning a house, and achieving a middle-class lifestyle while working one's way up and/or laboring in a blue-collar, unionized job. During the neoliberal era that began in the 1980s, the aspiration of a middle-class life that typified the American Dream became linked, however precariously, to the completion of college and entry into a white-collar occupation. That trajectory is no longer assured, especially for Latino and African American college graduates who actually suffered a *drop* of between 28 and 56 percent in overall net worth between 1992 and 2013 (Cohen 2015).

The Struggle over Purposes and Practices

Present mainstream policy discourse regarding public higher education, according to University of Delaware sociologist Gerald Turkel, offers three responses to the fiscal crisis facing higher education: "1) a view that cutting government support would actually be beneficial; 2) a view toward balancing public and private spending; 3) a view toward maximizing government support by providing for free higher education" (Turkel 2006, 18). The first approach creates a politics of intensifying austerity that disproportionately affects poor students, especially students of color. The second policy redirects money away from public higher education, as it encourages political resistance to increased public investment or progressive taxation. Economic growth alone will not "lift all boats" or, in this instance, the budgets of public agencies. Even when economic growth has been achieved during the last two decades, greater public investment in higher education has not followed. Rather, such growth has more often than not produced increased corporate or individual tax reductions, thus contributing to the long-term diminishment of public budgets and leaving policies of austerity intact. The third option, although the most politically unlikely, is also the only policy frame offering a path toward actual resource redistribution. A political commitment to free tuition offers concrete hope of stemming the rapid expansion of student debt. Free tuition must be accompanied by an increase in public resources to replace its loss. Only in this way can it not linger as a policy dictate joined to an unfunded mandate. The latter approach would only serve to intensify the existing fiscal crisis in higher education by drying up its most reliable and increasingly largest revenue stream—tuition—without using public revenue to replace it.

Free tuition is no longer a "pie-in-the-sky" policy fantasy. In the first half of 2015 it was a viable policy option. President Obama's 2015 State of the Union address, which promised to invest $60 billion to achieve the goal of free tuition in community colleges, altered political discourse regarding who should pay for public higher education (Stripling 2015b; Shear 2015). The president targeted community colleges, where the greatest concentrations of poor and working-class students were situated and the lowest per-capita public investments were made. The federal commitment to increase spending was linked to a mandate for greater state investment (Stripling 2015b). We will more fully elaborate the content of this policy initiative and further explain its potential to recast the politics of higher education later in the chapter. At this point, though, it is important to view it as an alternative to austerity. It signals that alternatives to austerity are both politically possible and economically necessary. Free tuition offers a major redistributive alternative to disinvestment.

Two of the nation's overriding policy objectives—the hope of developing a critically informed citizenry and evolving a workforce capable of meeting the many challenges of the twenty-first century—are inextricably linked to creating a robust system of public higher education. The shaping of a modern system of public higher education between the 1930s and the 1970s involved political struggle to address these two educational objectives. The evolution of interdisciplinary work; scientific breakthroughs in computer science; mapping of the genome; the astrophysics of launching satellites and spacecraft; and heightened attention to the hitherto subordinated knowledge of race, ethnicity, gender, sexuality, and class in part mark the recent history of higher education. It is important not to romanticize this history, however. Much of the effort to elevate subordinated knowledge in the social sciences and humanities emerged out of pitched political battles both inside and outside the university. Access to a university education during this time was not universal—race, gender, sexuality, and class identities influenced individuals' capacities to enter and complete a college education. Equally important, public investment varied depending on the status of the school and the historical achievements of the student body and faculty. Finally, students and the communities in which universities are embedded had little if any opportunity to influence the direction of institutional decision making related to curricula. This was the case particularly when course materials were badly out of date or were outright racist, sexist, or homophobic. The lack of such community participation was especially troubling when institutions threatened to remake historic neighborhoods or failed to disseminate their expertise in ways that could benefit the surrounding community's physical health or economic development.

The public university, even in the halcyon years of the 1960s—a time of rapid expansion and heightened access and investment—was a site of struggle, often failing to meet even the most basic needs of its students and the larger community. At the same time, it was a place where access to a quality higher education occurred with greater frequency for those who historically had little hope of achieving a college education and where hearts, minds, and lives were often reinvented and redefined. Thus we have two truths, both salient to the evolution of public higher education in our own time.

Achieving Emancipatory Education

The rebuilding of public higher education is only in part about a quantitative redistributive investment in working-class and poor Americans' educations. Policy makers must also address the critical and complementary question of *how* to invest the money. What kinds of investments are necessary to provide not merely access, but also a quality educational experience? New School critical theorist Nancy Fraser describes three approaches that influence the formation of a public good: marketization, or the evolution of state services that are either outsourced to the private sector or mimic its practices; quantitative dollars earmarked for the provision of base-line protective services (for example, welfare, income entitlements, or higher education tuition subsidies); and the qualitative development of services that do not simply offer protections from the market but instead provide forms of emancipatory experience (for example, course work that elevates issues such as race, gender, and sexuality as a way of clarifying, situating, and explaining individual or group experiences) (Fraser 2013). These approaches that contribute to the formation of a public good also produce critical contradictions. Fraser points out that "even as it overcomes domination, emancipation may help dissolve the solidary ethical basis of social protection, thus clearing a path for marketization" (Fraser 2013, 129). The neglect of experiences of emancipation in thinking about public goods, and almost exclusive attention to conflicts between marketization and social protection, has contributed to the underdevelopment of a progressive agenda for state services and, more specifically, higher education. Too often right-wing or conservative forces have used a language of choice, freedom, and liberation from soaring bureaucratic costs as synonyms for emancipation. This paves the way for a rollback of state-based protectionist policies associated with the provision of everything from tuition subsidies in higher education, to expanded public housing, to regulation of the prescription drug industry and the environment. Any campaign for public higher education must address the social protection needs of students (for example, minimizing or eliminating tuition costs) and emphasize an emancipatory educational experience intended to reshape their intellectual capacities and aspirations. Each of these demands is essential in promoting a different vision and purpose for the public university as it contests marketization reforms. This struggle must also be firmly identified with class, gender, sexuality, and racial issues and identities. Policies of disinvestment and the consequent decline in quality are occurring when access costs to public higher education for poor students, especially those of color, have been greatly increased. That is a central contradiction of present austerity policy in public higher education.

To at least begin to sketch the character of an emancipatory, quality public higher education we will briefly address in turn the following four questions: What types of strategic investments are most likely to contribute to a quality educational experience? How should we direct or target these investments to create the kind of university labor force necessary to best assure a quality education? What should be the auspices for organizing and administering the public good of higher education? How can digital technology best be deployed to enhance the quality of teaching and learning in public higher education?

What Types of Strategic Investments Are Needed?

Any joining of quality higher education to strategic public investment unsurprisingly must begin with the creation of robust instructional/ learner relationships between faculty and students. This is best accomplished through smaller classes and expanded time dedicated to contact or encounter inside and outside the classroom. Public institutions also need to invest in academic support and instructional technology services implemented and controlled by faculty that are necessary to improve student writing and critical thinking skills, including creative and strategic use of digital resources such as ePortfolios, "flipped" classrooms, and student blogging. Increased expenditures on academic guidance and mental health services are also essential to the academic development of students. A diverse and expanded range of course offerings spanning the humanities, natural sciences, and social sciences helps insure that students will have access to the classes they require to graduate on time and the breadth of intellectual experience necessary to become informed citizens. An expanded curriculum is also essential to building the advanced instruction critical to master complex bodies of knowledge, orient students to the constructive and appropriate uses of digital resources that are reshaping academic research and writing, and envisioning a trajectory that will carry them to the next stage of their intellectual development, more independent learning.

In addition, expanded investments in remedial instruction need to be made, targeting those students who have historically experienced underinvestment in both their K–12 and their higher education, the way CUNY's pioneering SEEK program once did for poorly prepared students of color in the 1960s and 1970s. The failures of the public K–12 system, frequently, although not entirely, traced to policies of austerity, undermine higher education course work and cannot be ignored or deflected through narrow metrics of graduation rates, time to degree, and sink-or-swim practices. Instructors and students cannot be expected to address basic math, writing, and reading challenges without the provision of critical learning supports. This can be accomplished through programs like CUNY's ASAP, which "substantially improved students' academic outcomes over three years, almost doubling graduation rates" (Scrivener et al. 2015, 3). This was accomplished through investment in intensified forms of instruction, including advising and smaller classes, as well as tuition subsidies. Researchers at the Manpower Demonstration Research Corp. note that "at the three-year point, the cost per degree was lower in ASAP than in the control condition. Because the program generated so many more graduates than the usual college services, the cost per degree was lower despite the substantial investment required to operate the program" (3). Clearly, we know how to effectively educate even the most challenged students through targeted program investment. We also know that the benefits of investment relative to cost are high as measured by efficiency measures of graduation and time to degree. Yet we continue to ignore the need for such investment while blaming public universities and particularly community colleges for low graduation rates in the midst of both declining investment and increasing numbers of academically underprepared students.

Building a Better Knowledge Workforce

If scholars and teachers are expected to evolve or invent an emancipatory education, they must be provided the social protections of job security, livable wages, and decent working conditions that promote the engagement and employment continuity necessary to enrich student learning. Many part-time faculty and staff laboring in the university must cobble together multiple adjunct jobs, which pay poverty wages and offer no job security. This stripped-down version of academic employment predictably leads too often to stripped-down forms of higher education. As part-time instructors run from class to class, time to engage students outside the classroom is an increasingly scarce commodity. Instructor exhaustion in the classroom is an epidemic as the continuing struggle to do the piece work necessary to stitch together a bare living grows ever more difficult for many. Finally, the insecurity of having no assurances of future employment beyond the single course or series of single courses being taught constrains academic freedom, as it is increasingly identified as a disappearing privilege of job stability. This causes many contingent instructors to steer their classroom discussions away from the controversies of politics, or complex ideas, or a discourse of dissent in relationship to dominant ideas. To correct for this diminished instructional capacity to engage relationally and substantively with students, necessary targeted correctives of increased pay and job security for part-time faculty and teaching assistants also need to be made.

Where Should Public Higher Education Be Situated?

The auspices for development of public higher education must be governmental and not the private sector. Public bureaucracy and, more specifically, universities have rightly been critiqued as having organizational inclinations that limit their productivity. These administrative predispositions include:

- generating costly and largely unproductive red tape;
- insulating itself from competition and innovation;
- elevating elite or narrowly framed forms of knowledge while subordinating often distinctive but relatively undervalued or invisible knowledge to the edges and lowest rungs of the academy; and
- limiting democratic participation in decision making to administrators and, to a lesser degree, faculty; the influence of surrounding communities and students in decision making is at best marginalized and at worst nonexistent.

No doubt these predispositions individually and cumulatively narrow the ambition of emancipatory learning projects in public higher education. By locating the governance and financing of public good in the public sphere, however, their ultimate character is more likely to be shaped by the push and pull of democratic debate and conflict between stakeholders than it is or has been in the private sector.

For-profit higher education institutions' drive for profit making affects how they organize themselves. Efficiencies of lower labor costs and maximization of revenue attached to increased student enrollments are more likely to define the character of a restructured, privatized service. This conclusion is powerfully illustrated by the actual experiences of for-profit higher education, which have resulted in relatively low graduation rates, near-total reliance on technology and distance learning for instruction, instructional labor forces almost exclusively comprised of part-time instructors, and heavy dependence on low-income students taking out federally guaranteed loans to pay tuition as a way to generate and guarantee institutional profits. Alternatively, the public sphere is more likely to invest its resources in developing ambitious learning trajectories consonant with its nonprofit, democratic mission and character. These two sets of objectives cannot be reconciled. Either we have an education that maximizes investment for a longer-term public good or one that emphasizes the organization of investment to increase private gain. Choosing redistributive forms of social protection and emancipatory investment rather than profit making as a basis for organizing public higher education is more likely to contribute to the larger social good by helping narrow various kinds of inequality. For these reasons and despite the often contradictory impulses of public bureaucracies regarding quality, innovation, and democratic decision making, we strongly support an exclusive siting of public higher education governance, financing, and instruction under the aegis of state or local governments.

Deploying Technology to Improve Teaching and Learning

University faculty members across the country have fought back against austerity-inspired efforts to automatize the process of teaching and learning and to reduce or deskill the academic workforce. But faculty resistance to administration-imposed technology "solutions" is not mere knee-jerk Luddism, nor has it been faculty members' only response to academic technology. Rather, university faculty have also actively embraced the use of a range of digital technologies to help reimagine and enhance the quality of their teaching and their students' learning outcomes.

The digital affordances employed and sometimes even conceived, designed, and developed by university faculty, staff, and graduate students have largely been built around inclusive notions of openness and collaboration, both hallmarks of good scholarship and effective pedagogy. One key attribute of this idea of openness has been the faculty rejection of proprietary software typically favored by administrators and the adoption instead of free and open-source software that has helped fundamentally redefine contemporary computing since its 1980s emergence. That movement was predicated on the belief that computer software should be freely and openly shared, worked on and updated collaboratively, and widely used without having to pay for such use (Benkler 2007, 64–67). This free and open-source philosophy functioned as a kind of principled countercultural/counterhegemonic opposition to the venture capital/ profit-driven sensibilities that animated the digital entrepreneurs and their university enablers.[1] The embrace of open-source software in many universities, especially by faculty and students, occurred in parallel to the increasing popularity of social media platforms (e.g., Facebook, Twitter, and Wikipedia) after 2005. Social media helped transform the daily online experience of hundreds of millions of ordinary people worldwide, linking them in a series of vast and distributed digital networks in what Harvard political theorist Yochai Benkler has described as the "networked information economy" (52–56). Contemporary college students are usually quite comfortable using the Internet and a variety of social media software to share and discover information and ideas, which orients them to the pedagogical uses of digital media in the learning process. Such developments in open source and social media computing led many public university faculty members over the past decade to search for innovative ways to incorporate digital tools into their academic research and, most importantly for our purposes here, into college curricula.

Luke Waltzer, a CUNY colleague, offers insight into the ways digital technology helped him transform the teaching and learning process in his undergraduate history classroom:

> Teaching with technology was about exploring and embracing new possibilities rather than reinforcing existing structures. They [his fellow users of academic technology] showed me that there was as much to learn from breaking down and reflecting upon the processes by which we produce knowledge as there was in using technology to engage deeply with content. They sharpened my understanding of experiential learning, and got me to focus more on nurturing sustained [student] engagement. (Waltzer 2010)

We point to two digital initiatives as illustrative of such efforts to enhance classroom teaching and encourage active learning by students, developed by faculty, staff, and graduate students at various campuses of the City University of New York, where both authors work. These initiatives are emblematic of larger national and even international trends in higher education to use digital tools and open-source software to improve teaching and learning. Especially salient are emerging "hybrid" educational models that combine traditional face-to-face classroom instruction with asynchronous uses of digital tools to encourage and sustain student engagement, active learning, and, more broadly, intellectual growth (Picciano, Dziuban, and Graham 2013).

THE CUNY ACADEMIC COMMONS

Created in 2009 by a group of CUNY faculty members, CUNY Academic Commons (CAC) is designed as a free-standing digital space and unified platform outside of central CUNY administrative control that allows faculty and graduate students to engage in collaborative work and to exchange information and ideas across the dispersed twenty-four-campus CUNY system. CAC is actively governed by a committee of CUNY faculty, staff, and technology administrators and is built in WordPress and BuddyPress, two widely used open-source software programs that encourage and facilitate online communication and collaboration.

CAC was conceived and is operated "to support," in the words of one of its founding documents, "faculty initiatives and build community through the use(s) of technology in teaching and learning. The free exchange of knowledge among colleagues across the university is central to better educating the student body and expanding professional development opportunities for faculty research and teaching" (CUNY Academic Commons 2009; Brier 2012, 396–97). In the seven years since its 2009 launch, CAC has garnered more than eight thousand CUNY faculty, staff, and graduate students who use its group sites, blogs, and wikis to find one another; to share information and ideas; to support and enhance the teaching of graduate-level courses, thus avoiding the CUNY-mandated use of the far more limited Blackboard proprietary learning management system; to collaborate on digital and other types of academic projects; and to form and sustain intellectual, political, cultural, and social communities.[2] In an era of increasing austerity in public institutions such as CUNY, CAC has served as an important communications tool to link faculty, staff, and graduate students together in common intellectual, pedagogical, and political issues and struggles. CAC has contributed immeasurably to building a sense of community and active intellectual engagement across the diverse and often fragmented multicampus CUNY system. And, in the spirit of the open-source idea, the CAC team has made the underlying software platform and computer code available for free to all potential users worldwide in its "Commons in a Box" program (Commonsinabox.org, n.d.).

Three out of four entering CUNY students received their high school diplomas from the New York City public schools. Because of the long-term failure of New York City public schools to properly prepare for college many of the tens of thousands of students who graduate, the CUNY system has had to provide academic support to entering undergraduates who need a significant amount of remedial help in basic reading, writing, and mathematics. One important remedial initiative at CUNY has been the Writing across the Curriculum (WAC) program, created in the late 1990s. WAC grew significantly over the next decade, with as many as 150 doctoral students employed each year as WAC fellows. The fellows use a variety of teaching methodologies to improve the basic writing skills of new undergraduates across all courses and academic programs at CUNY's community and senior colleges. WAC represents a continuation of CUNY's historic commitment, dating back to the 1960s, as described in chapter 3, to teach writing skills as a critical component of educating CUNY's working-class student body. This commitment is still sorely needed but more difficult to achieve half a century after its initial introduction, especially given the straitened financial circumstances of a large public institution like CUNY that faces persistent political pressure to "do more with less" (Brier 2012, 393).

Almost from the outset of WAC, CUNY writing fellows helped integrate digital technologies into WAC pedagogy. This includes Baruch College, home to CUNY's business school. WAC launched Blogs@Baruch in 2008, an online publishing and academic networking platform built in WordPress and BuddyPress, like CAC. Blogs@Baruch is used for course weblogs, student journals and publications, curriculum development, administrative communication, and faculty development (Brier 2012, 393–94). The key purpose of Blogs@Baruch is simply expressed: "College students should write regularly in all disciplines and in a variety of formats and genres" (Blogs@Baruch 2015). Good writing, critical reading, and informed discussion are the hallmarks of an educated student body and essential to informed citizenship. Half a dozen CUNY writing fellows collaborate with several hundred Baruch faculty members, supporting 250 WordPress course sites with a total enrollment of three to five thousand students during each academic year. Since its inception, Blogs@Baruch has set up more than four thousand WordPress faculty and student sites and served more than twenty thousand Baruch students. Faculty users of Blogs@Baruch have noted increased student engagement with all aspects of their learning, especially in their ability to use writing to communicate complex ideas and information (Francoeur 2014; Jones 2009). The blogging platform has also been used successfully to help first-year Baruch students enrolled in the college's SEEK program to improve their basic writing skills, aided by the highly interactive writing and peer reader community that blogging generates (Kreniske 2015). Blogs@Baruch is an instance of a public university committing itself despite its limited financial resources to deploy digital affordances thoughtfully to improve teaching and the educational success as well as the capacity of its working-class student body.

These two CUNY digital technology projects are offered as illustrative of the digital tools that emancipate college faculty, staff, and graduate students to develop more effective instructional approaches and strategies in the contemporary public university. CUNY is not unique in this regard, as the existence of important and innovative digital programs, projects, and tools created at public schools such as George Mason University, the universities of Virginia and Connecticut, and UCLA indicate. This digital work in public universities is not driven forward by a desire to save or make money by cutting labor costs in an era of austerity, as it is for far too many academic administrators and university trustees. Nor is it solely focused on distance learning. Rather, it is about using digital technology creatively and in a mixed-method, hybrid model to facilitate active and engaged learning by undergraduates and graduate students and to improve their communication skills, learning outcomes, and understanding of the world they inhabit.

As the development and growing uses of CAC and Blogs@Baruch indicate, good teaching and successful student learning in twenty-first-century public universities cannot be achieved without real financial expenditures, including on thoughtful and pedagogically appropriate deployment of digital technology. Engaged learning, one of the key attributes of democratic education, should not simply be cheapened to realize budget cuts via reduced labor costs and increased class size. The digital transformation of public higher education that we envision does not comply with the dictates of an austerity regime that will in the end only diminish the quality of that education. To the contrary, as the above examples suggest, concrete and useful alternatives do exist to joining of austerity, digital technology, and reduced quality of public higher education. These alternatives have been achieved because of the commitment of faculty and staff to experiment and dedicate the time and intellectual energy necessary to implement new and creative uses of digital technology. To evolve such platforms and pedagogy on a larger scale, however, faculty and staff will require greater financial and institutional support, not less.

Political Choice and Struggle

A public good is a complex and contradictory entity at once embedded in organizations, dependent on professional skill, profoundly shaped by the quality of relationships between providers and seekers of services, created through state investment, and ultimately configured and refigured on the basis of class forces. The last point is especially important. Public goods are not phenomena derived from a naturalized political environment or products of the *noblesse oblige* of dominant economic interests. To the contrary, public goods such as Unemployment Insurance, Social Security, and Medicaid have emerged, matured, and decayed in the heat of political struggles of working-class citizens seeking protection from the harsh outcomes of the market. Equally important, public goods such as higher education emerge less out of a desire for survival than an aspiration for mobility and transformation. As noted earlier, higher education investment is also linked to the production of economic multipliers, yielding a more competitive workforce and increased mobility. It has also been a gateway to reinventing individual identity, one's relationship to the world, and the life of the mind. These more qualitative and subtle experiences of higher education are inextricably linked with both its long history and its current articulated mission. How much is invested in either the economic or the intellectual development of working people through public higher education, however, is and always has been an open political question.

The levels and types of investment made in public goods are neither predetermined nor consequences simply of expertise or rational decision making. Rather, they are political choices and struggles determined in large part by the relative power of different class interests and the consequent distribution of scarce resources. While other factors such as the status of a nation's international competitiveness and the consequent shifting social reproduction needs of the labor force have important implications in the production of a public good, ultimately power and class interest are the most critical explanatory variables in determining the level of investment and the actual content of public goods such as higher education. In the 1930s and the 1960s, social movements influenced both investment levels and the types of public goods created. The political push-and-pull between social movements and a reluctant state tethered to dominant economic interests yielded greater levels of investment in public goods than would otherwise have been made available. The choice for greater investment in social services, the expansion of collective social protections, and qualitative changes in programs and organizations, such as the emergence of ethnic and gender studies programs in universities and colleges in the 1970s, occurred because of a movement politics that demanded it.

We are quite clear that it is in the interest of working people to have public goods flow from a context of economic redistribution rather than austerity. Economic investment is critical to creating robust services that can meaningfully improve the life circumstances of working people. However, simply increasing the volume of resources, although necessary, is not sufficient. They must be invested wisely and strategically.

Conversely, austerity aligns with dominant economic class interests. It is legitimated through the logic of the market and practices of accountability based on metrics in service of the radical restructuring of what are deemed flawed and failed public goods. It is within this context that choices are being made to recompose public goods such as higher education in ways that yield less cost, limit demands for progressive taxes, and promote greater possibilities for profit making. Such choices have implications regarding who wins and who loses in the twenty-first century as the larger economy, the state, and public goods are remade.

Fault Lines in Current Struggles

Various sites of struggle exist in the continuing effort to implement, consolidate, and expand austerity policy. Austerity policy makers promise that better public goods can be produced more cheaply by transferring public functions to the market. Technology is a key in unlocking the puzzle of how to at once save money and increase quality. Michael Crow, for example, has proposed that all of the university's freshmen requirements be offered online in MOOC-like courses in collaboration with the edX consortium. He expects this new instruction transmission belt to increase access and improve the overall quality of the curriculum (Stripling 2015a). No matter the promise of quality instruction and social justice afforded by greater access, we must remember that austerity has in fact been the primary force in technological reform across time. Austerity, or disinvestment, intensifies the need for labor-saving forms of technology to remake the university as it is less and less able to depend on public money or a downsized and contingent academic labor force to generate the revenue needed to pay its bills. Austerity is the larger context that shapes the uses of the technology in the public arena.

The critical question is whether distance-learning technology tethered to for-profit companies and/or MOOCs better meets the academic needs of students than other possible forms of instruction, especially the needs of poor students of color. Is this the kind of education that affluent parents would countenance for their children in an ever more competitive economy? Does this kind of education represent the best fit for academically challenged students entering college? These questions are rarely raised in policy-making circles driven by the economics of reducing costs while sustaining access. What is lost in current policy discourse regarding higher education is attention to matters of quality and the diverse learning needs of students. We would assert that the default position of mass distance learning for poor and working-class students in an era of austerity, especially when it is linked to profit-making companies, is most fundamentally a political decision of disinvestment rather than a choice based on the actual pedagogical needs of the students.

Another fault line in the struggle for public higher education is located at the conjunction between public investment and student outcomes. Policies of performance-based funding and attendant metrics of accountability have been implemented in a cross section of states, including Ohio and Tennessee. After-graduation job placements, graduation rates, and time to degree are increasingly important in assessing the performance of public universities. These policies also share a concern for maximal use of scarce resources to best meet projected demands of the labor market. Market volatility in combination with austerity policies produce in turn the logic of tuition-paying students increasingly being targeted for public investment based on the probability they will generate more productive yields (for example, shorter time to graduation, greater academic readiness for high-paying market jobs, and/or higher standardized test scores).

This formulation in part explains policies of increased per capita investment in students as we examine the higher education hierarchy from community colleges and senior public colleges to private colleges (Carnevale and Strohl 2010). Suffice it to say at this point in our analysis that where investment lags, class size soars, the number of part-time faculty expands, and distance learning increasingly dominates. In turn, the quality of education will decline and so too will the potential career trajectories afforded by the college experience. The bundling of metrics of academic achievement with public investment and the consequent deleterious impact on poor students, especially of color, have never been clearer. Is this bet on short-term economic yield, however, the right formulation for organizing and investing in public higher education? This is not simply a technical choice regarding targeting of investment but rather a way of illuminating potential sites of struggle to evolve a public higher education most likely to serve the needs of the broadest cross section of students.

There is currently a diminished state interest and investment in public higher education as a site for educating a citizenry to possess political analytical skills, critical faculties, and the character to dissent from established orthodoxies. The diminished political tolerance for academic political dissent is one outcome of proposals for greater investment in the STEM fields and reduced investment in "irrelevant" social science and humanities fields such as anthropology, sociology, and even English. Some part of this argument for differential investment is the likelihood of greater economic impact. Enhanced market productivity is forecast for students majoring in STEM and far less for those concentrating in the humanities or social sciences (Berrett 2015; Davey and Lewin 2015; Eagleton 2015; Fausset 2015). This effort to contain and diminish the role of "soft" disciplines, however, has political intentions and consequences. The courses and faculty most likely to promote new and more critical ways of understanding the world, thus contributing directly to an altered politics and reimagined citizenship role, are in the social sciences and humanities.

The conjunction between policies of disinvestment or austerity and reduced curriculum offerings is also evident in the rollback of remedial courses and the restructuring of general education. In the last decade, general education curricula in a number of universities have been reengineered to create better alignment between community colleges and four-year colleges and to compress requirements and dilute the demands of course work, all when there is intense pressure to increase graduation rates and improve time to degree. Alignment of course requirements between community colleges and four-year colleges as an efficiency measure has obvious merit for students. As more uniform general education classes are created to expedite the efficient transfer of course credits from community to senior colleges and remedial courses are eliminated, there is an unfortunate and corresponding reduction in the range, rigor, and quality of offerings (Bowen 2012). Finally, these trends have an especially powerful impact on poor students, especially those of color, who disproportionately attend community colleges and need the support provided by remedial course work (Mitchell and Leachman 2015). These policies have resulted in both a dilution of the rigor of general education and disinvestment in access to remedial education. By diluting general education standards or quality, and deflecting students in need of remedial education away from college, these practices are expected to lead to spikes in graduation rates and reduced costs, or greater capacity to do more with less. Policies of targeted economic disinvestment in general education and remedial course work combined with an ideological commitment to diminish the academy's curricular offerings in critical social inquiry are not natural or inevitable. Rather, they are part of a policy agenda that comports with elite economic and political interests while simultaneously undermining working-class and poor students' exposure to the ideas and supports often essential to transforming their lives and minds. And so curricular reforms associated with distance learning technologies, outcomes metrics, and public investments targeted to disciplines promising greater economic return on the dollar are not benign or necessary innovations, but rather adaptations to a politically invented resource scarcity undermining working-class and poor students' access to high-quality education. The policy choices being made are more and more explicitly wedded to dominant economic interests, not the larger public good.

The past two decades have witnessed expansion of managerial centralization over basic operations of universities. These centralizing or corporatizing tendencies have been accompanied by a 28 percent increase in the number of academic administrators between 2000 and 2012 and the introduction of more comprehensive and intrusive information technology systems tracking faculty and staff behavior and productivity as well as student progress (Carlson 2014). As the size of the administrative workforce and reach of information technology grow, so too do their share of university resources. The promise of this investment is linked to anticipated savings extracted from greater managerial oversight of scarce resources achieved through economies of scale. Especially salient to the growth in managerial authority and function is the displacement of decentralized forms of faculty governance and control. Such reach into academic decision making has occurred in any number of ways, including, but not limited to, department chairs working directly for management (rather than selected by faculty), legal decisions eroding faculty authority over curriculum, and courses being devised by corporate donors in alliance with administrators who are looking for ways to generate new revenue streams. It is important not to romanticize the role that faculty have played in shaping curricula, given historical evidence of their frequent resistance to needed or demanded curricular changes. At the same time, it is clear that the current trend promises to subordinate a relatively decentralized, complex discipline-based academic expertise to the fiscal exigencies of austerity and managerial authority. This transaction erodes the faculty's role in knowledge production and the work of educating both undergraduate and graduate students. The irony, of course, is that expertise developed over decades of advanced education to promote the intellectual development of students within universities is increasingly supplanted by academic managers, many drawn from the private and governmental sectors, who often have little if any curricular expertise or teaching experience. This tension is elemental to implementing a regimen of austerity. It is also a point of tension between working-class students' access to a high-quality education and elite interests in reducing costs. This curricular redesign is described as a necessary technical intervention, better aligning university resources with the contemporary needs of students while simultaneously deriving needed cost savings. This rationale, however, strips away from these practices the political-economic context of austerity that drives it.

Historically, austerity policies have not met the educational needs of poor and working-class students. Inner-city K–12 public education students, as we have suggested, too often leave or graduate from high school and enter college with marginal academic skills. Alternatively, the best hope for transforming curricula to meet the developmental needs of these students and disciplinary standards of faculty is not to further technical engineering to derive savings. Rather, what is needed is a political struggle joining students with faculty and staff to press for a redistribution of resources sufficient to underwrite the necessary supports, reduced class size, rigor, and curricular complexity to assure expanded access, more timely graduation, and, perhaps most importantly, a high-quality education.

Grassroots Struggles and Educational Policy Reforms

Organizing campaigns have emerged across the country to reverse the present direction of higher education reorganization. The discussion that follows will focus on both defensive campaigns to preserve the size of university budgets, faculty rights, or class size, and the efforts to extend the boundaries of current discourse and policy making through aggressive faculty- and student-led organizing campaigns. Examples of successful efforts in each of these arenas are abundant. We have selected a number of critical examples to illustrate campaigns and initiatives currently underway in higher education. They depict struggles to increase investment in student supports, improve the quality of instruction, student debt relief, and a fight for a livable wage for part-time faculty. Second, campaigns for universal access to public higher education are described. Faculty, student, and community resistance to the shutting down of San Francisco City College on the basis of failure to meet accreditation standards, for example, will be briefly explored. Third, political, faculty-led struggles around control over and improvement of curriculum will be examined. Perhaps the most notable example of such organizing occurred at CUNY around the central administration's Pathways initiative (Vitale 2014).

Each of these snapshots of struggle has been chosen because of its significance to the larger national fight to save public higher education. However, these campaigns are local or university-wide rather than national. That limitation must be addressed in the near future. The effort to reshape public higher education is, of necessity, a national project. Therefore, to successfully advance an alternative platform for the restoration of programs, redistribution of public resources, and creation of an emancipatory educational agenda, local organizing work must cohere into a national movement that fights for public higher education. The organizing work in public higher education also cannot occur in a political vacuum; it must be linked to a range of potentially complementary campaigns in K–12 education, health care, environmental justice, and development of low- to moderate-priced housing.

Student Debt and the Choice to Strike

Expanding student debt to help underwrite the costs of attending public universities is a growing trend. Student groups are increasingly pushing back against debt financing and loan indenture. An especially dramatic and important example of student debt organizing involved fifteen Corinthian Colleges students who took the collective and dramatic step of undertaking a debt strike to make clear that they would not repay their loans. The student debt strike emerged out of the financial setbacks experienced by the for-profit corporation resulting most recently in Corinthian Colleges filing for bankruptcy protection early in 2015 (Blumenstyk and Fabris 2015). The consequences have been especially troubling for Corinthian students. At its height, the colleges enrolled one hundred thousand students. More recently, according to a *New Yorker* report, "all fourteen of Corinthian's Canada campuses have been shut down. In the U.S., more than fifty campuses have been sold off; a dozen have been closed" (Vara 2015). The students who have made the choice to undertake a debt strike have launched "what appears to be an unprecedented collective action against [their] debt" (Vara 2015). The fifteen strikers believe they have both the legal and the ethical grounds for resisting repayment of their federally insured student loans. As documentary filmmaker Astra Taylor editorialized in the *New York Times*, the Corinthian 15 are "committing a new kind of civil disobedience: a debt strike. They refuse to make any more payments on their federal student loans" (Taylor 2015, A-17; Strike Debt, n.d., 26; Lewin 2015b).

The debt strikers are making a powerful statement about the $1.2 trillion of student debt burdening millions of students and the larger economy. The Corinthian student strikers are part of Rolling Jubilee, a debt collective that emerged in 2012 (Taylor 2015, A-17). Rolling Jubilee was organized to explore alternatives to the weight of individual debt as the basis for financing public goods that in the past were largely subsidized by government. Taylor indicated that policies of austerity have altered the historic compact between citizens seeking, for example, health care or education, and public investment (A-17). The debt strikers are reasserting the responsibility of the state to subsidize education by transferring responsibility from the individual back to the state. In effect the students are saying: "Instead of collecting [our debts], we abolish them, operating under the belief that people shouldn't go into debt for getting sick or going to school" (A-17). The choice to go on debt strike therefore not only raises the question of who should pay for public higher education, but also whether the state should assure free tuition for every individual seeking a college education, as in some western European countries. Proposed federal policies introduced by President Obama and actual efforts in states such as Tennessee indicate the first halting steps being taken toward free tuition in community colleges (Kelderman 2015a; McCambridge 2014; Porter 2015). For-profit universities' greater dependence on public loans, low graduation rates, high incidence of dropouts, modest levels of postgraduation employment, and an avalanche of student indebtedness are especially notable. However limited student strikes are presently, the numbers have recently grown to more than a thousand in the case of the Corinthian fiscal meltdown. In June 2015, according to a *New York Times* report, Arne Duncan, secretary of education, announced that the US Department of Education would forgive the federal loans of tens of thousands of students who attended Corinthian Colleges. He also indicated that "the department planned to develop a process to allow any student—whether from Corinthian or elsewhere—to be forgiven their loans if they had been defrauded by their colleges" (Lewin 2015a, A11). This is a remarkable outcome given the modest scope of the original Corinthian strike and is, to some extent, a testament to the power of this tactic. But the question of student debt extends far beyond for-profit universities such as Corinthian.

A thousand students located at one for-profit school are not going to change laws severely restricting nonrepayment options for the largest majority of college students declaring bankruptcy. More to the point, these bankrupt students have generally not attended universities that explicitly and illegally engaged in fraudulent activity. To change both the law and university policies, larger and larger cohorts of current students and recent graduates will need to undertake strikes. Like parents resisting austerity policies in public K–12 education who are willing to take the step of noncompliance by opting out of standardized testing of their children, debt strikers' political power will be determined by the number of students they can draw to the campaign.

Free Tuition and Community Colleges

The Tennessee Promise—"the program guaranteeing that the state will cover tuition and required fees for two years of community or technical college for . . . every graduating high-school senior in the state"—is the most expansive local experiment increasing public spending to subsidize student college tuition (Kelderman 2015b, A6). Eric Kelderman, a reporter for *CHE,* reported, "It's a large-scale experiment, and higher-education experts and policy makers across the nation will be watching to see if the lure of tuition-free college attracts students—and keeps them in college long enough to complete a degree or vocational program" (A6). Shortly after implementation of the Tennessee Promise, President Obama announced a corollary American College Promise initiative to nationally invest "about $60-billion dollars over 10 years. That [public investment] would cover three-quarters of the anticipated cost [of community college tuition] saddling participating states with the rest of the tab" (Stripling 2015b, A-4; Shear 2015). Short on details, the Obama initiative tied federal spending to matching funds provided by participating states. The federal intention to incentivize increased state spending on higher education through matching funds was to reverse the trend of continual disinvestment by states. Christopher Loss, a Vanderbilt faculty member, compared the president's proposal to sweeping policy initiatives like the GI Bill that were part of the "grand narrative of educational access, of the federal government taking pretty significant steps to adapt the educational system to the realities of a changing world" (Stripling 2015b, A-4; Shear 2015). Although partially correct, what Loss fails to acknowledge is that this wider access would not have occurred without the federally sponsored GI Bill being accompanied by the heightened state-level investment to expand public universities. It is interesting to note that the "free college" movement has also gained some traction early in the 2016 presidential campaign, at least with respect to plans offered by the three major Democratic Party candidates. Each of the candidates' proposals goes beyond President Obama's original "free community college" idea to focus on government grants replacing student loans (Hillary Clinton) and/or entirely tuition-free public higher education (Bernie Sanders) (Healy 2015; Bosman and Lewin 2015).

The emphasis on free tuition is also generating interest outside the DC Beltway. Obama's proposal largely emerged out of policy debates unfolding inside and outside of Washington, DC about the rising costs of college and diminished student access. The coalition for free tuition, Redeeming America's Promise, emerged from this discourse. Its founder and president, Morley Winograd, an advisor to former vice president Gore, says he "wants to start a national conversation about college, 'sort of like the conversation Horace Mann started' [in the mid-nineteenth century] that led to universal elementary and secondary education" (Blumenstyk 2014a, A15). The coalition consists of dozens of government, think-tank, and foundation officials. It has drawn a spectrum of political interest groups to the "large tent" coalition, including "Common Sense Action, an organization of Millennials, John Blanchard a former governor of Michigan and a former head of the Association of Private Colleges and Universities Harris Miller" (A15). Prominent Republicans have also signed on. Academics like Sara Goldrick-Rab, a professor at the University of Wisconsin, have influenced this policy-making process. Goldrick-Rab's and President Obama's proposals are "'first dollar' programs that cover tuition upfront and allow other aid to be used for living expenses" (Stripling 2015b, A-6). There are also differences in their aspirations: the federal proposal only covers community colleges, while Goldrick-Rab, Bernie Sanders, and others are advocating for free tuition at four-year colleges as well.

The shift in policy discussion inside the Beltway is important precisely because it got the president to "put college and free in the same sentence" (Mangan and Supiano 2015). This new framing counters the politics and economics of austerity by challenging its most essential assumption. It asserts that the cost of public services should shift from the individual to the state through redistributive taxation. However, proposals emanating from policy insiders advancing an agenda of free tuition are also fraught with problems. Joni Finney, director of the University of Pennsylvania's Institute on Higher Education has argued that "the president's use of the bully pulpit [may not] change the fact that many taxpayers see college as a private benefit for individuals rather than a broader public good," so "they are willing to tolerate these costs being pushed more and more to students," an essential aspect of the conservative argument against public higher education (Stripling 2015b, A4).

Glenn Altschuler, the dean of continuing education at Cornell, distinguishes between the historic push for access to higher education in the 1940s and the current politics of universal free tuition when he notes, "The G.I.'s were seen as having earned this benefit and therefore it had a different meaning" (Stripling 2015b, A4). He also suggested that "President Obama faces obstacles in Congress that President Franklin D. Roosevelt who signed the GI Bill into law, did not" (A4). Columnists like Eduardo Porter of the *New York Times* have questioned whether federal and state dollars should be invested in free tuition or student support programs like CUNY's ASAP. Porter notes, "Whether his [Obama's] plan ultimately delivers on its promise, however, will depend less on how many students enter than how many successfully navigate their way out" (Porter 2015, B2). Porter also argues that "it's past time we paid attention. Community colleges have been consistently ignored by policy makers who equate higher education with a bachelor's degree—mostly ignoring the fact that a very large group of young Americans are not prepared, either financially, cognitively or socially for that kind of education" (B2).

The relatively narrow political and economic framing of the present tuition-versus-public-investment debate on higher education is in part explained by professional interest groups, academics, policy makers, and politicians regulating the terms of the problem's definition and their proposed agenda for change. These actors have helped move the question of who should pay for college tuition into the public arena. The proposals have received media attention and resulted in several legislative proposals. However, the absence of a larger mass movement of students, faculty, and community groups to advance a wider vision and broaden the struggle has restricted what can be achieved. Proposals regarding free tuition are essential to any rethinking of the balance between individual and public financial responsibility for attending college. A public investment in tuition, however, must be accompanied by a simultaneous sweeping strategic reinvestment in the decaying core functions of instruction and support services necessary to assure a quality education. Otherwise, as noted throughout our analysis, students will find they have greater access to colleges while experiencing a rapidly declining quality of education.

Significant reversal of the austerity policy agenda in higher education cannot emerge from insider policy discussions and legislative proposals alone. Insider work demands the pressure of outside social movements to both enlarge the policy conversation and build power commensurate with that of dominant economic and political interests advancing a sweeping austerity agenda. Insiders alone have neither the power nor the resources to significantly reverse present austerity policy. And so the lesson of the policy struggles regarding free tuition is that insider legislative and academic proposals are substantively necessary, but still politically and analytically insufficient.

Increasing Wages and Job Protections for Part-Time Faculty

The campaigns for a livable wage and job security for part-time faculty are especially powerful current examples of national organizing efforts in higher education. They have been underwritten by both local faculty and staff unions committed to meeting the basic needs of their contingent members and the Service Employees International Union (SEIU), which has launched a national campaign in cities across the country and a "metropolitan strategy" to unionize adjuncts in private and public universities (Schmidt 2014b). At the University of Oregon, for example, United Academics, a faculty union, signed a one-year contract in 2013 assuring greater job protection so that, according to a report in *Labor Notes*, "teachers hired into career, non-tenure track positions can be offered one-year appointments for only their first three years. Starting with their fourth year, their appointments will have to be for a minimum of two years (or three years if the teacher is promoted). . . . Current employees with more than three years of service will have their positions reviewed for reclassification as a career" (Ostrach 2013). Members of the University of Illinois at Chicago United Faculty went on strike in 2013 for a "fair and honest contract" emphasizing critical demands for adjuncts, including increased salaries, job security, and pathways to a career. Because of a court decision "the union must . . . negotiate two separate contracts for non-tenure-track and tenure-track faculty" (Burns 2013, 2). At CUNY, the Professional Staff Congress, the union of faculty and staff, has secured a number of contractual rights for part-time faculty over the past decade, including membership in the city's health insurance program for those who teach two courses a semester, one credit of pay for an office hour for those who teach at least two courses on one campus in a given semester, and a development fund to support research and teaching interests (New Caucus 2015).

This is not an exhaustive list; other faculty unions from SUNY's United University Professions (UUP) to the California Faculty Association (CFA, the union in the CSU system) have advanced contractual demands and organizing agendas that highlight part-time faculty needs. Equally important, in 2014 a key committee of the Colorado legislature passed model legislation that promised to remove pay inequity and preserve education quality for part-time faculty. Peter Schmidt reported in *CHE* that "the measure's long term prospects for passage are far from certain. The price estimates . . . ranged from $86-million to well over $110-million, and Republican lawmakers and community-college administrators disputed assertions by Representative Fischer that the colleges would be able to free up such funds by rethinking their spending priorities." As one advocate stated, "at the end of the day whatever happens with it, it is going to call attention to the horrendous conditions of contingent faculty at community colleges, and that can only be a good thing" (Schmidt 2014a).

These local union campaigns for equity for part-time faculty represent a diverse patchwork of change platforms and strategies. Alternatively, SEIU has developed a coherent national strategy and campaign to improve adjunct pay, benefits, and working conditions. The organizing strategy is to unionize adjuncts and low-wage workers in general throughout an entire metropolitan area. SEIU's "higher-education campaign, Adjunct Action, has spread to 10 metropolitan areas, where it has formed, or is working to form, unions at more than 30 campuses employing a total of about 25,000 adjuncts." By late 2014 "it had already unionized about 70 percent of adjuncts in colleges in Washington, D.C. and . . . gained footholds in Boston, Los Angeles and around Seattle" (Schmidt 2014b). Organizing campaigns are also underway in Pittsburgh, St. Louis, and Philadelphia, the latter of which involves both the American Federation of Teachers (AFT) and SEIU (Schmidt 2014b).

The organizing assumption of the SEIU Metropolitan Campaigns as described by Malini Cadambi Daniel, director of the SEIU national higher education campaign, is that "it will take only the unionization of a substantial share—perhaps not even half—of adjuncts in a given metropolitan area to leverage market wide improvements in working conditions" (Schmidt 2014b). A recent contract victory at Tufts University and a successful vote in favor of unionization at Lesley University suggest that Boston may be especially responsive to such a campaign. The vote at Bentley University, where part-time faculty rejected unionization by one hundred to ninety-eight, however, indicates that achieving the labor density necessary to raise market wages in Boston remains a continuing challenge. Boston has a number of assets that suggest it is a best bet for early significant success in a national campaign. To begin with, Boston's "geographically confined layout . . . enables adjuncts to teach at multiple campuses, leaves them more choices of where to work, and will make it easier for union organizers to network and spread the word of any victories" (Schmidt 2014b). Equally important, the culture and politics of Boston are relatively friendly to organized labor. "The city councils of Boston and Cambridge have passed resolutions urging colleges not to stand in the way of adjunct unionization efforts" (Schmidt 2014b). And the *Boston Globe* recently endorsed the unionization of adjuncts with an editorial headline that declared, "For Northeastern Adjuncts Organizing Is a No-Brainer." The editorial concluded, "Improving the status of adjunct faculty is a cause that benefits the entire university community, and all should embrace it" (*Boston Globe* 2014). Even in Boston, where the convergence of geographic, political, and media organizing assets are likely greatest, however, it remains "unclear whether the SEIU can unionize enough Boston-area colleges for its metropolitan strategy to have a market-wide effect" (Schmidt 2014b). SEIU has indicated that no matter the short-term setbacks or challenges, "we are here to stay" (Schmidt 2014b). Success, if achieved in Boston, could help other metropolitan campaigns gain traction by rallying members and guiding campaigns.

There are a variety of dilemmas associated with organizing adjunct faculty either on local campuses, across metropolitan areas, or in a national campaign. The heterogeneity of adjunct faculty can undermine organizing campaigns. Those part-time workers who have full-time jobs elsewhere or are retirees receiving pensions are relatively advantaged economically. Consequently, their willingness to commit to campaigns to fight for job security or increased wages that will disproportionately benefit part-time faculty, who have to cobble together an entire livelihood through university adjunct teaching, presents a daunting challenge for organizers. But organizing the segment of the adjunct labor force holding other jobs that pay relatively well and include benefits is essential as they represent a majority of part-time instructors. Any hope of achieving labor density depends on bridging this economic and social divide. Exposure of job-insecure adjunct faculty to reprisals is another obstacle facing organizers. The willingness of adjunct faculty to participate in any organizing campaign will largely depend on the degree to which they feel protected while taking necessary individual risks. The push and pull between risk and exposure is explosive and consequently has the potential to create a significant drag on adjunct organizing campaigns.

The long-term fiscal viability of SEIU's metropolitan campaigns is also a growing concern. The low wages of part-time faculty constrain potential dues revenue to the union, while the costs of organizing or servicing part-time faculty are substantial. The contradiction between low dues-paying capacity and union costs in the short term is likely to produce a deficit for both local and national unions engaged in adjunct organizing. Metropolitan density of membership and consequent significant wage gains are the best hopes for achieving the long-term fiscal viability for such organizing. Clearly this is a long-term project, and much-needed victories on both the fiscal and organizing sides of the equation will not be easily achieved.

Yet another dilemma is associated with stand-alone, part-time faculty chapters requiring subsidies from both national and state federations to support even the most basic organizing campaign or services. The alternative is to create inclusive faculty unions in which full- and part-time instructors are members of the same chapter. In such "wall-to-wall" chapters, full-time members' dues generally subsidize services and other investments in part-time or adjunct faculty organizing. The trade-off from the point of view of part-time faculty is that in these combined chapters, the voices and needs of contingent labor are often not sufficiently heard by union leaders. Clearly every organizing campaign produces contradictions and dilemmas. The higher the stakes, the larger the scope of the campaign, and the more pronounced the contradictions; the metropolitan strategy of SEIU is no exception. That being said, the SEIU effort is the most ambitious, imaginative, and comprehensive campaign to date attempting to improve the working conditions of contingent labor in higher education.

Cross-Sector Campaigns and Increased Investment

A number of state campaigns largely financed by public unions and in alliance with community groups have advanced platforms calling for increased taxation. In Minnesota and Oregon, taxes have been raised to supplement public higher education while freezing tuition costs (Post 2013; Fain 2015a). The political positioning of a tuition freeze in conjunction with investment in the core functions of the public university needs to be mapped onto every higher education campaign. Such a proposal breaks with the present policy and political trend pushed by both Republican and Democratic legislators of freezing tuition while continuing the long-term trend of disinvesting in public higher education. Tuition freezes without additional public investment, although they might potentially sustain access, further erode the quality of the educational experience in an era of austerity. Policy initiatives in both Minnesota and Oregon seek to reverse this trend in part because they emerged out of alliances of students, unions, and community groups with shared interests in both increasing access and improving quality.

The most ambitious example of statewide organizing for progressive redistributive taxes was carried out in California. The Courage Campaign, which emerged in 2010 from the Restoring California Coalition, spearheaded organizing on a referendum for the "Millionaires Tax," a permanent levy on seven-figure California incomes. The campaign was supported by the California Federation of Teachers, Occupy Education, and various community groups. Over time, however, support for the maximal progressive measure waned as an alternative compromise proposal, combining elements of the Millionaires Tax with a more regressive sales tax, gained political support. The counterproposal was made by Governor Brown, who argued that "his plan was more responsible and would not inspire concerted business opposition" (Eidelson 2012). The plan was quickly endorsed by much of organized labor, including SEIU, UAW, AFSCME, and the NEA-affiliated California Teachers Association (Eidelson 2012). The governor's proposed taxes were temporary, with the income tax lasting seven years and the sales tax, four. The final labor compromise with the governor disappointed many progressive groups which were part of the movement campaign and ended up splitting the coalition.

The split could be directly traced to both the regressive sales tax and the lack of a transparent process in reaching a compromise with Governor Brown. The push-pull between "real politics" and the aspiration to achieve a significant redistributive corrective to austerity were always at the center of the campaign. The "splitting off" of many unions at an earlier stage, however, eroded the power and organizing momentum necessary to achieve more sweeping tax reform. It is within this context that Josh Pechthalt, the president of the AFT state federation (CFA), concluded that a "united effort behind the overwhelmingly progressive current compromise will fare better than a push for the more progressive version in the absence of broad labor support and the support of the Democratic Party" (Eidelson 2012). The pushback by community groups, although substantial, did not prevail. Ultimately, unions made the decision to compromise with the governor and business groups because the failure to pass a referendum in the midst of the state's budget shortfall would have produced deep cuts, affecting every public agency. It was within this context that public unions made a unilateral decision to reach a deal with Governor Brown. Josh Pechthalt commented that "we may have had community support [, but] . . . at the end of the day, there are a group of people who put their resources and their organizations behind the thing, they're the ones who have to call the shots" (Eidelson 2012). He also noted that "the old 'Millionaires Tax' guaranteed that some revenues would be used for higher education. The new one doesn't." Pechthalt continued, "We asked the governor's staff to include such a guarantee in the compromise but [were] rebuffed because legislative leaders first wanted to . . . address 'programs for the poor' and then turn to education" (Eidelson 2012).

The tension between short-term budget crises, political compromise necessitated by the limited power of the mass movement, and the schism that emerges when end-game decision making is controlled by dominant institutions is sadly all too predictable. Early in the campaign, unions other than the CFA agreed to a compromise proposal because the situation "got complicated for folks who have business before the state and the governor" and did not want to "find themselves feeling as if they were on the opposite side of him" (Eidelson 2012). The gravitational pull of union self-interest in the first stage of the campaign and pragmatic assessment of power and probability of winning in the second half does not come without a cost in building the kinds of foundational relationships essential to a larger movement's power. The campaign produced a victory, which is critically important. However, the tension between a visionary, transformative movement politics and the pragmatism of coalition campaigns ultimately organized to achieve specific, concrete gains will not disappear.

The crisis of disinvestment in public institutions endures. At the same time, if we are to move beyond essential stopgap measures toward broader and more sweeping change, greater movement power must be built. Movement power, however, can only emerge from an enduring collaboration between dominant partners like unions and students, as well as community groups. In turn, that kind of partnership is solidified through a deep sense of mutual need and trust over the short- and long-term.

Any hope of reversing disinvestment and austerity through redistributive tax policies is larger than the power of either a diminished labor movement or the fragmented, often isolated circumstances of community groups. Together, though, community groups and labor stand a chance of blunting the momentum of austerity policies and creating an alternative politics of public investment as a basis for justice and equity. For this to occur movement structures must have authority to assure community groups a greater voice in decision making, despite their relative lack of resources; support the reflective work of tactically assessing the trade-offs of short-term and long-term decisions; and initiate both the development and the implementation of campaigns. Only this kind of robust collaboration grounded in political campaigning can produce a movement politics rather than isolated, discontinuous examples of pushback, whether effective or ineffective. As the California referendum struggle suggests, this will not be easy to achieve, but it is the only way to create a power commensurate with that of the forces presently supporting austerity policies. In the words of Karen Lewis, the president of the Chicago Teachers Union, "it is the only way we can even begin to think about facing down and beating the enemy that would take everything from us (Fine and Fabricant 2014, 19).

Sustaining and Expanding Universal Access

The CFHE, an allied national group of university faculty and staff working to develop a progressive policy platform and accurate reporting of the contemporary challenges facing higher education, issued a report in 2012 entitled "Closing the Door, Increasing the Gap: Who's Not Going to Community College?" The report indicated that "after an enrollment surge from 2006 to 2009, enrollments of first-time, traditional age students in community colleges declined by 5.1 percent from 2009 to 2010" (Rhoades 2012, 5). The National Student Clearing House amplifies this finding: "Institutional capacity continues to be 'strained' by the enrollment surge, and there continues to be strong student demand, despite the enrollment decline" (2). In California, perhaps the most extreme examples of diminished access have been reported. The California Community Colleges noted that "133,000 first time students had been unable to enroll even in a single course in the 2009–10 academic year." That same year the president of the Community College League of California indicated that "we expect to see a decline of nearly 250,000 students enrolled this time next year" (2). In numerous states, including Florida, Michigan, Illinois, Maine, Arizona, and Texas, demand for higher education access continues to outstrip supply. What we are witnessing is a gradual contraction of access and rationing of opportunity in community colleges, which is in turn largely redrawing the boundaries of opportunity along racial and class lines.

Perhaps the most dramatic example of the struggle around access is occurring at City College of San Francisco (CCSF). In 2013 the Accreditation Commission for Community and Junior Colleges (ACCJC) voted to terminate or revoke by July 2014 the accreditation of CCSF, which enrolls eighty thousand students. The decision was part of a broader effort by ACCJC, one of six regional commissions, to put a quarter of all California community colleges on sanction. The sanctions, according to the commission, were necessary because of low graduation rates and extended time to degree (Gardner 2014, A-13). The record of CCSF became part of a larger public debate in 2014 about the motivations of the commission, the reasonableness or overreach of its termination decision, and the relationship between outcomes such as graduation rates and public investment. Resistance to the Accreditation Commission's agenda was led by a group of CCSF faculty and students, which demanded among other things to "end push out policies" and "reaffirm the Open Access commitment of the California Master Plan of 1960," and to invest in and rebuild the college (Save CCSF Research Committee 2013, 2–3). The Save the City College Coalition developed an organizing campaign and systematically scaled it up from the campus to the surrounding community and the city at large. Over time, online campaign literature and faculty leaders traveled across the country to spread the word about the closure threats and create national support from other labor unions and community groups. The coalition also enlisted political and legal support from state legislative allies.

The commission moved quickly to restructure the CCSF Board of Trustees and centralize college decision making. It proposed the elected

City College Board of Trustees be replaced by a super trustee nominated by the CCC Board of Governors. The CCSF Coalition argued that the unilateral authority of a super trustee in the present political climate would likely speed up the "downsizing of the college, cutting out students, faculty, staff . . . rid[ing] roughshod over the unions; impos[ing] a higher ratio of part-time to full time faculty with downgraded job security, pay and benefits; and open the door for more outsourced contractors" (Save CCSF Research Committee 2013, 2–3; Fisher 2014).

After a year of intensifying escalation tactics on both sides, a judge blocked the commission from terminating accreditation in the short term to await the outcome of a lawsuit. At the same time "Officials at other California community colleges sent a letter to the commission this week saying that the San Francisco college had made '95 percent' of the necessary changes and urging the Commission to give it more time" (Gardner 2014, A-13). Powerful congressional representatives such as Nancy Pelosi encouraged the commission to rethink its decision, while other legislators, including Jackie Speier, a US representative, were harsher and more public in their assessment of the ACCJC's record, indicating that the "problem with any institution like the commission is that it's self-regulated, self-appointed, and accountable to no one." Speier concluded that this is "a recipe for disaster and abuse" (A-13). In the early summer of 2014, the commission retreated, allowing CCSF up to two more years to restructure (A-13).

The struggle over the future of CCSF, however, has not ended. The ACCJC indicated that "this is not just a blank check for more time, but a careful process of holding the college accountable for bringing in new practices that do meet the standards within two years" (Gardner 2014, A-13). This brief statement is a powerful reminder that the forces arrayed against CCSF will continue to press for reforms emphasizing an austerity regimen. The implications regarding quality of education, learning objectives, and citizenship development are not evident in ACCJC's concerns regarding restructuring, standard setting, and outcomes assessment. And so whether the coalition's victory is pyrrhic or enduring will largely depend on its capacity to create a power base that shifts from the short term and critical defensive victory of stopping immediate closure to the proactive, aggressive campaign needed to increase education investment and quality as a matter of justice for poor students, especially those of color. In the absence of this broader campaign for equity, the doors of the college may remain open, but learning and instruction are likely to be diminished. A central dilemma in the San Francisco campaign and beyond is not to lose sight of how austerity combined with access creates a chimera of both efficiency and justice. This sheen of relying on policies of "efficiency" or rededicating existing money to produce greater equity regarding outcomes such as graduation rates is largely an illusion. This dynamic represents a straight path to eroding both core functions of the university. It also erodes the less visible but equally powerful intention of transformation and emancipation that has at least been part of the promise, if not the experience, of higher education in the United States since the end of World War II.

Resisting Curriculum Dilution

Universities in South Dakota, Nebraska, and other states are reducing the number of credits needed for graduation. The University of North Carolina is considering the elimination of "low-productivity" disciplines, including history and political science, while the University of Southern Maine is contemplating dropping courses in physics (Pratt 2013). Equally important, the governors of both North Carolina and Wisconsin have indicated that continued state investment in public universities that teach the humanities disciplines may be part of an era whose time has passed (Bosman 2015; Ovaska 2015). The conjunction between these trends and broader austerity policies is reasonably clear. The drive to impose efficiencies has resulted in the elimination of courses or whole disciplines not clearly aligned with concrete market needs and, thus, declared unproductive. These efficiency measures are also expected to move more students more quickly to graduation by either rearranging or reducing long-established credit requirements. Performance-based funding, linking public financing to student graduation rates, is being proposed by President Obama (Stewart 2015). States such as Ohio and Tennessee have been especially aggressive in this area; an *Inside Higher Ed* report noted "4/5 of base support in the two states is now being linked to performance indicators" (Fain 2014).

Slippage in graduation rates is clear. Presently 56.1 percent of college students at four-year schools graduate within six years (Pratt 2013). Advocates for performance-based funding and similar initiatives make the seemingly plausible argument that faculty "who resist it have an obvious stake in a status quo that doesn't work" (Pratt 2013). Two questions about the fit between these higher education policies and factors accounting for the problem remain largely unaddressed, however: How is the slowed rate of graduation linked to policies of disinvestment, debt, and institutional decay? And how are policies of performance-based funding affecting the quality of what is being taught? We have spent much time in earlier chapters addressing the first question. The shift in policy emphasis to metrics of graduation within a context of declining public investment will by definition produce aftershocks to the curriculum. Those aftershocks, according to Debra Humphreys, vice president of the Association of American Colleges and Universities, are likely, with greater frequency, to "mak[e] a bad situation worse if we don't look at the impact of not only how many students get through, but what they learn" (Pratt 2013). Humphreys concludes, "There is too little known about whether efforts to create more college graduates are affecting the quality of what is being taught" (Pratt 2013).

It is within this context that faculty at CUNY enunciated the need to protect the quality of their curriculum and organized to do so. The organizing campaign was a partnership between faculty governance bodies and the faculty staff union, the PSC. In essence, the anti-Pathways campaign was structured to resist management's assumption that it had the authority to initiate curriculum reform.

The problem as articulated by administrators was that "of CUNY's 240,000 undergraduates, more than 10,000 transfer from one college to another each fall." A high-level CUNY administrator noted that "for more than 40 years, students' difficulty in transferring their credits was a recognized difficulty that sometimes delayed and even derailed their graduation, a common problem in American higher education" (Logue 2015, A-52).

CUNY management organized faculty outside university governance structures to promote Pathways. As Alexandra Logue, executive vice chancellor for academic affairs, noted, "more than 70 Pathways-related meetings were held with central administration and campus personnel just in the early stages of developing the program." She continues, "However, the work was done mostly by the CUNY central administration, because it had the people with the needed expertise and time" (Logue 2015, A-52). Administrative claims to the expertise and authority to initiate changes in CUNY's curriculum were questioned by faculty. Consequent resistance to Pathways became one of the most galvanizing and unifying campaigns of CUNY faculty in decades.

At the very earliest stages in the implementation of Pathways, members of the Queensborough Community College (QCC) chapter of the PSC and QCC's faculty senate united in their efforts to halt its implementation. The most aggressively resistant departments, English and foreign languages, were slated for significant curriculum redesign as a result of Pathways. Specifically, English composition courses were to be reduced from four credits to three despite the complex writing problems of QCC students and consequent labor-intensive work required of instructors. Foreign language courses were also subject to credit reduction; their status as required courses was also diminished (Sailor 2015; Vitale 2014). Some science faculty joined the campaign because course credit for lab time was also eliminated. The uniform application of three credits for general education courses no matter the variation in content was a primary source of conflict between CUNY faculty and administrators.

The imposition of the Pathways structure and the attendant diminishment of quality and faculty authority over curriculum were at the heart of the resistance. It was within this context that Barbara Bowen, the president of the PSC, noted: "Pathways and its analogues in other states are a means of rationing higher education. . . . That's why the battle at Queensborough is so significant. There, one department's faculty took a stand against the rationing of education for their students. For that they were threatened with everything from cancellation of courses to firing of untenured faculty. Yet now faculty across the University are preparing to take a similar stand" (Bowen 2012).

This resistance at QCC quickly spread across the CUNY system. Union organizing at a number of campuses focused on establishing a moratorium in the implementation of Pathways. Many CUNY campuses—including Brooklyn, Baruch, and Queens colleges; the Borough of Manhattan, LaGuardia, and Hostos community colleges; and the College of Staten Island—passed governance resolutions calling for an immediate halt in Pathways' implementation. The partnership between the union and faculty governance bodies regarding faculty authority over curriculum was an encouraging development. This partnership extended to a lawsuit challenging Pathways as a management- rather than a faculty-initiated reform, concluding that the initiative was unlawful (Vitale 2014).

In the late winter and fall of 2013, the PSC increased both the scope and the intensity of its organizing by creating a more public campaign (Vitale 2014). This public campaign, amplified through major media outlets including the *New York Times,* increased the visibility of faculty dissatisfaction with Pathways because of its threat to the quality of a CUNY education. CUNY countered with its own advertising campaign.

Throughout the controversy, the CUNY chancellor claimed wide and deep support for Pathways among faculty. The legitimacy of that claim was tested and failed when two-thirds of the entire CUNY faculty voted and 92 percent of those voting registered no confidence in Pathways (Vitale 2014). The systematic organizing by the union to rally faculty was at the heart of the public campaign. In a matter of months, thousands of organizing conversations occurred among members. Union leaders visited every one of CUNY's campuses, rallying support for the vote of no confidence. Governance leaders also convened meetings to get out the vote while also advising faculty senators to go back to their departments and educate members about the need for a negative vote. The unity of faculty in announcing its collective resistance to Pathways was both clear and decisive.

This long-term campaign, although unifying faculty across historic boundaries of governance, union, academic discipline, individual campus, and ideology, did not halt or significantly slow the implementation of Pathways. Over time the moratoriums on all but a few campuses were rescinded. The claims of the Pathways lawsuit were rejected by the lower court in which it was tried. That decision was appealed and the lower court's judgment upheld. Finally, the referendum, although chilling and destabilizing for CUNY administrators, did not dramatically alter the implementation pace of Pathways. Faculty governance structures slowly acceded to management's curricular reforms because their campuses were threatened with financial and other hardships if they resisted. A few campuses like Brooklyn College and the College of Staten Island maintained their moratoria, and as a result revealed the emptiness of CUNY management's threats. Union leaders have also been stonewalled by management regarding further discussion of Pathways. But the resistance to Pathways has not ended. Its disfiguring impact on CUNY's undergraduate curriculum continues to unite the union and governance bodies on a number of campuses. A new report by Kevin Sailor, a Lehman College (CUNY) psychology professor, on Pathways, bolstered by the most rigorous methodology and data collection to date on student transfer in CUNY, persuasively challenges its basic rationale (Sailor 2015). The Sailor report's primary findings are that "(1) the influence of the size of the general education curriculum on senior colleges appears to have a minimal impact on the overall number of credits earned and the number of credits not accepted during the transfer process, (2) transfer students (outside CUNY) and native matriculants (within CUNY) earn approximately the same number of credits, (3) institutional transfer caps or residency requirements are significant contributors to lost credits." The analysis concludes that the Pathways initiative is unlikely to have a large impact on the outcomes it was designed to address. It further suggests one might deduce from these findings that "Pathways' focus on general education curriculum to solve problems of transfer credits was at best misguided and at worst a misrepresentation of the University's intentions" (1).

Despite this empirical confirmation of the union's and governance bodies' critiques, the report is not likely to halt or slow Pathways' implementation. Argument and data alone will not prevail. It must be joined to the growing power of faculty, staff, and students to impose their agendas on management regarding curriculum through existing governance structures. The streamlining and standardization of curriculum as embodied by Pathways is largely driven by the stress on the institution, and in turn management, to meet the budgeting and accountability demands of austerity. It is in the melding of fiscal retreat and aggressive forms of new accountability that inventions such as Pathways are shaped. As noted throughout this book, powerful economic and political forces are aligned with this agenda. Therefore, it will take nothing less than a sustained, expansive campaign of faculty and students advancing an alternative agenda not simply of resistance, but of an enriched curriculum better able to meet the complex academic learning needs of CUNY's primarily poor students of color to reverse course. The issues of race and class and the broader mission of public higher education will need to be at the heart of such a campaign.

The Pathways campaign is a local, notable effort to resist austerity-driven curricular reform. To date, the Pathways resistance has not succeeded because of legal barriers, the failure to sustain a faculty-led campaign across the university, and the lack of an alternative platform for change. Faculty members cannot win locally or scale up their fight for improved quality of education until they join race, class, inequality, and public investment with a specific curriculum reform platform and/or proposal. The Pathways campaign never sketched such an alternative because of the urgency of resistance, differences in perspective between various stakeholders, and the complexity of the project. This was clearly not the only reason for the failure of the campaign to achieve a decisive victory. And yet the need to arrive at a single platform offering a large tent for diverse faculty interests could not be greater than it is in this moment. Faculty must come to understand the stakes of the present struggle over curriculum, the need to articulate and collectivize an alternative, and the daily need to organize and evolve into something more than frustrated bystanders in the remaking of the public university. To create enduring higher education campaigns, constituent groups can only be enlisted for the long haul if they understand what they are resisting and what they are fighting to win.

Scaling Up and Drilling Down

A politics of public higher education cannot win in isolation from the wider social and economic currents that course through our national and local politics. Any social movement that emerges over the next decade to challenge and reverse the present politics of austerity, market inequalities, and privatization of state services must scale up its power. That scaling up is necessary if the economic and political might needed to stop resources being directed away from the neediest communities and redirected to sites of concentrated wealth is to coalesce. Growing struggles over minimum subsistence wages, the deaths of unarmed black men at the hands of police, moderate and low-income housing, quality K–12 education for all children, and the deleterious impact of various ecological disasters have a common thread. Each of these campaigns is most fundamentally about a fight over redistributive justice. Justice for poor black men experiencing a degraded public education system while bearing the growing wounds of underinvestment and consequent toxins of dead end jobs, stultifying work, and subminimum wages is but one example. Penned into their neighborhoods as a result of growing poverty, poor education, and racism, aggressive and destructive policing intensifies. These policing practices cannot be separated from the greater anxiety of political and economic governing groups intent upon containing the escalating, legitimate anger of poor communities of color. It is within this context that violent encounters between police and black men repeatedly occur. On the other side of the race and class divide, middle-class, white communities largely in rural areas are threatened with environmental spoilage on a grand scale produced by aggressive and destructive forms of mineral extraction. From fracking to mountain top coal removal, to heedless oil extraction, energy companies operating in an increasingly deregulated political environment have an opportunity to maximize their short-term profits as a result of weakened or nonexistent regulatory policies.

From jobs, to housing, to health care, to policing, to education (both K–12 and higher), and the physical environment, the future prospects for most citizens for a healthful, productive, and safe life grow ever dimmer. Much of this is already understood by increasing numbers of Americans. However, it remains unknown what to do about it. How do we establish a coherent language and politics that penetrate beyond the surface of individual, destabilizing events to their unjust collective essence? Other questions that must be addressed include the following:

- How can the historic divides of race, class, gender, and sexuality be crossed within the ever hotter, fragmented political environment of anger and reaction?
- How can the requirement for successful campaigns in the midst of urgent need be balanced against the inefficiencies of the democratic process?
- How can movement campaigns partner with labor and national human rights organizations?
- Who are the legislative champions prepared to take the political risks to align with a movement politics?
- How do we elect movement champions?
- What are the prospects of a strong social movement radically altering the priorities of the state, as presently configured, in an era of austerity?

Clearly these questions can only be raised and partially answered in the midst of campaigns struggling to grow their power. We are not in that circumstance. The question that we must ask first is: how do we get there? This we do know: It must grow out of continuing local organizing struggles to scale up, link up, and win, in turn producing variant forms of redistributive justice and an emancipatory education. Different approaches to realizing these twin ends will be tested in the swirl of movement practice and politics. To offer anything more in this text would be misguided and would stray far beyond what we know. But we will suggest some of the ways in which these larger issues have already begun to play out and will continue to play out in the realm of public higher education, to which we turn in the epilogue.

Epilogue

We believe that public higher education struggles must be situated within a larger movement politics and, at the same time, have an independent life and a coherent voice. We have described local campaigns organizing to guarantee access, to support government rather than private auspices for the provision of higher education, for quality instruction, and for redistributive investment. Each of these dimensions of struggle, although essential to building a robust public higher education, is not sufficient. Throughout this book we have taken the risk of saying that an emancipatory education is essential to rebuilding public higher education. Many would critique such an assertion as both vague and in the ether of abstract pedagogy and/or instruction, offering little that is concrete or useful in mapping a way forward for public higher education. Although this critique is not without merit, we stand by our assertion that an emancipatory education is an essential public responsibility.

It is not enough to open access or invest in public higher education; we must simultaneously ask how we wish to reinvent it. Our belief is that higher education must enable students to locate what and how they are learning within the context of their experience. Ideas must travel back and forth between their history, a larger social context, and the independent life of an idea or body of ideas. Without such a progressive trajectory, learning is stagnant and unlikely to be dynamic or of enduring value. The ingestion of ideas in biology challenging historic and contextual assumptions about creationism or scientific racism, for example, have powerful learning reverberations. This kind of discourse shared in classrooms rethinks assumptions held as "truth," both by students and by the world at large. It is in the evidence, the careful reading of texts, interpretive analyses, and, perhaps most importantly, the conscious ped-agogical choice to incorporate students' own narratives into the various threads of discussion that new forms of thinking and learning can begin to occur. This open-classroom culture is the one most likely to nurture critical thinking, the articulation of ideas, and transmission of learning from the classroom to the larger world of work, community, and politics. These learning experiences can help facilitate new forms of student agency, risk-taking, and individual as well as collective trajectories outside the classroom.

At its best, a public higher education should offer students the oppor-tunity to build the confidence and expertise necessary to engage intel-lectual ideas and the work world from a critical and analytical perspective. Emancipatory forms of education have a standpoint. They place the student at the center of the experience and invest in both the disruption of historical and standard judgments, replacing them with critical in-quiry. Such experiences require both quantitative investment of public funds and qualitative commitment to experiment with alternative bodies of knowledge. This experimentation must search for the kinds of peda-gogy, curricula, and collaboration that are most likely to foster emanci-patory forms of education. The change we are proposing is complex. It begins and ends with a number of assumptions:

- investment in public higher education must grow dramatically;
- unequal public investment by race, class, gender, and sexuality cannot be tolerated, and investment should be greater in those institutions educating the most academically challenged students;
- the growing contingency of the instructional workforce is a wound that has spread across all of public higher education requiring the necessary corrective of increased wages, benefits, and job security—anything less undermines both the teachers and the quality of instruction they provide;
- public higher education cannot be financed by student debt, because such debt financing for those least able to afford it, a form of regressive taxation, is an especially toxic consequence of public disinvestment and austerity policies;
- new forms of technology to distribute and organize knowledge must be constructed and utilized to meet the needs of a public, not

private, good and decoupled from projects intended to shrink labor costs or generate profits;

- the content of courses must be largely shaped by faculty expertise and decision-making autonomy. Both students and administrators must also have voices in this process. Student participation is especially important if emancipatory forms of education are to be created.

These assumptions may appear to be quixotic precisely because they challenge almost every aspect of the contemporary remaking of public higher education. We do not begin or end this book with the notion that the changes we propose are politically benign, largely a matter of technique, or possible without a transformative and redistributive public investment. To the contrary, we have a political and economic perspective that we have tried to make evident. We believe that the breadth of the required changes must offer a sweeping corrective to the politics of austerity and disposability. Increasing access without the political will to invest is a cynical exercise, signaling that an ever more hollow college education is available to anyone who wants one.

And so the politics of austerity is largely a politics of disposability for populations historically defined as disposable. Paradoxically, institutions of public higher education that have helped to alter life trajectories for students and communities are now increasingly reinforcing, deepening, and extending experiences of disposability. The alternative—a politics of redistributive investment, emancipatory education, and, most importantly, social justice—may seem romantic or even threatening at this moment. It is a vision, however, upon which a platform for political change can and should be built. To move that vision or platform forward in campaigns for a just public higher education will require significant political power.

The present reform agenda built on austerity policies and practices is intended to downsize, privatize, and deprofessionalize all public goods, including higher education. The "austerity reformers" agenda for public higher education and K–12 is sold as a campaign of high ideals and redistributive justice. We have argued otherwise. As in the past, redistributive justice can only be achieved through collective actions and social movements organized by working-class and poor people.

We have begun to see the sprouting of some of these seeds of political possibility in several contemporary events and struggles on public university campuses. Two of them are especially salient to our analysis of what it will take to construct an emancipatory education and a successful fight for redistributive justice: student activism in the fall of 2015 around racial and ethnic issues, embodied particularly by events at the University of Missouri and the struggle within the CUNY system for a decent contract that addresses the economic and educational needs not only of full-time, tenure-track faculty, but also of university staff and graduate students.

The University of Missouri and Beyond

A series of campus-based struggles during the fall of 2015 revealed the ongoing political, economic, racial, and intellectual tensions, fed by larger national struggles over neoliberal practices and conservative policies, disproportionately affecting communities of color. In response to racist incidents on campuses as disparate as the University of Oklahoma and Yale, coalitions—led largely by black students and linked directly to the larger Black Lives Matter movement that emerged nationally after the August 2014 police killing of Michael Brown in Ferguson, Missouri— brought the issue of racism on campuses to public consciousness (Berrett and Hoover, 2015; Miller and Stuckey-French 2015).

The situation on the thirty-five-thousand-student campus of University of Missouri (UM) in Columbia was emblematic of these larger developments and the one that received the most public attention. A series of racist incidents triggered the growth of a militant student movement led by Concerned Student 1950 (named for the year the first black student was admitted to the university) (Sherwin, Gallion, and Sherman 2015; Sherwin, Edwards, and Wortman 2015). The head of the multicampus UM system, the president, Timothy M. Wolfe, a former IBM executive with no prior academic experience, was installed by the Republican-controlled state legislature.[1] Wolfe was hired in part to cut the university's budget, which included closing the longstanding university press and eliminating health benefits for graduate student assistants (Berrett and Hoover 2015; Miller and Stuckey-French 2015). The cuts in health care pushed graduate students to organize a union and to launch a series of campus protests in the early fall of 2015 (O'Connor 2015; Brehe 2015).

At the same time, in response to pressure from Republican state legislators, UM administrators canceled the university's longstanding contract with Planned Parenthood to provide reproductive health services at the UM hospital. In response a broad coalition of students and faculty organized a large campus rally in late September in support of Planned Parenthood (Weinberg 2015a, 2015b).

Wolfe, along with the campus's chancellor, R. Bowen Loftin, proved remarkably tone-deaf and slow in responding to the spiraling number of racist incidents on the Columbia campus. In early October the Concerned Student 1950 issued a series of demands (which included calls for the immediate removal of President Wolfe and for the UM administration to meet "the Legion of Black Collegians' demands that were presented in 1969 for the betterment of the black community" (Weinberg and Blatchford 2015).[2] This conscious linkage by Concerned Student 1950 to historic student struggles at UM against racism is important and striking. In this intensifying campus student campaign Jonathan Butler, a graduate student, began a public hunger strike in late October to protest administrative actions (or inactions) in response to campus racism (Oide 2015). Butler's brave political act inspired the black players on the college's football team to publicly endorse the campaign. When thirty black football players joined the larger student body's demand for the ouster of the president by threatening to boycott an upcoming game (which would have cost the university a $1 million forfeiture fee), the board of curators forced Wolfe to resign; shortly thereafter Lofton also tendered his resignation (Eligon and Pérez-Peña 2015). Wolfe was quickly replaced by a recently retired African American UM administrator, Michael Middleton (who ironically had been one of the founding undergraduate members of the Legion of Black Collegians in 1969 noted earlier) (Gaines/ Oldham Black Culture Center 2015; University of Missouri 2013). No doubt the Board of Curators hoped Middleton would cool down student activism on the campus (Pérez-Peña 2015). The UM student movement's tactics, which led to intensifying political pressure, heightened media visibility, and the deepening involvement of the UM student body and faculty, quickly became a referent point for university activists across the country, spurred on by widespread use of social media (Jaschik 2015b). The Twitter hashtags #StandwithMizzou, #BlackonCampus, and #StudentBlackOut created to support the UM movement and to spread the message to other college campuses, have been deployed across the country to focus continued discussions about structural racism on college campuses (Jaschik 2015c). These tools and tactics are also being adapted on campuses to fight back against various forms of austerity-driven politics and policies undermining public educational institutions. As this is being written, it is simply too soon to tell if this upsurge of college student/campus activism will have as significant a long-term impact as the student movement did half a century ago. Nonetheless, it is an encouraging sign.

And in the spring of 2015, after five years without a contract and having exhausted every other option, the CUNY PSC planned an escalating organizing campaign. The campaign was designed to join issues of faculty and staff working conditions, including increased wages, with opposition to the diminishment of quality education. The continuing impasse over a new contract was producing a migration of some of the best faculty out of the university and ever greater difficulty in recruiting scholars to CUNY (Vilensky 2015). The issues of faculty workload, overreliance on part-time instructors, and ever greater dependence on increasing tuition to sustain CUNY were highlighted during the campaign as factors affecting both the quality of an education and the access of working-class and poor students, especially students of color, to a college education. These are not unfamiliar issues outside of CUNY or in the larger world of public higher education. For example, the CFA recently had a strike authorization vote in which 80 percent of its instructors voted and 93 percent approved a strike. At the CCFS a call for a strike is being built in alliance with student and community groups. What distinguishes the CUNY experience is the length of the impasse, the level of resistance of the PSC to the stark regimen of austerity, and the emergent alliance of community residents, students, and other New York City union members to defend CUNY in a moment of crisis. The campaign also maintained a consistent focus on student access issues and wage freezes that were linked to an overarching politics of austerity and diminishment of the quality of education. These linkages in turn were inflected in the design of the contract campaign.

The targets of the campaign were the chancellor of the university, seen as ineffective in securing the needed resources for CUNY, and the New York governor, who actively pursued policies that assured a continuing decline in the per capita investment in the state's public university students (Vilensky 2015). Actions over a two-month period included a "Wake Up" rally at the Chancellor's private residence, civil disobedience and arrests of fifty-four faculty and staff in front of the CUNY administration offices, and a mass meeting to announce and organize for a strike authorization vote. A student postcard campaign directed at the governor was also launched across the state and resulted in the collection of about forty thousand, which were delivered at a press conference in Albany. The postcard campaign involved a coalition of groups including the SUNY union (UUP), the state federation of teachers (NYSUT), and the New York Public Interest Research Group (NYPIRG), representing students.

The civil disobedience produced significant media attention and an immediate contract offer from CUNY administrators of 6 percent over six years, woefully inadequate but a starting point for negotiations, given the previous five years of silence from the CUNY leadership (Chapman 2015). The work of building alliances to defend CUNY concretely involved joining community and student interests with those of union members. In turn, this organizing focused on the need to promote a quality, accessible education. The campaign called for increased public investment to enhance public higher education while freezing tuition to insure continued access. The larger intention of the campaign was to highlight the ways austerity undercuts CUNY's historic aspirations to educate poor and working-class students across the city.

The continuing work of building a broader alliance to defend CUNY will hopefully extend beyond this contract fight and offers a framework for building more powerful campaigns in defense of public higher education across the country. Most importantly this organizing practice joins a call for a redistributive investment of public dollars in higher education supported by faculty and staff with the justice work of enlarging the life possibilities for poor and working-class students especially of color (Ruiz 2015). The cauldron of an ever more intense contract fight has created not simply a conception of how to build power, but a beginning practice that offers a different arc of possibility in reversing austerity policies more generally.

The recent struggles at UM and CUNY offer us distinct possibilities for cross-racial and cross-class alliance building in public universities. The task of such movement building, inside and outside of the academy, must be actively attended to if we are to save public higher education and make it a robust public good. If these efforts fail, we will watch as the achievements of past struggles for redistributive justice and likely even the aspirations for quality college education for all citizens are washed away by market and state forces. The choice is ours. The choice, as always, is political, whether we work in the academy or at a car wash. Finally, the choice must be to create the movement power necessary to secure a more just future. Some part of our aspiration must be, in the inspiring words of the Tunisian organizer Fathi Ben Haj Yahia, to find "that common denominator in which people can recognize themselves, in a fiction, in a hope, that draws people toward a horizon" (Gall 2015, A-5).

[ACKNOWLEDGMENTS]

We have many people to acknowledge and thank for their help, both intellectual and emotional. We benefited from the hard work of three research assistants. Craig Hughes asked important questions at key stages of the manuscript's development and provided astute research suggestions and editorial assistance. Equally important, his work on the California case study in chapter 5 provided the data and much of the language for that discussion. His contributions were timely, precise, and thoughtful. Natalie Demyan helped to organize and systematically review the book's references and citations. She also made a major contribution to the final copyediting of the volume. We appreciated her consistent thoroughness, accuracy, and commitment to the project. And Rachel Thompson did important research work and uncovered primary and secondary sources for the history and technology chapters.

Steve Burghardt, Betsy Fabricant, and Michelle Fine reviewed and offered valuable comments on chapters 1 and 4 at an early stage in the manuscript's development. Additionally, conversations with Eric Zachary, Barbara Bowen, Steve London, Debbie Bell, Naomi Zauderer, and Robert Fisher over many years helped to shape chapters 5 and 7. These chapters were also influenced by the thinking of the leaders in the Campaign for the Future of Higher Education and the AAUP. Julie List offered key editing suggestions in the introduction and caught numerous infelicities in the prose. The historical chapters (2 and 3) benefited from the close reading and thoughtful comments and suggestions of Jon Amsden, Josh Brown, Tahir Butt, Josh Freeman, Jerry Markowitz, David Nasaw, Ellie Shermer, and Paul Worthman. Chapter 6 on the history of educational technology was improved by the comments and astute suggestions of George Otte and Luke Waltzer. We also want to acknowledge the insightful comments on the draft manuscript offered by the two anonymous outside readers for Johns Hopkins University Press. We also want to thank our indexer, Jim O'Brien, for his careful reading of the page proofs.

Finally, we want to thank Gregory Britton, our Johns Hopkins University Press editor, who believed in the book from the very beginning. His wise counsel regarding the structure of the book and careful reading of the draft provided an essential touchstone for the development and refinement of our analysis. Equally important, his flexibility and support provided the ballast and backup necessary to allow us to complete the book.

Chapter 2 • The State Expansion of Public Higher Education

1. Morrill, who was still serving in the Senate, would expand the original act twenty-eight years later to support the building of the sixteen historically "black" colleges across the South.

2. The more conservative final framing of the GI Bill may also have had a great deal to do with the Roosevelt administration's ongoing need to curry favor with racist and reactionary southern Democrats, especially Congressman John Rankin of Mississippi, who controlled a key committee essential to the passage of legislation during and immediately after the war (Katznelson 2005, 114, 123).

3. In New York City's four municipal colleges, which were tuition-free, the final GI Bill, thanks to Mayor Fiorello LaGuardia's intervention with Congress, included a provision to pay up to $500 to reimburse the city for "instructional costs" for each veteran who attended tuition-free municipal colleges. By 1946–47, federal funds from the GI Bill already comprised one-quarter of NYC's municipal colleges' revenues (Glazer 1981, 207–10).

4. Female college students achieved parity with male college students nationally around 1980, after which women's college enrollments exceeded 55 percent of the national student total.

5. George Zook, who was the Commission chair, was Roosevelt's Commissioner of Education at the beginning of the New Deal and had served as head of the American Council on Education since 1934.

6. Truman finally legally desegregated the army and navy by executive order in July 1948.

7. The board was officially known as "The Regents of the University of the State of New York," a confusing title, given that New York did not found its state university system until 1948.

8. Ezra Cornell agreed to put up $500,000 personally to help finance the new university. The only concession the new school had to make to secure the state's lucrative land grant was to agree to admit one "free" student a year from each assembly district in New York. To this day, Cornell University, an essentially private institution, maintains the fig leaf of a distinctly public purpose through its schools of Forestry, Agriculture, and Industrial and Labor Relations.

9. Two new municipal colleges were founded in Brooklyn (1930) and Queens (1937).

10. The New York City Board of Higher Education was created in 1926 to govern and coordinate the activities of the two municipal colleges, CCNY and Hunter.

11. The passage of FEPA hardly solved all problems of discrimination in higher education, as evidenced by the five-day strike in spring 1949 by thousands of CCNY students protesting the anti-Semitic and racist attitudes and actions of two senior faculty members (Dyer 1990, 47–48).

12. The BHE was also consumed in these years by growing paranoia about Communist influence among the faculty and students in the existing municipal colleges, which led to a series of investigative hearings in Albany and New York City in the 1940s and early 1950s by the Rapp-Coudert joint committee of the New York State legislature. These hearings contributed significantly to the McCarthyite witch hunts that soon followed (Gordon 1975, 60; Schrecker 1986).

13. Heald was the head of the Ford Foundation and the former New York University president. The committee included only two other members: Marion Folsom, former treasurer of the Eastman Kodak Company and former secretary of health, education, and welfare in the Eisenhower administration; and John Gardner, president of the Carnegie Corporation of New York. All three, not surprisingly, were from the private sector.

14. The Heald report also argued that two new doctoral programs should be established at SUNY, but none in New York City (Axelrod 1974, 131–45; Gordon 1975, 113–15, 120–21).

15. John Aubrey Douglass's history of California public higher education has significantly influenced our understanding in this chapter (Douglass 2000).

16. Wisconsin, like California, experienced intense battles over financial resources and educational mission between its state university system, led by the flagship Madison campus (established in 1848), and its nine state colleges. The state legislature finally intervened, setting up a coordinating committee in 1955 to develop a higher education strategic plan similar to California's more widely known Master Plan that emerged five years later (Snider 1999, 117; Wendt 1975, 95; Fellman 1975, 105; Penniman 1975, 113–15).

Chapter 3 • Students and Faculty Take Command

1. Sheila Gordon's and Judith Glazer's excellent unpublished dissertations on CUNY's history have been invaluable resources for this section of the chapter. It should be noted that the municipal colleges began charging tuition to students attending part-time and evening programs early in the twentieth century, a practice that would continue after CUNY's creation (Butt 2014).

2. State funding support for the city's municipal colleges had come in 1959–60, when the state agreed to supply one-third of the operating costs of educating students in the senior municipal colleges during the first two years of their undergraduate study, plus fiscal support from the state for one-half of the debt service for the municipal colleges' capital costs (Gordon 1975, 84; Glazer 1981, 222–23).

3. Rockefeller signed into law in 1968 Bundy Aid (named for McGeorge Bundy, president of the Ford Foundation and chair of the committee Rockefeller appointed to design the program), which provided $400 to private colleges for every degree they awarded. Total Bundy Aid in 1969, the program's first year, totaled $25 million, which would quickly jump by 1973 to $69 million, almost half the total amount New York State provided CUNY in that year (Connery and Benjamin 1979, 315–23).

4. In a 1979 interview after he had decamped from CUNY to become the chancellor of UC Berkeley, Bowker, in responding to the BHE's dogged defense of free tuition, suggested that "Nobody on the [BHE] understood the philosophical shift occurring in the nation or in the state of New York to equalize educational opportunities" (Glazer 1981, 266).

5. The only other state to grant that kind of constitutional independence to its state university system was Michigan (Kolins 1999, 61).

6. The donation was not entirely altruistic. It helped launch a building boom on the surrounding Irvine Ranch land (including the newly created city of Irvine), all controlled by the Irvine Company, the corporate entity that controlled the ranch.

7. Kerr was not alone in entering university administration from a background as a labor mediator and labor economist. Derek Bok, president of Harvard (1971–91); William Bowen, president of Princeton (1972–88); and Michael Sovern, president at Columbia (1980–93), followed Kerr's career trajectory as well. Thanks to Josh Freeman for this insight.

8. The notable exception is Kerr's prescient acknowledgment of the "incipient revolt of undergraduate students," who increasingly "look upon themselves more as a 'class'; some may even feel like a 'lumpen proletariat'" in response to the degradation of undergraduate instruction (Kerr 1963, 103–4).

9. Though first published in 1963, Kerr published no fewer than four revised editions of *The Uses of the University* over the next four decades, each time massaging and reshaping his analysis and his prose to fit changing circumstances and to explain and justify his own actions.

10. Full disclosure: one of the authors (Brier) was an eighteen-year-old sophomore at UC Berkeley who was in Sproul Plaza that day, and, with some of his friends, occupied the right front wheel of the police car.

11. Kathleen Frydl argues that this large lecture method traces its origins back to the US Army during World War II, which she claims UCB and other public institutions adopted because of the postwar shortage of qualified faculty members (Frydl 2009, 316).

12. The UCB administration had adopted punch cards supposedly to streamline student registration. Mario Savio once stated, "At Cal, you're little more than an IBM card" (Cohen 2009, 205; Lubar 1992).

13. Stanley Aronowitz makes a similar point about Savio's conscious manipulation of Kerr's industrial imagery to undermine the UC president's evocation of the contemporary multiversity (Aronowitz 2000, 33–34).

14. Similar increases in college attendance by white, working-class students under state open admissions policies occurred across the country in the 1960s, according to educational theorist K. Patricia Cross (Nasaw 1979, 219).

15. The "1,595 votes" presumably referred to the number of BMCC students who graduated that day.

Chapter 4 • *The Making of the Neoliberal Public University*

1. This material was drawn from anonymous personal communications to the authors in 2014 by a number of CUNY administrators and staff members.

2. Joseph Schumpeter, an influential early twentieth-century Austrian philosopher and economist who ended his career in the 1930s at Harvard, described the market's

proclivity to rapidly destroy obsolete industries and their workers in the wake of innovations producing new technology and forms of production, as well as the reduction of market-driven wages.

3. Julia Wrigley was CUNY's associate university provost and chaired the committee that issued the 2010 Pathways report.

4. There is a growing academic literature on successful uses of hybrid forms of instruction, as indicated by a number of the studies in *Blended Learning: Research Perspectives, Volume 2* (Picciano, Dziuban, and Graham 2013).

Chapter 5 • The Public University as an Engine of Inequality

1. The authors thank Jacob Jackson of the Public Policy Institute of California for drawing their attention to this report.

Chapter 6 • Technology as a "Magic Bullet" in an Era of Austerity

1. Much of the institutional and policy history of educational technology summarized in this and following sections draws from the encyclopedic work of Paul Saettler, whose *Evolution of American Educational Technology* is the standard reference work on US educational technology in the pre–World Wide Web era.

2. *Continental Classroom* won a prestigious Peabody Award for "Television Education" in its premier season. In 1957 CBS launched *Sunrise Semester*, in collaboration with NYU, which, like *Continental Classroom*, televised early morning credit-bearing courses, taught by notable NYU faculty members. The program lasted for a quarter century, ending its run in 1982 (NYU Bobst Library webpage, n.d.).

3. Historian and columnist Jill Lepore has written a critical analysis of Christensen and the disruptive innovation concept in the *New Yorker* (Lepore 2014). See also Evan Goldstein's article on critiques of Christensen in the *Chronicle of Higher Education* (Goldstein 2015).

4. Noble's three online articles appeared in *First Monday* in 1998 (Noble 1998), which he expanded and published as *Digital Diploma Mills: The Automation of Higher Education* (2001).

5. The UCLA AITB was replaced in 2000 by the Information Technology Planning Board (ITPB), "a joint Administration-[Faculty] Senate committee" whose charge to advise and consult on all IT-related matters clearly reflected the administration's overreach in the THEN-OLN brouhaha (UCLA ITPB 2001 webpage).

6. Walsh's 2011 book *Unlocking the Gates: How and Why Leading Universities Are Opening Up Access to Their Courses*, which includes extensive interviews with key administrative players, is an essential source for understanding the online mania that swept higher education in these years, and we have drawn on it extensively in this chapter.

7. Crow and William B. Dabars co-authored *Designing the New American University* (2015), which argues for a fundamental restructuring of the contemporary research university, a rethinking and rebranding of Clark Kerr's fifty-year-old original multiversity idea. Christopher Newfield has written a thoughtful review of the book in the *Los Angeles Review of Books* (Newfield 2015).

8. The Ithaka S+R, self-described as a "strategic consulting and research service," published an entirely positive evaluation of Michael Crow's public higher education vision and its implementation at ASU in January 2015. The fifteen interviews that form the

basis of the Ithaka report were conducted solely with senior administrators and department chairs, none of whom offers an iota of criticism of Crow or the current direction of ASU. Not a single student or rank-and-file faculty member was included among the interviewees (Guthrie, Mulhern, and Kurzweil 2015).

9. Despite its elite roots at Harvard and MIT, edX has worked hard to capture many of the elite colleges and universities, including the universities of Michigan and Pennsylvania, originally linked to Coursera's and Udacity's MOOC projects, agreeing to provide edX MOOC courses for a substantial fee (Schaffhauser 2015; Straumsheim 2015c).

Chapter 7 • *Fighting for the Soul of Public Higher Education*

1. The spread of collaboration and open-source ideals was significantly aided by the emergence of the Creative Commons movement after 2001, which produced a series of online copyright licenses designed to help individuals and institutions make their works freely available online and/or dedicate those works to free digital use and reuse in the public domain (Lessig 2005, 282–86).

2. See Jim Groom and Brian Lamb's excellent *EDUCAUSE Review* article "Reclaiming Innovation" for five arguments against the use of mandated learning management system software such as Blackboard (Groom and Lamb 2014).

Epilogue

1. Wolfe's hiring appears to be part of a general trend that saw boards of trustees hiring politicians or business leaders, with little or no university experience, as public university heads. The former category includes David Boren (Oklahoma), Mitch Daniels (Purdue), Janet Napolitano (University of California), and Margaret Spellings (North Carolina); the latter category includes Bruce Harreld (Iowa), another former IBM executive (Nelson 2014; Kelderman 2015; Brown 2015; Jaschik 2015a).

2. UM's independent student newspaper, the *Maneater*, produced a useful illustrated timeline, including links to various issues of the online paper detailing the fall 2015 events on the UM–Columbia campus (Weinberg and Blatchford 2015). A current student group on the campus also took the name of the original 1969 student group, calling itself the Legion of Black Collegians and suggesting that it was "the only Black Student Government in the country" (University of Missouri 2015).

Introduction

Blyth, Mark. 2013. *Austerity: The History of a Dangerous Idea.* New York: Oxford University Press.

Bradsher, Keith. 2013. "Next Made-in-China Boom: College Graduates." *New York Times*, January 16. http://www.nytimes.com/2013/01/17/business/chinas-ambitious-goal-for-boom-in-college-graduates.html.

Nylander, Johan. 2015. "China's Investment in Elite Universities Pays Off: New Ranking." *Forbes*, September 14. http://www.forbes.com/sites/jnylander/2015/09/14/chinas-investment-in-elite-universities-pays-off-new-ranking/.

Szalai, Jennifer. 2015. "The Tough Love of 'Austerity.'" *New York Times Magazine*, August 9. http://www.nytimes.com/2015/08/09/magazine/the-tough-love-of-austerity.html.

Chapter 1

Alexander, Michelle. 2010. *The New Jim Crow: Mass Incarceration in the Age of Colorblindness.* New York: New Press.

American Social History Project. 2008. *Who Built America? Working People and the Nation's History.* Vol. 2. New York: Bedford/St. Martin's.

Biondi, Martha. 2006. *To Stand and to Fight: The Struggle for Civil Rights in Postwar New York City.* Cambridge, MA: Harvard University Press.

Blumenstyk, G. 2014. "'Risk Adjusted' Metrics for Colleges Get Another Look." *The Chronicle of Higher Education*, April 28. http://chronicle.com/article/Risk-Adjusted-Metrics/146193/.

Braverman, Harry. 1975. *Labor and Monopoly Capital: The Degradation of Work in the Twentieth-Century.* New York: Monthly Review Press.

Brown, Edmund, Jr. 2013. "2013–14 Governor's Budget Summary." January 10. http://www.ebudget.ca.gov/2013-14/pdf/BudgetSummary/FullBudgetSummary.pdf.

Carnevale, Anthony P., and Jeffrey Strohl. 2013. *Separate and Unequal: How Higher Education Reinforces the Intergenerational Reproduction of White Privilege.* Washington, DC: Georgetown Policy Institute. https://georgetown.app.box.com/s/zhi9ilgzba9ncmri6ral.

Desrochers, Donna, and Rita Kirshstein. 2012. *College Spending in a Turbulent Decade: Findings from the Delta Cost Project.* A Delta Data Update 2000–2010. Washington,

DC: American Institutes for Research. http://www.deltacostproject.org/sites
/default/files/products/Delta-Cost-College-Spending-In-A-Turbulent-Decade
.pdf.

Eaton, Charles, Cyrus Dioun, Daniela Gracia Goboy, Adam Goldstein, Jacob
Habinek, and Robert Osley-Thomas. 2014. *Borrowing against the Future: The
Hidden Costs of Financing US Higher Education.* Berkeley: The Center for Culture,
Organizations and Politics, UC Berkeley Institute for Research on Labor and
Employment.

Fabricant, Michael. 2010. *Organizing for Educational Justice: The Campaign for Public
School Reform in the South Bronx.* Minneapolis: University of Minnesota Press.

Fabricant, Michael, and Michelle Fine. 2013. *The Changing Politics of Education:
Privatization and the Dispossessed Lives Left Behind.* Boulder, CO: Paradigm.

Fain, Paul. 2013. "Complete College America Report Tracks State Approaches to
Performance Based Funding." *Inside Higher Ed*, October 30. https://www
.insidehighered.com/news/2013/10/29/complete-college-america-report-tracks
-state-approaches-performance-based-funding.

Field, Kelly. 2014. "In Health Care, Lessons for Obama in Rating Colleges." *The
Chronicle of Higher Education*, April 25. http://chronicle.com/article/In-Health
-Care-Lessons-for/146089/.

Folbre, Nancy. 2010. *Saving State U: Why We Must Fix Public Higher Education.* New
York: New Press.

Foroohar, Rana. 2013a. "Davos Wisdom, 2013: Five Lessons from the Global Forum."
Time, January 26. http://business.time.com/2013/01/26/davos-wisdom-2013-five
-lessons-from-the-global-forum.

———. 2013b. "Why the Elites Are Losing Sleep." *Time*, January 31. http://business
.time.com/2013/01/31/why-the-elites-are-losing-sleep/.

Frazier, Nancy. 2014. "Behind Marx's Hidden Abode: For an Expanded Conception
of Capitalism." *New Left Review* 86:55–72.

Ghani, Ashraj, and Clare Lockhart. 2008. *Fixing Failed States: A Framework for
Rebuilding a Fractured World.* New York: Oxford University Press.

Giroux, Henry. 2014. *Neoliberalism's War on Higher Education.* Chicago: Haymarket
Books.

Goldstein, Matthew. 2011. "Rational Tuition Policy: A Primer." *The Chancellor's Desk*
(blog), October 12. http://www1.cuny.edu/mu/forum/2011/10/12/the-chancellors
-desk-rational-tuition-policy-a-primer/.

Guttenplan, D. D. 2013. "Vying for a Spot on the World's A List." *New York Times*,
April 14. http://www.nytimes.com/2013/04/14/education/edlife/university-rankings
-go-global.html?_r=0.

Hacker, Jacob, and Paul Pierson. 2011. *Winner Take All Politics: How Washington Made
the Rich Richer—and Turned Its Back on the Middle Class.* New York: Simon and
Schuster.

Harvey, David. 2003. *The New Imperialism.* New York: Oxford University Press.

———. 2005. *A Brief History of Neoliberalism.* New York: Oxford University Press.

Henig, J. R. 2009. *Spin Cycle: How Research Is Used in Policy Debates: The Case of
Charter Schools.* New York: Russell Sage.

Jansson, Bruce. 2012. *The Reluctant Welfare State: Engaging History to Advance Social Welfare Practice*. Belmont, CA: Wadsworth.

Katz, Cindi. 2001. "Vagabond Capitalism and the Need for Social Reproduction." *Antipode* 33 (4): 717–24.

Klein, Naomi. 2007. *The Shock Doctrine: The Rise of Disaster Capitalism*. New York: Picador.

———. 2014. *This Changes Everything: Capitalism vs. the Climate*. New York: Simon and Schuster.

Kolowich, Steve. 2013. "SUNY Signals Major Push toward MOOCs and Other New Educational Models." *The Chronicle of Higher Education*, March 20. http://www.highereducation.org/crosstalk/pdf/ct_1209.pdf.

Lanier, Jaron. 2013. *Who Owns the Future?* New York: Simon and Schuster.

Lewin, Tamar. 2013. "Obama's Plan Aims to Lower Cost of College." *New York Times*, August 22. http://www.nytimes.com/2013/08/22/education/obamas-plan-aims-to-lower-cost-of-college.html.

Marcus, Jon. 2009. "Overcrowded and Underfunded: New York's Public University Systems, and Beleaguered Students, Are an Extreme Example of National Trends." *National Crosstalk* 17:2. http://www.highereducation.org/crosstalk/pdf/ct_1209.pdf.

McCoy, Alfred. 2010. "Tomgram: Alfred McCoy, Taking Down America." *TomDispatch* (blog), December 5. http://www.tomdispatch.com/post/175327/.

McDermott, Casey. 2013. "US Higher Education System Perpetuates White Privilege, Report Says." *The Chronicle of Higher Education*, July 31. http://chronicle.com/article/US-Higher Education System/140631.

McGettigan, Andrew. 2013. *The Great University Gamble: Money, Markets and the Future of Higher Education*. New York: Pluto.

Mettler, Susan. 2014. *Degrees of Inequality: How the Politics of Higher Education Sabotaged the American Dream*. New York: Basic Books.

Moltz, David. 2009. "No Vacancy." *Inside Higher Ed*, July 21. https://www.insidehighered.com/news/2009/07/21/california.

Morozov, Evgeny. 2013. *The Folly of Technological Solutionism: To Save Everything Click Here*. New York: Public Affairs.

New York City Department of Education. 2014. "DOE Overview—Funding Our Schools." http://schools.nyc.gov/AboutUs/funding/overview/default.htm.

New York Times Editorial Board. 2014. "The College Faculty Crisis." *New York Times*, April 14. http://www.nytimes.com/2014/04/14/opinion/the-college-faculty-crisis.html.

Piketty, Thomas. 2014. *Capital: In the Twenty-First Century*. Cambridge, MA: Belknap of Harvard University Press.

Piven, Francis Fox, and Richard Cloward. 1993 [1971]. *Regulating the Poor: The Functions of Public Welfare*. New York: Vintage.

Quinterno, John. 2012. *The Great Cost Shift: How Higher Education Cuts Undermine the Future Middle Class*. New York: Demos. http://www.demos.org/sites/default/files/publications/TheGreatCostShift_Demos_0.pdf.

Selingo, Jeffrey. 2013. *College (Un)Bound: The Future of Higher Education and What It Means for Students*. Boston: New Harvest.

Simon, Stephanie, and Stephanie Banchero. 2010. "Putting a Price on Professors: A Battle in Texas over Whether Academic Value Can Be Measured in Dollars and Cents." *Wall Street Journal*, October 22. http://online.wsj.com/articles/SB100014240 52748703735804575536322093520994.

Stiglitz, Joseph. 2012. *The Price of Inequality: How Today's Divided Society Endangers Our Future*. New York: W. W. Norton.

Stripling, Jack. 2013. "President's Proposal Renews Debate over How to Measure College Quality." *The Chronicle of Higher Education*, September 5. http://chronicle .com/article/Presidents-Proposal-Renews/141391/.

Toch, Thomas. 2009. *Sweating the Big Stuff: A Progress Report on the Movement to Scale up the Nation's Best Charter Schools*. http://scholasticadministrator.typepad.com/files /sweating060309.doc.pdf.

Treschan, Lazar, and Apurva Mehrotra. 2012. *Unintended Impacts: Fewer Black and Latino Freshmen at CUNY Senior Colleges after the Recession*. The Community Service Society Reports. New York: Community Service Society. http://b.3cdn.net /nycss/2e01feab246663d4a8_1hm6b94lq.pdf.

US Senate. Health, Education, Labor, and Pensions Committee. 2012. *For Profit Higher Education: The Failure to Safeguard the Federal Investment and Ensure Student Success, Executive Summary*. http://www.help.senate.gov/imo/media/ for_profit _report/ExecutiveSummary.pdf.

Warren, Mark R., and Karen L. Mapp. 2011. *A Match on Dry Grass: Community Organizing as a Catalyst for School Reform*. Oxford: Oxford University Press.

Welen, Richard. 2013. "Open Access, Megajournals, and MOOCs: On the Political Economy of Academic Unbundling." *SAGE Open* 3:1–16.

Wilkinson, Richard, and Kate Pickett. 2009. *The Spirit Level: Why Greater Equality Makes Society Stronger*. New York: Bloomsbury.

Chapter 2

Abbott, Frank C. 1958. *Government Policy and Higher Education: A Study of the Regents of the University of the State of New York, 1784–1949*. Ithaca, NY: Cornell University Press.

American Social History Project. 2008. *Who Built America? Working People and the Nation's History*. 3rd ed., vol. 2. New York: Bedford/St. Martin's.

Aronowitz, Stanley. 2000. *The Knowledge Factory: Dismantling the Corporate University and Creating True Higher Learning*. Boston: Beacon.

Axelrod, Donald. 1974. "Higher Education." *Proceedings of the Academy of Political Science* 31:131–45.

Bowen, William G., and Eugene M. Tobin. 2015. *Locus of Authority: The Evolution of Faculty Roles in the Governance of Higher Education*. Princeton, NJ: Princeton University Press.

Brown, Edmund G. 1965. "Public Higher Education in California." In *Emerging Patterns in American Higher Education*, edited by Logan Wilson, 104–9. Washington, DC: American Council on Education.

Cardozier, V. R. 1993. *Colleges and Universities in World War II*. Westport, CT: Praeger.

Carmichael, Oliver, Jr. 1955. *New York Establishes a State University*. Nashville, TN: Vanderbilt University Press.

Clark, John B., W. Bruce Leslie, and Kenneth P. O'Brien, eds. 2010. *SUNY at Sixty: The Promise of the State University of New York*. Albany: State University of New York Press.

Connery, Robert H., and Gerald Benjamin. 1979. *Rockefeller of New York: Executive Power in the Statehouse*. Ithaca, NY: Cornell University Press.

Denning, Michael. 1996. *The Cultural Front*. New York: Verso.

Douglass, John Aubrey. 2000. *The California Idea and American Higher Education: 1850 to the 1960 Master Plan*. Stanford, CA: Stanford University Press.

Dyer, Conrad. 1990. "Protest and the Politics of Open Admissions: The Impact of the Black and Puerto Rican Students' Community (of City College)." PhD diss., CUNY Graduate Center.

FDR Library. n.d. "Message to Congress on the Education of War Veterans, October 27, 1943." Accessed July 1, 2014. http://docs.fdrlibrary.marist.edu/odgiced.html.

Fellman, David. 1975. "Faculty Governance, 1949–1974." In *The University of Wisconsin: One Hundred and Twenty-Five Years*, edited by Allan G. Bogue and Robert Taylor, 99–112. Madison: University of Wisconsin Press.

Frydl, Kathleen. 2009. *The G.I. Bill*. New York: Cambridge University Press.

Gilbert, Amy M. 1950. *ACUNY, the Associated Colleges of Upper New York: A Unique Response to an Emergency in Higher Education in the State of New York*. Ithaca, NY: Cornell University Press.

Glazer, Judith. 1981. "A Case Study of the Decision in 1976 to Initiate Tuition for Matriculated Undergraduate Students in the City University of New York." PhD diss., New York University.

Glenny, Lyman. 1965. "State Systems and Plans for Higher Education." In *Emerging Patterns in American Higher Education*, edited by Logan Wilson, 86–103. Washington, DC: American Council on Education.

Gordon, Sheila. 1975. "The Transformation of the City University of New York, 1945–1970." PhD diss., Columbia University.

Halstead, D. Kent. 1974. *Statewide Planning in Higher Education*. Washington, DC: Government Printing Office.

Harlow, James G. 1953. "Five Years of Discussion." *Journal of Higher Education* 24:17–24.

Ingraham, Mark H. 1975. "The University of Wisconsin, 1925–1950." In *The University of Wisconsin: One Hundred and Twenty-Five Years*, edited by Allan G. Bogue and Robert Taylor, 38–78. Madison: University of Wisconsin Press.

Katsinas, Stephen G., J. Leland Johnson, and Lana G. Snider. 1999. "Two-Year College Development in Five Midwestern States: An Introduction and Overview." *Community College Journal of Research and Practice* 23:1–17.

Katznelson, Ira. 2005. *When Affirmative Action Was White: An Untold History of Racial Inequality in Twentieth Century America*. New York: W. W. Norton.

Loss, Christopher. 2012. *Between Citizens and the State: The Politics of American Higher Education in the 20th Century*. Princeton, NJ: Princeton University Press.

Mettler, Suzanne. 2005. *Soldiers to Citizens: The G.I. Bill and the Making of the Greatest Generation*. New York: Oxford University Press.

———. 2014. *Degrees of Inequality: How the Politics of Higher Education Sabotaged the American Dream*. New York: Basic Books.

Nasaw, David. 1979. *Schooled to Order: A Social History of Public Schooling in the United States*. New York: Oxford University Press.

National Center for Education Statistics. 1993. *120 Years of American Education: A Statistical Portrait*. Washington, DC: National Center for Education Statistics. http://nces.ed.gov/pubs93/93442.pdf.

Ottman, Tod. 2010. "Forging SUNY in New York's Cauldron." In *SUNY at Sixty: The Promise of the State University of New York*, edited by John B. Clark, W. Bruce Leslie, and Kenneth P. O'Brien, 15–28. Albany: State University of New York Press.

Penniman, Clara. 1975. "The University of Wisconsin System." In *The University of Wisconsin: One Hundred and Twenty-Five Years*, edited by Allan G. Bogue and Robert Taylor, 113–30. Madison: University of Wisconsin Press.

Rudolph, Frederick. 1962. *The American College and University: A History*. New York: Vintage Books.

Schrecker, Ellen. 1986. *No Ivory Tower: McCarthyism and the Universities*. New York: Oxford University Press.

Schrum, Ethan. 2007. "Establishing a Democratic Religion: Metaphysics and Democracy in the Debates over the President's Commission on Higher Education." *History of Education Quarterly* 47:277–301.

Smelser, Neil. 1974. "Growth, Structural Change, and Conflict in California Higher Education, 1950–1970." In *Public Higher Education in California*, edited by N. Smelser and G. Almond, 9–142. Berkeley: University of California Press.

Snider, Lana G. 1999. "The History and Development of the Two-Year Colleges in Wisconsin: The University of Wisconsin Colleges and the Wisconsin Technical College System." *Community College Journal of Research and Practice* 23:107–28.

US Census Bureau. 2014. "Table 19. California—Race and Hispanic Origin: 1850 to 1990." *Historical Census Statistics on Population Totals*. http://www.census.gov/population/www/documentation/twps0056/twps0056.html.

Wechsler, Harold. 2010. "The Temporary Commission Survey Bias in Admissions." In *SUNY at Sixty: The Promise of the State University of New York*, edited by John B. Clark, W. Bruce Leslie, and Kenneth P. O'Brien, 29–38. Albany, NY: State University of New York Press.

Wendt, Kurt F. 1975. "The Growth of the University's Physical Resources, 1949–1975." In *The University of Wisconsin: One Hundred and Twenty-Five Years*, edited by Allan G. Bogue and Robert Taylor, 87–96. Madison: University of Wisconsin Press.

Zook, George F. 1947. "The President's Commission on Higher Education." *Bulletin of the American Association of University Professors*, 33:10–28.

Zook, George, et al. 1947. *President's Commission on Higher Education for Democracy, A Report of the President's Commission on Higher Education*. Vols. 1–6. Washington, DC: Government Printing Office.

Chapter 3

American Social History Project. 2008. *Who Built America? Working People and the Nation's History*. 3rd ed., vol. 2. New York: Bedford/St. Martin's.

Aronowitz, Stanley. 2000. *The Knowledge Factory: Dismantling the Corporate University and Creating True Higher Learning*. Boston: Beacon.

Axelrod, Donald. 1974. "Higher Education." *Proceedings of the Academy of Political Science* 31:131–45.

Berrett, Dan. 2015. "The Day the Purpose of College Changed." *The Chronicle of Higher Education*, January 27. http://chronicle.com/article/The-Day-the-Purpose -of-College/151359.

Biondi, Martha. 2012. *The Black Revolution on Campus*. Berkeley: University of California Press.

Bowen, William G., and Eugene M. Tobin. 2015. *Locus of Authority: The Evolution of Faculty Roles in the Governance of Higher Education*. Princeton, NJ: Princeton University Press.

Butt, Tahir. 2014. "Free Tuition and Expansion in New York Public Higher Education." *TRAUE*. http://traue.commons.gc.cuny.edu/volume-iii-issue-1-fall-2014/free -tuition-expansion-new-york-public-higher-education/.

CCNY Libraries. 2009. *"Five Demands": The Student Protest and Takeover of 1969* (exhibition). New York: City College of New York (CUNY).

Cohen, Robert. 2009. *Freedom's Orator: Mario Savio and the Radical Legacy of the 1960s*. New York: Oxford University Press.

Connery, Robert H., and Gerald Benjamin. 1979. *Rockefeller of New York: Executive Power in the Statehouse*. Ithaca, NY: Cornell University Press.

Demac, Donna, and Philip Mattera. 1976. "Developing and Underdeveloping New York: The 'Fiscal Crisis' and the Imposition of Austerity." *Zerowork 2: Political Materials*, 113–39. https://libcom.org/library/developing-underdeveloping-new-york -fiscal-crisis-imposition-austerity.

Dyer, Conrad. 1990. "Protest and the Politics of Open Admissions: The Impact of the Black and Puerto Rican Students' Community (of City College)." PhD diss., CUNY Graduate Center.

Ferguson, Roderick A. 2012. *The Reorder of Things: The University and Its Pedagogies of Minority Difference*. Minneapolis: University of Minnesota Press.

Freeman, Joshua. 2000. *Working Class New York: Life and Labor since World War II*. New York: New Press.

Frydl, Kathleen. 2009. *The G.I. Bill*. New York: Cambridge University Press.

Garson, Marvin. 1965. *The Regents*. Berkeley, CA: Free Speech Movement.

Glazer, Judith. 1981. "A Case Study of the Decision in 1976 to Initiate Tuition for Matriculated Undergraduate Students in the City University of New York." PhD diss., New York University.

Gordon, Sheila. 1975. "The Transformation of the City University of New York, 1945–1970." PhD diss., Columbia University.

Jordan, June. 1989. "Black Studies: Bringing Back the Person." *Moving towards Home: Political Essays*. London: Virago.

Kerr, Clark. 1963. *The Uses of the University*. New York: Harper and Row.

———. 1991. *The Great Transformation in Higher Education 1960–1980*. Albany: State University of New York Press.

Kolins, Craig A. 1999. "Michigan's Community Colleges: The Fulfillment of Civic Sovereignty." *Community College Journal of Research and Practice* 23:61–78.

Lubar, Steven. 1992. "'Do Not Fold, Spindle or Mutilate': A Cultural History of the Punch Card." *Journal of American Culture* 15:43–55.

Lustig, Jeff. 2004. "The Mixed Legacy of Clark Kerr: A Personal View." *Academe* 90:51–53.

Molloy, Sean. 2015. "CUNY SEEK and OA Oral Histories." *CompComm* (blog), November 24. http://compcomm.commons.gc.cuny.edu/cuny-oral-histories/.

Nasaw, David. 1979. *Schooled to Order: A Social History of Public Schooling in the United States.* New York: Oxford University Press.

Newt Davidson Collective. 1974. *Crisis at CUNY.* New York: Newt Davidson Collective.

Persico, Joseph E. 1982. *The Imperial Rockefeller: A Biography of Nelson A. Rockefeller.* New York: Simon and Schuster.

Rudolph, Frederick. 1962. *The American College and University: A History.* New York: Vintage Books.

Smelser, Neil. 1974. "Growth, Structural Change, and Conflict in California Higher Education, 1950–1970." In *Public Higher Education in California,* edited by N. Smelser and G. Almond, 9–142. Berkeley: University of California Press.

Tabb, William K. 1982. *The Long Default: New York City and the Urban Fiscal Crisis.* New York: Monthly Review.

Traub, James. 1994. *City on a Hill: Testing the American Dream at City College.* New York: Addison-Wesley.

UC Berkeley Bancroft Library. 2014. "Free Speech Movement Chronology." http://bancroft.berkeley.edu/FSM/chron.html.

Wechsler, Harold. 1977. *The Qualified Student: A History of Selective College Admission in America.* New York: Wiley.

Chapter 4

Alonso, Carlos J. 2010. "Paradise Lost: The Academy Becomes a Commodity." *The Chronicle of Higher Education,* December 12. http://www.chronicle.com/article/Paradise-Lost the Academy-as/125669/.

Berrett, Dan. 2014. "In Clashes over Curriculum, Completion Goals Vie with Quality." *The Chronicle of Higher Education,* March 19. http://chronicle.com/article/In-Curricular-Clashes/145385/.

Blow, Charles M. 2013. "A Dangerous 'New Normal' in College Debt." *New York Times,* March 9. http://www.nytimes.com/2013/03/09/opinion/blow-a-dangerous-new-normal-in-college-debt.html.

Bound, John, Michael Lovenheim, and Sarah Turner. 2007. *Understanding the Decrease in College Completion Rates and the Increased Time to Graduation to the Baccalaureate Degree.* Population Studies Center, Report 07-626. http://www.psc.isr.umich.edu/pubs/pdf/rro7-626.pdf.

Bowen, Barbara. 2012. "Austerity Education: The Real Agenda of Pathways." In *Clarion: Newspaper of the Professional Staff Congress/City University of New York,* October. http://www.psc-cuny.org/sites/default/files/clarion_pdfs/Clarion%20October%202012%20olr _o.pdf.

Brown, Phillip, Hugh Lauder, and David Ashton. 2011. *The Global Auction: The Broken Promises of Education, Jobs and Incomes.* New York: Oxford University Press.

Carlson, Scott. 2014. "Administrator Hiring Drove 28% Boom in Higher-Ed Work Force Report Says." *The Chronicle of Higher Education*, February 5. http://chronicle .com/article/Administrator-Hiring-Drove-28-/144519/.

Carnevale, Anthony P. 2012. "The Great Sorting." *The Chronicle of Higher Education*, July 2. http://chronicle.com/article/The-Great-Sorting/132635/.

Chomsky, Noam. 2014. "The Assault on Public Education." *Nation of Change*, July 7. http://www.nationofchange.org/print/11816.

Chung, Andrew. 2015. "Apple's Newest Courtroom Foe Is Patent-Savvy University." *Business Insider*, October. http://www.businessinsider.com/r-apples-newest -courtroom-foe-is-patent-savvy-university-2015-10.

City University of New York. 2014a. "How Credits Transfer." http://www.cuny.edu /academics/initiatives/pathways/credit-transfer.html.

———. 2014b. "Accelerated Study in Associate Programs." http://www.cuny.edu /academics/programs/notable/asap/about.html.

College Affordability and Transparency Center. 2014. "College Scorecard." http:// www.whitehouse.gov/issues/education/higher-education/college-score-card.

Collini, Stefan. 2013. "Sold Out." Review of *Everything for Sale? The Marketisation of UK Higher Education* by Roger Brown, with Helen Carasso, and *The Great University Gamble: Money, Markets and the Future of Higher Education* by Andrew McGettigan. *London Review of Books*, October 24. http://lrb.co.uk/v35/n20/stefan -collini/sold out.

Cooper, Sandi. 2013. "The Road to Pathways." *Academe*, May–June. http://www.aaup .org/article/road-pathways.

Curtis, John W., and Saranna Thornton. 2013. "Here's the News: The Annual Report on the Economic Status of the Profession." *Academe,* March–April: 4–19.

DeParle, Jason. 2012. "For Poor, Leap to College Often Ends in a Hard Fall." *New York Times*, December 22. http://www.nytimes.com/2012/12/23/education/poor -students-struggle-as-class-plays-a-greater-role-in-success.html.

Desrochers, Donna, and Rita Kirshstein. 2012. *College Spending in a Turbulent Decade: Findings from the Delta Cost Project*. A Delta Data Update 2000–2010. Washington, DC: American Institutes for Research. http://www.deltacostproject.org/sites /default/files/products/Delta-Cost-College-Spending-In-A-Turbulent-Decade.pdf.

Eaton, Charles, Cyrus Dioun, Daniela Gracia Goboy, Adam Goldstein, Jacob Habinek, and Robert Osley-Thomas. 2014. *Borrowing against the Future: The Hidden Costs of Financing US Higher Education*. Berkeley: The Center for Culture, Organizations and Politics, UC Berkeley Institute for Research on Labor and Employment.

Equal Justice Works. 2013. "Student Loan Act Could Mean Higher Federal Profits." *US News and World Report,* August 14. http://www.usnews.com/education/blogs /student-loan-ranger/2013/08/14/student-loan-act-could-mean-higher-federal -profits.

Erwin, Andrew, and Marjorie Wood. 2014. *The One Percent at State U: How Public University Presidents Profit from Rising Student and Low Wage Faculty Labor*. Washington, DC: Institute for Policy Studies. http://www.ips-dc.org/wp-content /uploads/2014/05/IPS-One-Percent-at-State-Universities-May2014.pdf.

Fernandez, Manny, and Richard Pérez-Peña. 2014. "Deal Allows University of Texas President to Keep Job for Now." *New York Times*, July 9. http://www.nytimes.com /2014/07/10/us/deal-is-reached-in-clash-over-university-of-texas-president.html.

Field, Kelly. 2013. "Obama Plan to Tie Student Aid to College Ratings Draws Mixed Reviews." *The Chronicle of Higher Education*, August 22. http://chronicle.com /article/Obama-Plan-to-Tie-Student-Aid/141229/.

Fischer, Karen, and Jack Stripling. 2014. "An Era of Neglect: How Public Colleges Were Crowded Out, Beaten Up and Failed to Fight Back." *The Chronicle of Higher Education*, March 3. http://chronicle.com/article/An-Era-of-Neglect/145045/.

Foderaro, Lisa W. 2011. "CUNY Adjusts Amid Tide of Remedial Students." *New York Times,* March 3. http://www.nytimes.com/2011/03/04/nyregion/04remedial.html.

Folbre, Nancy. 2010. *Saving State U: Why We Must Fix Public Higher Education.* New York: New Press.

Giroux, Henry A. 2014. *Neoliberalism's War on Higher Education.* Chicago: Haymarket Books.

Goldstein, Matthew. 2013. "Remarks at CUNY Financial Management Conference: The Future of Higher Education." http://www1.cuny.edu/mu/chancellor/2013 /01/29/remarks-at-cuny-financial-management-conference-the-future-of-higher -education/.

Gonen, Yoav. 2013. "Nearly 80% of City Public High School Grads at CUNY Community Colleges Require Remediation for English or Math." *New York Post,* March 7. http://nypost.com/2013/03/07/nearly-80-of-city-public-high-school-grads -at-cuny-community-colleges-require-remediation-for-english-or-math/.

Guttenplan, D. D. 2013. "Vying for a Spot on the World's A List." *New York Times,* April 12. http://www.nytimes.com/2013/04/14/education/edlife/university -rankings-go-global.html.

Hechinger, John. 2012. "Obama Relies on Debt Collectors Profiting from Student Loan Woe." *BloombergBusiness,* March 26. http://www.bloomberg.com/news/articles/2012 -03-26/obama-relies-on-debt-collectors-profiting-from-student-loan-woe.

House Committee on Education and the Workforce, Democratic Staff. 2014. *The Just in Time Professor.* U.S. House of Representatives, January. http://democrats .edworkforce.house.gov/sites/democrats.edworkforce.house.gov/files/documents /1.24.14-AdjunctEforumReport.pdf.

Jaschik, Scott. 2005. "The Missing Black Men." *Inside Higher Ed,* December 5. https:// www.insidehighered.com/news/2005/12/05/blackmale.

Kamenetz, Anya. 2013. "System Failure: The Collapse of Public Education." *Village Voice,* April 3. http://www.villagevoice.com/2013-04-03/news/system-failure-the -collapse-of-public-education/.

Kelderman, Eric. 2013. "Luminda Foundation Adopts New Tactics to Reach College- Competition Goal." *The Chronicle of Higher Education*, January 10. http://chronicle .com/article/Lumina-Foundation-Adopts-New/136551/.

Kendzior, Sarah. 2013. "Academia's Indentured Servants." *Aljazeera,* April 11. http:// www.aljazeera.com/indepth/opinion/2013/04/20134119156459616.html.

Kirp, David. 2014. "How to Help College Students Graduate." *New York Times,* January 9. http://www.nytimes.com/2014/01/09/opinion/how-to-help-college -students-graduate.html.

Lederman, Doug. 2010. "3 Million and Counting." *Inside Higher Ed*, August 26. https://www.insidehighered.com/news/2010/08/26/enroll.

Leef, George. 2012. "The Problem Is Elsewhere." *The Chronicle of Higher Education*, July 2. http://chronicle.com/article/The-Problem-is-Elsewhere/132629/.

Lewin, Tamar. 2011. "Public Universities Relying More on Tuition Than State Money." *New York Times*, January 24. http://www.nytimes.com/2011/01/24/education/24tuition.html.

———. 2013. "Student Loan Rate Set to Rise, Despite Lack of Support." *New York Times*, April 8. http://www.nytimes.com/2013/04/09/education/student-loan-rate-set-to-rise-despite-lack-of-support.html.

———. 2014. "Student Debt Grows Faster at Universities with Highest-Paid Leaders, Study Finds." *New York Times*, May 19. http://www.nytimes.com/2014/05/19/education/study-links-growth-in-student-debt-to-pay-for-university-presidents.html.

Logue, Alexandra. 2015. "CUNY's Pathway to Shared Governance." *The Chronicle of Higher Education*, January 23. http://chronicle.com/blogs/conversation/2015/01/23/cunys-pathways-to-shared-governance/.

Lowery, Annie. 2013. "Student Debt Slows Growth as Young Spend Less." *New York Times*, May 11. http://www.nytimes.com/2013/05/11/business/economy/student-loan-debt-weighing-down-younger-us-workers.html.

Lumina Foundation. 2014. *Students on the Move*, May 12. http://www.luminafoundation.org/resources/students-on-the-move.

Mangan, Katherine. 2013. "Florida Colleges Make Plans for Students to Opt out of Remedial Work." *The Chronicle of Higher Education*, September 23. http://chronicle.com/article/Some-Florida-Colleges-Plan-for/141783/.

Martell, Terrence. 2012. "The Real Motivation for Pathways? It Can't Be Transfer." *UFS* (blog), December 5. https://sites.google.com/site/universityfacultysenatecuny/UFS-blog/pleasesendcommentstocunyufsgmailcom.

McGettigan, Andrew. 2013. *The Great University Gamble: Money, Markets and the Future of Higher Education*. New York: Pluto.

Mitchell, Michael, Vincent Palacios, and Michael Leachman. 2014. *States Are Still Funding Higher Education Below Pre-Recessionary Levels*. Washington, DC: Center of Budget and Policy Priorities, May 1. http://www.cbpp.org/files/5-1-14sfp.pdf.

Moser, Richard. 2014. "Overuse and Abuse of Adjunct Faculty Members Threaten Core Academic Values." *The Chronicle of Higher Education*, January 13. http://chronicle.com/article/OveruseAbuse-of-Adjuncts/143951/.

Newfield, Christopher. 2008. *Unmaking the Public University: The Forty Year Assault on the Middle Class*. Cambridge, MA: Harvard University Press.

Otterman, Sharon. 2011. "Most New York Students Are Not College-Ready." *New York Times*, February 7. http://www.nytimes.com/2011/02/08/nyregion/08regents.html.

Pérez-Peña, Richard. 2012. "Ousted Head of University Is Reinstated in Virginia." *New York Times*, June 26. http://www.nytimes.com/2012/06/27/education/university-of-virginia-reinstates-ousted-president.html.

Picciano, A. G., C. Dziuban, and C. Graham, eds. 2013. *Blended Learning: Research Perspectives*. Vol. 2. New York: Taylor & Francis.

4

Pratt, Timothy. 2013. "We Are Creating Walmarts of Higher Education." *The Atlantic,* December 26. http://www.theatlantic.com/education/archive/2013/12/we-are-creating-walmarts-of-higher-education/282619.

Professional Staff Congress. 2014. *New York Has an Inequality Crisis: CUNY Is the Solution.* http://psc-cuny.org/sites/default/files/NYsInequalityCrisis.CUNYis%20the%20Solution.web_.pdf.

Quinterno, John. 2012. *The Great Cost Shift: How Higher Education Cuts Undermine the Future Middle Class.* New York: Demos. http://www.demos.org/sites/default/files/publications/TheGreatCostShift_Demos_0.pdf.

Sailor, Kevin. 2014. "Revisiting Transfer Data and Pathways at CUNY." Unpublished manuscript in authors' possession.

Schnoebelen, Ann. 2013. "College Enrollment Will Grow More Slowly, Education Department Projects." *The Chronicle of Higher Education.* http://chronicle.com/article/College-Enrollment-Will-Grow/136547/.

Selingo, Jeffrey J. 2013. "Colleges Struggles to Stay Afloat." *New York Times,* April 14. http://www.nytimes.com/2013/04/14/education/edlife/many-colleges-and-universities-face-financial-problems.html.

Statista. 2015. "Annual Inflation Rate in the United States From 1990 to 2014." http://www.statista.com/statistics/191077/inflation-rate-in-the-usa-since-1990/.

Strategy Labs. 2013. "Adopt Statewide Policies to Guarantee Transfer." http://strategylabs.luminafoundation.org/higher-education-state-policy-agenda/core-element-three/action-14/.

Supiano, Beckie. 2013. "7 in 10 Undergraduates Get Financial Aid, New Data from a Major Federal Study Show." *The Chronicle of Higher Education,* August 20. http://chronicle.com/article/7-in-10-Undergraduates-Get/141193/.

University of Wisconsin–Madison. 2014. "WARF grants more than $70 million to support UW-Madison." *University of Wisconsin–Madison News,* October 14. http://news.wisc.edu/23197.

U.S. Senate Health, Education, Labor, and Pensions Committee. 2012. *For-Profit Higher Education: The Failure to Safeguard the Federal Investment and Ensure Student Success, Executive Summary.* http://www.help.senate.gov/imo/media/for_profit_report/PartI-PartIII-SelectedAppendixes.pdf.

Vitale, Alex. 2014. "The Fight against Pathways at CUNY." *Academe,* September–October: 39. http://www.aaup.org/article/fight-against-pathways-cuny.

Wellman, Jane V. 2006. "Costs, Prices and Affordability." A Background Paper for the Secretary's Commission on the Future of Higher Education. https://www2.ed.gov/about/bdscomm/list/hiedfuture/reports/wellman.pdf.

Wrigley, Julia. 2010. "Improving Student Transfer at CUNY." Office of Academic Affairs, the City University of New York, October 22. www.cuny.edu/academics/initiatives/pathways/about/archive/archive/TransferReport.pdf.

Chapter 5

Bateman, Bradley. 2013. "The Wrong Ratings." *New York Times,* December 18, A29.

Baum, Sandy, Kristin Conklin, and Nate Johnson. 2013. "Stop Penalizing Poor College Students." *New York Times,* November 13, A31.

Berrett, Dan. 2014. "In Clashes over Curriculum, Completion Goals Vie with Quality." *The Chronicle of Higher Education*, March 28, A19.

Best, Eric, and Joel Best. 2014. "Forget Gainful Employment. For-Profits Should Restructure Instead." *The Chronicle of Higher Education*, April 14, A33.

Blumenstyk, Goldie. 2014. "Analysts Map Some of the Challenges a College-Ratings System Would Face." *The Chronicle of Higher Education*, February 6, A9.

Bohn, Sarah, Belinda Reyes, and Hans Johnson. 2013. *The Impact of Budget Cuts on California's Community Colleges*. The Public Policy Institute of California, March. http://www.ppic.org/content/pubs/report/R_313SBR.pdf.

California Community Colleges Chancellor's Office. 2015. "Annual/Term Student Headcount." http://datamart.cccco.edu/Students/Student_Term_Annual_Count.aspx.

California Faculty Association. 2010. "'Restructuring' the CSU or Wrecking It? What Proposed Changes Mean and What We Can Do about Them." CFA White Paper, Winter 2009/2010. http://www.calfac.org/sites/main/files/CFA_White_Paper-Restructuring_Winter09_10.pdf.

California Legislative Information. 2014. *AB-1456 Higher Education: Tuition and Fees: Study*, January 9. http://leginfo.legislature.ca.gov/faces/billNavClient.xhtml?bill_id=201320140AB1456.

California State Auditor. 2011. *University of California: Although the University Maintains Extensive Financial Records, It Should Provide Additional Information to Improve Public Understanding of Its Operations*. July 2011, Report 2010-105. https://www.auditor.ca.gov/pdfs/reports/2010-105.pdf.

California State University. 2014. "CSU Enrollment by Ethnicity Type." http://www.calstate.edu/as/stat_reports/2014-2015/feth14.htm.

Campaign for the Future of Higher Education. 2015. "Back to School in Higher Ed: Who Needs Faculty?" CFHE Working Paper, September 16. http://futureofhighered.org/wp-content/uploads/2015/09/CFHE-Paper-Sept-2015.pdf.

Campos, Paul. 2015. "The Real Reason College Tuition Costs So Much." *New York Times*, April 4. http://www.nytimes.com/2015/04/05/opinion/sunday/the-real-reason-college-tuition-costs-so-much.html.

Carlson, Scott. 2014. "Administrator Hiring Drove 28% Boom in Higher-Ed Workforce, Report Says." *The Chronicle of Higher Education*, February 5. http://chronicle.com/article/Administrator-Hiring-Drove-28-/144519/.

Carnevale, Anthony P., and Jeffrey Strohl. 2010. "How Increasing College Access Is Increasing Inequality and What to Do about It." In *Highlights from Rewarding Strivers: Helping Low Income Students in College*, edited by Richard Kahlenberg, 71–137. New York: Century Foundation.

———. 2013. *Separate and Unequal: How Higher Education Reinforces the Intergenerational Reproduction of White Privilege*. Washington, DC: Georgetown Policy Institute.

Cauthen, Nancy. 2009. "The High Cost of Working Hard: Why Students Need to Work Less and Study More." *The American Prospect*, October 22. http://prospect.org/article/high-cost-working-hard.

Cohen, Patricia. 2015. "For-Profit Colleges Accused of Fraud Still Receive U.S. Funds." *New York Times*, October 12. http://www.nytimes.com/2015/10/13/business/for-profit-colleges-accused-of-fraud-still-receive-us-funds.html.

Curtis, John W. 2014. *The Employment Status of Instructional Staff Members in Higher Education, Fall 2011*. Washington, DC: American Association of University Professors. http://www.aaup.org/sites/default/files/files/AAUP-InstrStaff2011 -April2014.pdf.

DeParle, Jason. 2012. "For Poor, Leap to College Often Ends in a Hard Fall." *New York Times*, December 22, A1 and A30.

Desrochers, Donna, and Rita Kirshstein. 2012. *College Spending in a Turbulent Decade: Findings from the Delta Cost Project. A Delta Data Update 2000–2010*. Washington, DC: American Institutes for Research. http://www.deltacostproject.org/sites /default/files/products/Delta-Cost-College-Spending-In-A-Turbulent-Decade .pdf.

———. 2014. *Labor Intensive or Labor Expensive? Changing Staffing and Compensation Patterns in Higher Education*. Issue Brief. Washington, DC: Delta Cost Project, American Institutes for Research.

Dougherty, Chrys. 2014. *Catching Up to College and Career Readiness: The Challenge Is Greater for At-Risk Students*. Issue Brief. Iowa City, IA: ACT Research & Policy, May 2014. http://www.act.org/research/policymakers/pdf/CatchingUp -Part3.pdf.

Eaton, Charlie, and Jacob Habinek. 2013. "Why America's Public Universities and Not Just Their Students Have a Debt Problem." Scholars Strategy Network, Harvard University. http://www.scholarsstrategynetwork.org/brief/why-americas -public-universities-not-just-their-students-have-debt-problem.

Erwin, Andrew, and Marjorie Wood. 2014. *The One Percent at State U: How Public University Presidents Profit from Rising Student Debt and Low Wage Faculty Labor*. Washington, DC: Institute for Policy Studies. http://www.ips-dc.org/wp-content /uploads/2014/05/IPS-One-Percent-at-State-Universities-May2014.pdf.

Fain, Paul. 2013a. "Possible Probation for Phoenix." *Inside Higher Ed*, February 26. https://www.insidehighered.com/news/2013/02/26/university-phoenix-faces -possible-probation-accreditor#ixzz2Mowhp7QD.

———. 2013b. "Scorecard for Scorecards." *Inside Higher Ed*, October 29. https://www .insidehighered.com/news/2013/10/29/complete-college-america-report-tracks-state -approaches-performance-based-funding.

Fichtenbaum, Rudy. 2014. *Testimony Before the House State, and Veterans and Military Affairs Committee*. American Association of University Professors, February 3. http://bcaaup.org/wp-content/uploads/2009/12/FichtenbaumTestimony-on-HB14 -1154.pdf.

Field, Kelly. 2013. "Abrupt For-Profit Closures Surprises Regulators." *The Chronicle of Higher Education*, August 2, A3.

Fry, Richard. 2012. "A Record One-in-Five Households Now Owe Student Loan Debt." Pew Research Center, September 26. http://www.pewsocialtrends.org/2012 /09/26/a-record-one-in-five-households-now-owe-student-loan-debt/.

Gardner, Lee. 2013. "Berkeley Documentary Captures a Campus on the Cusp of Change." *The Chronicle of Higher Education*, September 27, A20.

Gipson, M. A. 2015. "Oversight Hearing Calls for Audit of UC Budget" (press release). February 9. http://asmdc.org/members/a64/news-room/press-releases /oversight-hearing-calls-for-audit-of-uc-budget.

Goldin, Claudia, and Lawrence F. Katz. 2007. "Long-Run Changes in the Wage Structure: Narrowing, Widening, Polarizing." NBER Working Paper No. 13568, Brookings Papers on Economic Activity, Economic Studies Program, Brookings Institution 38:135–68.

Hiltonsmith, Robert. 2013. "New York's Great Cost Shift: How Higher Education Undermines the Future Middle Class." Briefing Paper, Demos, New York. http://www.demos.org/sites/default/files/publications/NYGreatCostShift.pdf.

House Committee on Education and the Workforce Democratic Staff. 2014. *The Just-in-Time Professor: A Staff Report Summarizing eForum Responses on the Working Conditions of Contingent Faculty in Higher Education.* http://democrats.edworkforce.house.gov/sites/democrats.edworkforce.house.gov/files/documents/1.24.14-AdjunctEforumReport.pdf.

Huelsman, M. 2015. *The Debt Divide: The Racial and Class Bias behind the 'New Normal' of Student Borrowing.* New York: Demos. http://www.demos.org/sites/default/files/publications/The%20Debt%20Divide.pdf.

Johnson, H., M. C. Mejia, and K. Cook. 2015. *Successful Online Courses in California's Community Colleges.* San Francisco: Public Policy Institute of California. http://www.ppic.org/content/pubs/report/R_615HJR.pdf.

Johnson, Hans. 2012. *Defunding Higher Education: What Are the Effects on College Enrollment?* San Francisco: Public Policy Institute of California. http://www.ppic.org/content/pubs/report/R_512HJR.pdf.

———. 2014. *Making College Possible for Low-Income Students: Grant and Scholarship Aid in California.* San Francisco: Public Policy Institute of California. http://www.ppic.org/content/pubs/report/R_1014HJR.pdf.

Kaminer, Ariel. 2013. "Lists That Rank Colleges' Value Are on the Rise." *New York Times*, October 28, A1.

Kiley, Kevin. 2012. "The Other Debt Crisis." *Inside Higher Ed*, April 10. https://www.insidehighered.com/news/2012/04/10/public-universities-will-take-more-debt-states-decrease-spending-capital-projects.

———. 2013. "Can Funding Be Fair?" *Inside Higher Ed*, July 31. https://www.insidehighered.com/news/2013/01/31/university-california-rethinks-how-it-funds-campuses.

Kirkham, Chris. 2012. "For-Profit College Group Fights to Keep Students in Dark on Debt." *Huffington Post*, August 23. http://www.huffingtonpost.com/2012/08/23/for-profit-college-student-debt_n_1823215.html.

Lewin, Tamar. 2010. "For Profit Colleges Step-Up Lobbying against New Rules." *New York Times*, September 8, A16.

———. 2014. "Student Debt Grows Faster at Universities with Highest Paid Leaders, Study Finds." *New York Times*, May 19, A11.

Looney, Adam, and Constantine Yannelis. 2015. "A Crisis in Student Loans? How Changes in the Characteristics of Borrowers and in the Institutions They Attended Contributed to Rising Loan Defaults." Brookings Papers on Economic Activity, Brookings Institution, Fall. http://www.brookings.edu/about/projects/bpea/papers/2015/looney-yannelis-student-loan-defaults.

Mangan, Katherine. 2013. "Group Pushes 'Game Changing' Tactics for Improving College Completion." *The Chronicle of Higher Education*, October 8, A16.

Martin, Andrew. 2013. "Moody's Gives Colleges a Negative Grade." *New York Times*, January 16. http://www.nytimes.com/2013/01/17/business/moodys-outlook-on -higher-education-turns-negative.html?_r=0.

Medina, Jennifer. 2012. "California Cuts Threaten the Status of Universities." *New York Times*, June 1, A14.

Mettler, Susan. 2014. "Equalizers No More: Politics Thwart Colleges' Role in Upward Mobility." *The Chronicle of Higher Education*, March 3, 6–10.

Newfield, Christopher. 2013. "The Great University Gamble, Money Markets and the Future of Higher Education: The Counterreformation in Higher Education." *Los Angeles Review of Books*, October 19. http://lareviewofbooks.org/review/the -counterreformation-in-higher-education.

New York Times Editorial Board. 2014. "The College Faculty Crisis." *New York Times*, April 13, A22.

Nocera, Joe. 2013. "The Berkeley Model." *New York Times*, December 10, A19.

Piketty, Thomas. 2014. *Capital in the Twenty-First Century*. Cambridge, MA: Belknap of Harvard University Press.

Quinterno, John. 2012. *The Great Cost Shift: How Higher Education Cuts Undermine the Future Middle Class*. New York: Demos. http://www.demos.org/sites/default/files /publications/TheGreatCostShift_Demos_0.pdf.

Saul, Stephanie. 2015. "For-Profit College Chain Forgives Loans." *New York Times*, November 17, A17.

Selingo, Jeffrey. 2014. "Merit Aid Won't Help Colleges Survive." *The Chronicle of Higher Education*, May 5, A30.

Severns, Maggie. 2013. "The Student Loan Debt Crisis in 9 Charts." *Mother Jones*, June 5. http://www.motherjones.com/politics/2013/06/student-loan-debt-charts.

Shear, Michael, and Tamar Lewin. 2013. "On Business Tour Obama Seeks to Shame Colleges into Easing Costs." *New York Times*, August 23, A18.

Stratford, Michael. 2015. "Pointing a Finger at For-Profits." *Inside Higher Ed*, September 11. https://www.insidehighered.com/news/2015/09/11/study-finds-profit -colleges-drove-spike-student-loan-defaults.

Street, Steve, Maria Maisto, Esther Merves, and Gary Rhoades. 2012. "Who Is Professor 'Staff' and How Can This Person Teach So Many Classes?" Center for Higher Education Policy Report No. 2. https://www.insidehighered.com/sites /default/server_files/files/profstaff(2).pdf.

Stripling, Jack. 2013. "President's Proposal Renews Debate over How to Measure College Quality." *The Chronicle of Higher Education*, September 5, A2 and A4.

Stripling, Jack, and Andrea Fuller. 2011. "Presidents Defend Their Pay as Public Colleges Slash Budgets." *The Chronicle of Higher Education*, April 3, A1.

Tatum, A. 2014. "University of California Tuition Hikes: 5 Things You Must Know." California Common Sense, November 12. http://cacs.org/research/university-of -california-tuition-hikes-5-things-must-know/.

Thomason, Andy. 2013. "Student-loan Default Rates Continue Steady Climb." *The Chronicle of Higher Education*, October 1, A6.

Thompson, Vinton. 2013. "History Suggests College Ratings System a Losing Proposition." *Diverse: Issues in Higher Education*, December 16. http:// diverseeducation.com/article/59515/.

University of California. 2012. "Budget for Operations 2013–14." http://edsource.org
/wp-content/uploads/2013-14-budget.pdf.
———. 2015. "Fall Enrollment Headcounts." http://www.universityofcalifornia.edu
/infocenter/fall-enrollment-headcounts.
US Government Accountability Office. 2014. "Higher Education: State Funding
Trends and Policies on Affordability." Report to the Chairman, Committee on
Health, Education, Labor, and Pensions, United States Senate. http://www.gao
.gov/assets/670/667557.pdf.
US Senate Committee on Health, Education, Labor and Pensions. 2012. *For Profit
Higher Education: The Failure to Safeguard the Federal Investment and Ensure
Student Success.* http://www.help.senate.gov/imo/media/for_profit_report/PartI
.pdf.
Vendituoli, Monica. 2014. "At-Risk Students Who Fall Behind Struggle to Catch Up,
Study Finds." *The Chronicle of Higher Education*, May 30. http://chronicle.com
/blogs/headcount/at-risk-students-who-fall-behind-struggle-to-catch-up-report
-says/38447.
Wong, Marian. 2013. "Public Colleges' Quest for Revenue and Prestige Squeezes
Needy Students." *The Chronicle of Higher Education*, September 11, A16–17.

Chapter 6

Academic Partnerships. 2013. "Learn More about Academic Partnerships." *The
Chronicle of Higher Education.* September 23. http://chronicle.com/article/Learn
-More-about-Academic/141833/.
———. 2015. "Online Delivery of Higher Education Worldwide." AP. http://www
.academicpartnerships.com/.
Arenson, Karen W. 1999. "Columbia University Explores How to Profit from
Educational Offerings on the Internet." *New York Times*, April 3, sec. N.Y./Region.
http://www.nytimes.com/1999/04/03/nyregion/columbia-university-explores-profit
-educational-offerings-internet.html.
———. 2000. "Columbia Sets Pace in Profiting Off Research." *New York Times*,
August 2, sec. N.Y./ Region. http://www.nytimes.com/2000/08/02/nyregion
/columbia-sets-pace-in-profiting-off-research.html.
Arnone, Michael. 2002a. "Fathom Adds Training to Distance-Education Offerings."
The Chronicle of Higher Education, February 22. http://chronicle.com/article
/Fathom-Adds-Training-to/7148/.
———. 2002b. "Columbia Senate Questions Spending on Fathom." *The Chronicle
of Higher Education*, May 10. http://chronicle.com/article/Columbia-Senate
-Questions/25343/.
Bady, Aaron. 2009. "UC Governance and Blaming 'Sacramento.'" *History News
Network* (blog). December 4. http://historynewsnetwork.org/blog/120931.
Basken, Paul. 2015. "Stirring Fear and Hope, U. of Akron Mulls an Aggressive Move
Online." *The Chronicle of Higher Education*, July 15. http://chronicle.com/article
/Stirring-FearHope-U-of/231637/.
Bernhard, Meg. 2015. "Digital Platform Seeks to Match Employers, Job Seekers, and
Courses." *The Chronicle of Higher Education*, July 12. http://chronicle.com/article
/Digital-Platform-Seeks-to/231107/.

Best, Randy. 2015. "Essay on Ways MOOCs Helped and Hurt Debates about Future of Higher Education." *Inside Higher Ed*, January 9. https://www.insidehighered.com/views/2015/01/09/essay-ways-moocs-helped-and-hurt-debates-about-future-higher-education.

Bittner, Walton, and Hervey Mallory. 1933. *University Teaching by Mail: A Survey of Correspondence Instruction Conducted by American Universities.* New York: Macmillan.

Blume, Howard. 2010. "L.A. Charter School Supporters Austin and Arkatov Nominated to State School Board." *L.A. NOW* (blog). March 29. http://latimesblogs.latimes.com/lanow/2010/03/la-charter-school-supporters-austin-and-arkatov-nominated-to-state-school-board.html.

Blumenstyk, Goldie. 1999. "A Company Pays Top Universities to Use Their Names and Their Professors." *The Chronicle of Higher Education*, June 18. http://chronicle.com/article/A-Company-Pays-Top/9911/.

———. 2001. "Knowledge Is 'a Form of Venture Capital' for a Top Columbia Administrator." *The Chronicle of Higher Education*, February 9. http://chronicle.com/article/Knowledge-Is-a-Form-of/17565/.

———. 2012. "Change Takes Root in the Desert." *The Chronicle of Higher Education*, November 19. http://chronicle.com/article/Change-Takes-Root-in-the/135824/.

———. 2014. "Starbucks Plan Shines a Light on the Profits in Online Education." *The Chronicle of Higher Education*, June 27. http://chronicle.com/article/Starbucks-Plan-Shines-a-Light/147395/.

———. 2015. "Starbucks and Arizona State U. Will Expand Tuition-Discount Partnership." *The Chronicle of Higher Education*, April 6. http://chronicle.com/article/StarbucksArizona-State-U/229127/.

Blustain, Harvey, and Paul Goldstein. 2004. "Report on UNext and Cardean University." In *The E-University Compendium.* Vol. 1, *Cases, Issues and Themes in Higher Education Distance e-Learning*, edited by Paul Bacsich, with Sara Frank Bristow, chap. 11. New York: Higher Education Academy. http://www.virtualschoolsandcolleges.eu/index.php/Report_on_UNext_and_Cardean_University#Full_title.

Bok, Derek. 2004. *Universities in the Marketplace: The Commercialization of Higher Education.* Princeton, NJ: Princeton University Press.

Bolkan, Joshua. 2013a. "Stanford Partners with EdX to Improve Platform Ahead of Source Code Release." *Campus Technology*, April 3. http://campustechnology.com/articles/2013/04/03/stanford-partners-with-edx-to-improve-platform-ahead-of-source-code-release.aspx.

———. 2013b. "Massive: What Good Is the M in MOOC?" *Campus Technology*, May 2. http://campustechnology.com/articles/2013/05/02/massive-what-good-is-the-m-in-mooc.aspx.

Bowen, William G., and Eugene M. Tobin. 2015. *Locus of Authority: The Evolution of Faculty Roles in the Governance of Higher Education.* Princeton, NJ: Princeton University Press.

Brooks, David. 2012. "The Campus Tsunami." *New York Times*, May 3. http://www.nytimes.com/2012/05/04/opinion/brooks-the-campus-tsunami.html.

Business Wire. 1997. "The Home Education Network Appoints Former UCLA Vice Chancellor as President and CEO." *The Free Library*. http://www.thefreelibrary .com/The+Home+Education+Network+appoints+former+UCLA+vice +chancellor+as+ . . . -a019102154.

Campaign for the Future of Higher Education. 2013. "CFHE Working Papers Archives." *Campaign for the Future of Higher Education*. http://futureofhighered.org /workingpapers/.

"Cardean University Home." 2015. http://www.trinity.edu/rjensen/000aaa/prest/unext /cardean.htm.

Career Overview. 2015. "Cardean University Online MBA Degree Programs." CareerOverview.com. http://www.careeroverview.com/cardean-university.html.

Carlson, Scott. 2000. "Going for Profit and Scholarship on the WebAnn G. Kirschner." *The Chronicle of Higher Education*, May 5. http://chronicle.com/article /Going-for-Profit-and/24148/.

———. 2003. "After Losing Millions, Columbia U. Will Close Its Online-Learning Venture." *The Chronicle of Higher Education*, January 7. http://chronicle.com/article /After-Losing-Millions/110813/.

Chafkin, Max. 2013. "Udacity's Sebastian Thrun, Godfather of Free Online Educa- tion, Changes Course." *Fast Company*. December. http://www.fastcompany.com /3021473/udacity-sebastian-thrun-uphill-climb.

Columbia University. n.d. "Columbia Interactive—E-Courses: View All." Accessed August 16, 2014. http://ci.columbia.edu/ci/ecourses/view_all_c.html.

Community College Research Center. 2013. "What We Know about Online Course Outcomes." Teachers College, Columbia University. *Research Overview*, April. http://www.achievingthedream.org/sites/default/files/resources/Online-Learning -Practitioner-Packet.pdf.

Confessore, Nicholas. 1999. "The Virtual University." *The New Republic* 221 (14): 26–28.

Crow, Michael M., and William B. Dabars. 2015. *Designing the New American University*. Baltimore: Johns Hopkins University Press.

Crowley, Jeannie. 2013. "cMOOCs: Putting Collaboration First." *Campus Technology*, August 15. http://campustechnology.com/articles/2013/08/15/cmoocs-putting -collaboration-first.aspx.

Davidson, Randall. 2006. *9XM Talking: WHA Radio and the Wisconsin Idea*. Madison: University of Wisconsin Press.

Distance-Educator.com. 2001. "Sylvan Learning Systems Announces Formation of Online Higher Education Division; New Division Will Be Headed by Sylvan Veteran Paula Singer." Distance-Educator.com. July 18. http://distance-educator .com/sylvan-learning-systems-announces-formation-of-online-higher-education -division-new-division-will-be-headed-by-sylvan-veteran-paula-singer/.

Dunning, John. 1998. *On the Air: The Encyclopedia of Old-Time Radio*. New York: Oxford University Press.

Edmonds, Victor. 2008. "Video Vision." *EDUCAUSE Review*, September 15. http:// www.educause.edu/ero/article/video-vision.

edX. 2015. "Announcing Global Freshman Academy." edX. https://www.edx.org/gfa.

Fenton, William. 2015. "What Disruption? Online Education and the Status Quo." *PC Magazine*, May 19. http://www.pcmag.com/article2/0,2817,2484354,00.asp.

Ferster, Bill. 2014. *Teaching Machines: Learning from the Intersection of Education and Technology.* Baltimore: Johns Hopkins University Press.

Fischman, Josh. 2011. "The Rise of Teaching Machines." *The Chronicle of Higher Education*, May 8. http://chronicle.com/article/The-Rise-of-Teaching-Machines /127389/.

Foderaro, Lisa W. 2011. "CUNY Adjusts amid Tide of Remedial Students." *New York Times*, March 3. http://www.nytimes.com/2011/03/04/nyregion/04remedial.html.

Ford Foundation and Fund for the Advancement of Education (US). 1961. *Teaching by Television: A Report from the Ford Foundation and the Fund for the Advancement of Education.* New York: Ford Foundation. http://catalog.hathitrust.org/Record /001279820.

Fox, Steve. 2010. "Teaching Matters: Rethinking the Hybrid Course." *The Chronicle of Higher Education*, January 31. http://chronicle.com/article/Teaching-Matters -Rethinking/63788/.

Fredette, Michelle. 2013. "Who Owns College Courses?" *Campus Technology*, October 16. http://campustechnology.com/articles/2013/10/16/who-owns-college -courses.aspx.

Friedman, Thomas L. 2012. "Come the Revolution." *New York Times*, May 15. http://www.nytimes.com/2012/05/16/opinion/friedman-come-the-revolution.html.

Gajilan, Arlyn Tobias. 2000. "An Education Revolution? Investors Like Michael Milken and Larry Ellison Are Betting That Chicago's UNext Can Change the Face of College Online." *CNN Money*, December 1. http://money.cnn.com /magazines/fsb/fsb_archive/2000/12/01/294025/.

Goldberg, Carey. 2001. "Auditing Classes at M.I.T., on the Web and Free." *New York Times*, April 4. http://www.nytimes.com/2001/04/04/us/auditing-classes-at-mit-on -the-web-and-free.html.

Goldstein, Evan. 2015. "The Undoing of Disruption." *The Chronicle of Higher Education*, September 15. http://chronicle.com/article/The-Undoing-of-Disruption/233101/.

Grush, Mary. 2013. "50+Percent Off! The Walmart of Education—Campus Technology." *Campus Technology*, October 16. http://campustechnology.com/articles/2013/10 /16/the-walmart-of-education.aspx.

Guess, Andy. 2007a. "On YouTube, No Enrollment." *Inside Higher Ed*, October 4. https://www.insidehighered.com/news/2007/10/04/youtube.

———. 2007b. "Open Courses Open Wider." *Inside Higher Ed*, December 12. https://www.insidehighered.com/news/2007/12/12/openyale.

Guthrie, Kevin M., Christine Mulhern, and Martin A. Kurzweil. 2015. *In Pursuit of Excellence and Inclusion: Managing Change at Arizona State University.* New York: Ithaka S+R. http://www.sr.ithaka.org/wp-content/uploads/2015/08/SR_Report _Managing_Change_ASU_012015.pdf.

Gutman, Herbert. 1987. *Power and Culture: Essays on the American Working Class.* New York: Pantheon Books.

Hafner, Katie. 2010. "Higher Education Reimagined with Online Courseware— Education Life." *New York Times*, April 16. http://www.nytimes.com/2010/04/18 /education/edlife/18open-t.html.

Hilgerch. 2014. "xMOOC vs cMOOC? A Glossary of Common MOOC Terms Part 2." *ExtensionEngine*, September 12. http://extensionengine.com/xmooc-vs -cmooc-a-glossary-of-common-mooc-terms-part-2-2/.

Ho, Andrew Dean, Justin Reich, Sergiy O. Nesterko, Daniel Thomas Seaton, Tommy Mullaney, Jim Waldo, and Isaac Chuang. 2014. "HarvardX and MITx: The First Year of Open Online Courses, Fall 2012–Summer 2013." SSRN Scholarly Paper ID 2381263, Social Science Research Network, Rochester, NY. http://papers.ssrn.com /abstract=2381263.

Howard, Caroline. 2015. "Barista to Bachelor's: Starbucks-ASU Partnership Offers Full 4-Year Online College Degrees." *Forbes*, April 6. http://www.forbes.com/sites /carolinehoward/2015/04/06/from-barista-to-bachelors-starbucks-asu-partnership -offers-full-4-year-online-college-degrees/.

Huckabee, Charles. 2015. "Arizona State and edX Will Offer an Online Freshman Year, Open to All." *The Ticker* (blog), *The Chronicle of Higher Education*, April 23. http://chronicle.com/blogs/ticker/arizona-state-and-edx-will-offer-an-online -freshman-year-open-to-all/97685.

Jacobs, A. J. 2013. "Grading the MOOC University." *New York Times*, April 20. http://www.nytimes.com/2013/04/21/opinion/sunday/grading-the-mooc-university .html.

Jaschik, Scott. 2013. "Public Universities Move to Offer MOOCs for Credit." *Inside Higher Ed*, January 23. https://www.insidehighered.com/news/2013/01/23/public -universities-move-offer-moocs-credit.

———. 2015. "Without a Staff Does a University Press Exist?" *Inside Higher Ed*, July 31. https://www.insidehighered.com/news/2015/07/31/university-akron-says-it -hasnt-eliminated-its-university-press-has-eliminated-all.

Jenkins, Rob. 2014. "Straight Talk about 'Adjunctification.'" *The Chronicle of Higher Education*, December 15. http://chronicle.com/article/Straight-Talk-About/150881/.

Keller, Josh. 2012. "A College Leader Urges His Peers to Push for Radical Change." *The Chronicle of Higher Education*, March 11. http://chronicle.com/article/A -College-Leader-Urges-His/131139/.

Khan Academy. 2015a. "Khan Academy." http://www.khanacademy.org.

———. 2015b. "Content Creation and Curation Fellowship Program." Khan Academy. https://boards.greenhouse.io/khanacademy/jobs/67124.

Kim, Joshua. 2013. "Q and A with Randy Best on MOOC2Degree." *Technology and Learning* (blog). *Inside Higher Ed*, January 24. https://www.insidehighered.com /blogs/technology-and-learning/qa-randy-best-mooc2degree.

Kirschner, Ann. n.d. "Ann Kirschner on Marketing and Distribution of Online Learning." *Ubiquity*. Accessed April 5, 2015. http://ubiquity.acm.org/article.cfm?id =1008542.

Kolowich, Steve. 2012. "Experts Speculate on Possible Business Models for MOOC Providers." *Inside Higher Ed*, June 11. https://www.insidehighered.com/news/2012 /06/11/experts-speculate-possible-business-models-mooc-providers.

———. 2013a. "Universities Try MOOCs in Bid to Lure Successful Students to Online Programs." *Wired Campus* (blog). *The Chronicle of Higher Education*, January 23. http://chronicle.com/blogs/wiredcampus/universities-try-mooc2degree -courses-to-lure-successful-students-to-online-programs/41829.

———. 2013b. "Why Professors at San Jose State Won't Use a Harvard Professor's MOOC." *The Chronicle of Higher Education*, May 2. http://chronicle.com/article /Professors-at-San-Jose-State/138941/.

———. 2013c. "Scores Improve in New Round of San Jose State's Experiment with Udacity." *Wired Campus* (blog). *The Chronicle of Higher Education Blogs*, August 28. http://chronicle.com/blogs/wiredcampus/scores-improve-in-new-round-of-san -jose-states-experiment-with-udacity/45997.

———. 2013d. "Angered by MOOC Deals, San Jose State Faculty Senate Considers Rebuff." *The Chronicle of Higher Education*, November 18. http://chronicle.com /article/Angered-by-MOOC-Deals-San/143137/.

Lepore, Jill. 2014. "What the Gospel of Innovation Gets Wrong." *The New Yorker*, June 23. http://www.newyorker.com/magazine/2014/06/23/the-disruption -machine.

Lewin, Tamar. 2012. "Consortium of Colleges Takes Online Education to New Level." *New York Times*, July 17. http://www.nytimes.com/2012/07/17/education /consortium-of-colleges-takes-online-education-to-new-level.html.

———. 2013a. "Public Universities to Offer Free Online Classes for Credit." *New York Times*, January 23. http://www.nytimes.com/2013/01/23/education/public -universities-to-offer-free-online-classes-for-credit.html.

———. 2013b. "Colleges Adapt Online Courses to Ease Burden." *New York Times*, April 20. http://www.nytimes.com/2013/04/30/education/colleges-adapt-online -courses-to-ease-burden.html.

———. 2015. "Coursera Adds 17 Partner Universities, Including Brown and Colum-bia." *New York Times*, September 19. http://www.nytimes.com/2012/09/19 /education/coursera-adds-more-ivy-league-partner-universities.html.

Lewin, Tamar, and John Markoff. 2013. "California to Give Web Courses a Big Trial." *New York Times*, January 15. http://www.nytimes.com/2013/01/15/technology/california -to-give-web-courses-a-big-trial.html.

Lobosco, Katie. 2015. "Number of Starbucks Workers Getting Free Tuition Could Double." *CNN Money*, May 11. http://money.cnn.com/2015/05/11/news/companies /starbucks-college/index.html.

Lorenzo, George. 2013. "Reclaiming the Original Vision of MOOCs." *Campus Technology*, September 5. https://campustechnology.com/articles/2013/09/05 /reclaiming-the-original-vision-of-moocs.aspx.

Ma, Jennifer, and Sandy Baum. 2012. "Trends in Tuition and Fees, Enrollment, and State Appropriations for Higher Education by State." Trends in Higher Education Series, College Board Advocacy and Policy Center. http://trends.collegeboard.org /sites/default/files/analysis-brief-trends-by-state-july-2012.pdf.

Mangan, Katherine. 2012. "Study Shows Promise and Challenges of 'Hybrid' Courses." *Wired Campus* (blog). *The Chronicle of Higher Education*, May 22. http://chronicle.com/blogs/wiredcampus/study-shows-promise-and-challenges-of -hybrid-courses/36350.

Manjoo, Farhad. 2015. "Udacity Says It Can Teach Tech Skills to Millions." *New York Times*, September 17. http://www.nytimes.com/2015/09/17/technology/udacity-says -it-can-teach-tech-skills-to-millions.html.

Masterson, Kathryn. 2010. "College Leaders Share Ideas for 'Reinventing' Higher Education." *The Chronicle of Higher Education*, October 4. http://chronicle.com /article/College-Leaders-Share-Ideas/124815/.

Meisenhelder, Susan. 2013. "MOOC Mania." *Thought and Action*, 7–26. http://www .nea.org/home/61255.htm.

Mettler, Suzanne. 2014. *Degrees of Inequality: How the Politics of Higher Education Sabotaged the American Dream*. New York: Basic Books.

Meyer, Leila. 2013. "California Bill Allowing Credit for MOOCs Passes Senate." *Campus Technology*, June 6. http://campustechnology.com/articles/2013/06/06 /california-bill-allowing-credit-for-moocs-passes-senate.aspx.

Michels, Patrick. 2012. "Randy Best Is Going to Save Texas' Public Universities, or Get Rich Trying." *The Texas Observer*, August 29. http://www.texasobserver.org /randy-best-is-going-to-save-texas-public-universities-or-get-rich-trying/.

MIT. 2001. "MIT to Make Nearly All Course Materials Available Free on the World Wide Web." *MIT News*, April 4. http://newsoffice.mit.edu/2001/ocw.

Mooney, Carolyn. 2015. "250 MOOCs and Counting: One Man's Educational Journey." *The Chronicle of Higher Education*, April 20. http://chronicle.com/article /250-MOOCsCounting-One/229397/.

NCES. 2015. "The NCES Fast Facts Tool Provides Quick Answers to Many Education Questions." National Center for Education Statistics. https://nces.ed.gov /fastfacts/display.asp?id=75.

Negrea, Sherrie. 2014. "Massive, Open, Online, for Credit." *University Business Magazine*, March. http://www.universitybusiness.com/article/massive-open-online -credit.

Nelson, Sharleen. 2013. "MOOC Initiative Opens Doors to College Degree Programs." *Campus Technology*, January 23. http://campustechnology.com/articles/2013 /01/24/mooc-initiative-opens-doors-to-college-degree-programs.aspx.

Newfield, Christopher. 2015. "What Is New about the New American University?" *Los Angeles Review of Books*. https://lareviewofbooks.org/review/new-new-american -university.

New York Times. 2015. "Reshaping Arizona State, and the Public Model." April 10. http://www.nytimes.com/2015/04/12/education/edlife/12edl-12talk.html.

Noble, David F. 1998. "Digital Diploma Mills: The Automation of Higher Education." *First Monday* 3 (1). http://firstmonday.org/ojs/index.php/fm/article/view /569.

———. 2001. *Digital Diploma Mills: The Automation of Higher Eduction*. 1st ed. New York: Monthly Review.

Noer, Michael. 2012. "One Man, One Computer, 10 Million Students: How Khan Academy Is Reinventing Education." *Forbes*, November 19. http://www.forbes.com /sites/michaelnoer/2012/11/02/one-man-one-computer-10-million-students-how -khan-academy-is-reinventing-education/.

Noffsinger, John. S. 1926. *Correspondence Schools, Lyceums, Chautauquas*. New York: Macmillan.

NYU Bobst Library. n.d. "175 Facts about NYU." Accessed June 25, 2015. http://www .nyu.edu/library/bobst/research/arch/175/pages/sunrise.htm.

O'Neil, Megan. 2014. "Pushed by Lawmakers, U. of Florida Dives into Online Education." *The Chronicle of Higher Education*, May 23. http://chronicle.com/article /Pushed-by-Lawmakers-U-of/146767/.

Opencast. 2015. "About Opencast." http://opencast.org/.

Pappano, Laura. 2012. "Massive Open Online Courses Are Multiplying at a Rapid Pace." *New York Times*, November 2. http://www.nytimes.com/2012/11/04 /education/edlife/massive-open-online-courses-are-multiplying-at-a-rapid-pace .html.

Parker, Kim, Amanda Lenhart, and Kathleen Moore. 2011. *The Digital Revolution and Higher Education*. Washington, DC: Pew Research Center, Internet, Science and Technology. August 28. http://www.pewinternet.org/2011/08/28/the-digital -revolution-and-higher-education/.

Parry, Marc. 2009a. "Sloan Foundation Ends Major Grant Program for Online Education." *The Chronicle of Higher Education*, April 6. http://chronicle.com/article /Sloan-Foundation-Ends-Major/47158/.

————. 2009b. "Obama's Great Course Giveaway." *The Chronicle of Higher Education*, August 3. http://chronicle.com/article/Obamas-Great-Course-Giveaway/47530/.

Pizzo, Stephen P. 2001. "Barbarians at the University Gate—Forbes.com." Forbes .com. September 10. http://www.forbes.com/asap/2001/0910/064s01.html.

Poster, Elizabeth. 2013. "MOOCs and More: Expanding Online Access for Nurses." *EDUCAUSE Review*, August 5. http://www.educause.edu/ero/article/moocs-and -more-expanding-online-access-nurses.

Pulley, John L. 2005. "Raising Arizona." *The Chronicle of Higher Education*, November 18. http://chronicle.com/article/Raising-Arizona/15714/.

Read, Brock. 2006. "U. of California at Berkeley Offers Free Podcasts of Courses on iTunes." *The Chronicle of Higher Education*, April 26. http://chronicle.com/article/U -of-California-at-Berkeley/118437/.

Rivard, Ry. 2013a. "MOOCs Spread Quickly, Aided by No-Bid Deals with Public Universities." *Inside Higher Ed*, July 17. https://www.insidehighered.com/news/2013 /07/17/moocs-spread-quickly-aided-no-bid-deals-public-universities.

————. 2013b. "Citing Disappointing Student Outcomes, San Jose State Pauses Work with Udacity." *Inside Higher Ed*, July 18. https://www.insidehighered.com/news /2013/07/18/citing-disappointing-student-outcomes-san-jose-state-pauses-work -udacity.

Rosenzweig, Roy. 1998. "Wizards, Bureaucrats, Warriors, and Hackers: Writing the History of the Internet." *The American Historical Review* 103 (December): 1530–52.

Saettler, Paul. 2004. *The Evolution of American Educational Technology*. Greenwich, CT: IAP.

Schaffhauser, Dian. 2013a. "Desire2Learn Offers Alternative MOOC Platform, Integrates New Tools." *Campus Technology*, October 8. http://campustechnology .com/articles/2013/10/08/desire2learn-offers-alternative-mooc-platform-integrates -new-tools.aspx.

————. 2013b. "Faculty Coalition: It's Time to Examine MOOC and Online Ed Profit Motives." *Campus Technology*, October 9. http://campustechnology.com /articles/2013/10/09/faculty-coalition-its-time-to-examine-mooc-and-online-ed -profit-motives.aspx.

————. 2014. "Georgia Tech MOOC-Based Degree Program Turns Away Nearly 2,000 Applicants." *Campus Technology*, January 21. http://campustechnology.com /articles/2014/01/21/georgia-tech-mooc-based-degree-program-turns-away-nearly -2000-applicants.aspx.

————. 2015. "U Michigan Scales Up MOOC Missions." *Campus Technology*, October 7. https://campustechnology.com/articles/2015/10/07/u-michigan-scales-up-mooc -missions.aspx.

Schuman, Rebecca. 2013. "The King of MOOCs Abdicates the Throne." *Slate*, November 19. http://www.slate.com/articles/life/education/2013/11/sebastian _thrun_and_udacity_distance_learning_is_unsuccessful_for_most_students .html.

Selingo, Jeffrey J. 2014. "Demystifying the MOOC." *New York Times*, October 29. http://www.nytimes.com/2014/11/02/education/edlife/demystifying-the-mooc .html.

Siemens, George. 2012. "MOOCs Are Really a Platform." *Elearnspace* (blog). http://www.elearnspace.org/blog/2012/07/25/moocs-are-really-a-platform/.

SJSU Philosophy Dept. 2013. "'An Open Letter to Professor Michael Sandel from the Philosophy Department at San Jose State U.'" *The Chronicle of Higher Education*, May 2. http://chronicle.com/article/The-Document-Open-Letter-From/138937/.

Starbucks. 2015. "Applications Surge for Starbucks College Plan," May 10. https:// news.starbucks.com/news/asu-spring-2015-graduation.

Steinberg, Jacques, and Edward Wyatt. 2000. "THE NATION; Boola, Boola, E-Commerce Comes to the Quad." Week in Review. *New York Times*, February 13. http://www.nytimes.com/2000/02/13/weekinreview/the-nation-boola-boola -e-commerce-comes-to-the-quad.html.

Straumsheim, Carl. 2014a. "One Semester In, Students Satisfied with Unfinished Georgia Tech Online Degree Program." *Inside Higher Ed*, June 6. https://www .insidehighered.com/news/2014/06/06/one-semester-students-satisfied-unfinished -georgia-tech-online-degree-program.

————. 2014b. "Contract Reveals Arizona State U.-Starbucks Partnership Details." *Inside Higher Ed*, June 23. https://www.insidehighered.com/news/2014/06/23 /contract-reveals-arizona-state-u-starbucks-partnership-details.

————. 2014c. "Online Ed Skepticism and Self-Sufficiency: Survey of Faculty Views on Technology." *Inside Higher Ed*, October 29. https://www.insidehighered.com /news/survey/online-ed-skepticism-and-self-sufficiency-survey-faculty-views -technology.

————. 2015a. "Academic Partnerships to Pay Faculty Who Include Live Online Sessions in Their Courses." *Inside Higher Ed*, April 21. https://www.insidehighered .com/news/2015/04/21/academic-partnerships-pay-faculty-who-include-live-online -sessions-their-courses.

————. 2015b. "Arizona State, edX Team to Offer Freshman Year Online through MOOCs." *Inside Higher Ed*, April 23. https://www.insidehighered.com/news/2015 /04/23/arizona-state-edx-team-offer-freshman-year-online-through-moocs.

————. 2015c. "'Double-Dipping' with MOOCs." *Inside Higher Ed*, October 13. https://www.insidehighered.com/news/2015/10/13/colleges-explain-why-they -double-dipped-moocs.

Strauss, Valerie. 2012. "Khan Academy: The Revolution That Isn't." *Washington Post*, July 23. http://www.washingtonpost.com/blogs/answer-sheet/post/khan-academy -the-hype-and-the-reality/2012/07/23/gJQAuw4J3W_blog.html.

Stripling, Jack. 2008. "Breaking Up Is Hard to Do." *Inside Higher Ed*, December 9. https://www.insidehighered.com/news/2008/12/09/ellis.

———. 2009. "Tarnished Jewel." *Inside Higher Ed*, July 13. https://www.insidehighered .com/news/2009/07/13/tarnished-jewel.

———. 2010. "As the Crow Flies." *Inside Higher Ed*, July 16. https://www.insidehighered .com/news/2010/07/16/crow.

———. 2015. "The Making of a Higher-Ed Agitator." *The Chronicle of Higher Education*, April 24. http://chronicle.com/article/The-Making-of-a-Higher-Ed /229619/.

Sufrin, Julia. 2014. "Report: Global MOOC Market Continuing to Grow." *Campus Technology*, July 22. http://campustechnology.com/articles/2014/07/22/new-research -report-shows-mooc-market-to-grow-at-51.61-percent-cagr-by-2018.aspx.

Sullivan, Bob. 2014. "The Truth behind Starbucks' Tuition Plan." *Credit.com* (blog), June 27. http://blog.credit.com/2014/06/the-truth-behind-starbucks-tuition-plan -86125/.

Talbert, Robert. 2012. "The Trouble with Khan Academy—Casting Out Nines." *The Chronicle of Higher Education*, July 2. http://chronicle.com/blognetwork /castingoutnines/2012/07/03/the-trouble-with-khan-academy/.

The MOOC Guide. 2008. "03. CCK08—The Distributed Course." The MOOC Guide. https://sites.google.com/site/themoocguide/3-cck08—the-distributed -course.

Thompson, Clive. 2011. "How Khan Academy Is Changing the Rules of Education." *WIRED*, July 15. http://www.wired.com/2011/07/ff_khan/.

UCLA ITPB. 2001. "About the ITPB." August 20. http://www.itpb.ucla.edu/history /charter.htm.

Udacity. 2015. "About Us." https://www.udacity.com/us.

Veletsianos, George. 2015. "The Invisible Learners Taking MOOCs." *Higher Ed Beta* (blog). *Inside Higher Ed*, May 27. https://www.insidehighered.com/blogs/higher-ed -beta/invisible-learners-taking-moocs#.VWwyOyobv-8.gmail.

Walsh, Taylor, S+R Ithaka. 2011. *Unlocking the Gates: How and Why Leading Universities Are Opening Up Access to Their Courses.* Princeton, NJ: Princeton University Press.

Walters, Dan. 2015. "Governor Aims to Reform California's Higher Education System." *San Jose Mercury News*, January 29. http://www.mercurynews.com /opinion/ci_27418438/dan-walters-governor-aims-reform-californias-higher -education.

Waltzer, Luke. 2013. "Assessing Coursera, the LMS." *Bloviate* (blog), June 3. http:// lukewaltzer.com/assessing-coursera/.

Warner, John. 2015a. "ASU Is the 'New American University'—It's Terrifying." *Just Visiting* (blog). *Inside Higher Ed*, January 25. https://www.insidehighered.com /blogs/just-visiting/asu-new-american-university-its-terrifying.

———. 2015b. "The Problem ASU Is Solving." *Just Visiting* (blog). *Inside Higher Ed*, April 23. https://www.insidehighered.com/blogs/just-visiting/problem-asu-solving-0.

———. 2015c. "ASU=edX's." *Just Visiting* (blog). *Inside Higher Ed*, April 29. https://www.insidehighered.com/blogs/just-visiting/asu-edxs-cleaner.

Waters, John K. 2013a. "SJSU Takes a 'Breather' from MOOC Project." *Campus Technology*, July 18. http://campustechnology.com/articles/2013/07/18/sjsu-takes-a-breather-from-mooc-project.aspx.

———. 2013b. "What Will Happen to MOOCs Now That Udacity Is Leaving Higher Ed?" *Campus Technology*, December 11. http://campustechnology.com/articles/2013/12/11/what-will-happen-to-moocs-now-that-udacity-is-leaving-higher-ed.aspx.

Watters, Audrey. 2011. "Year-End Stats from MIT Point to Increasing Popularity of Open Educational Resources," *ReadWrite*, January 4. http://readwrite.com/2011/01/04/year-end_stats_from_mit_point_to_increasing_popula.

Webcast.berkeley. 2015. "Educational Technology Services." https://ets.berkeley.edu/about-webcastberkeley.

Wexler, Ellen. 2015. "What the Results of a Survey of Coursera Students Means for Online Learning." *The Chronicle of Higher Education*, September 22. http://chronicle.com/blogs/wiredcampus/what-the-results-of-a-survey-of-coursera-students-mean-for-online-learning/57401.

Woo, Elaine. 1997. "Virtual College." *Los Angeles Times*, July 20. http://articles.latimes.com/1997/jul/20/news/ss-14508.

Xu, Di, and Shanna Smith Jaggars. 2013. "Adaptability to Online Learning: Differences across Types of Students and Academic Subject Areas." CCRC Working Paper No. 54, Community College Resource Center, Teachers College, Columbia University, New York. http://ccrc.tc.columbia.edu/publications/adaptability-to-online-learning.html.

Young, Jeffrey R. 2008. "Study Finds Hybrid Courses Just as Effective as Traditional Ones." *Wired Campus* (blog). *The Chronicle of Higher Education*, September 16. http://chronicle.com/blogs/wiredcampus/study-finds-hybrid-courses-just-as-effective-as-traditional-ones/4242.

———. 2013. "California State U. Will Experiment with Offering Credit for MOOCs." *The Chronicle of Higher Education*, January 15. http://chronicle.com/article/California-State-U-Will/136677/.

———. 2015. "The Catch in Arizona State's Low-Cost Freshman Year Online: No Aid." *The Chronicle of Higher Education*, April 23. http://chronicle.com/article/The-Catch-in-Arizona-State-s/229617/.

Chapter 7

Anderson, Nick. 2015. "California and N.Y. Are Thinking Big on Higher Education. Will the Feds?" *Washington Post*, April 15. http://www.washingtonpost.com/news/grade-point/wp/2015/04/15/california-and-n-y-are-thinking-big-on-higher-education-will-the-feds.

Benkler, Yochai. 2007. *The Wealth of Networks: How Social Production Transforms Markets and Freedom*. New Haven, CT: Yale University Press.

Berrett, Dan. 2015. "The Day the Purpose of College Changed." *The Chronicle of Higher Education*, January 26. http://chronicle.com/article/The-Day-the-Purpose-of-College/151359.

Biemiller, Lawrence. 2015. "The Week." *The Chronicle of Higher Education*, March 30. http://chronicle.com/article/The-Week/228853.

Blogs@Baruch. 2015. "Mission Statement." http://blogs.baruch.cuny.edu/about -blogsbaruch/mission-statement/.

Blumenstyk, Goldie. 2014a. "What's Out: Student Debt. What's In: Free College." *The Chronicle of Higher Education*, June 11. http://chronicle.com/article/Whats-Out -Student-Debt/147023/.

———. 2014b. "5 Surprises in Writing a Book about What Ails Higher Education." *The Chronicle of Higher Education*, September 26, A12.

Blumenstyk, Goldie, and Casey Fabris. 2015. "Abrupt Closing of Corinthian Campuses Leaves 16,000 Students Scrambling." *The Chronicle of Higher Education*, April 28. http://chronicle.com/article/Abrupt-Closing-of-Corinthian /229717.

Bosman, Julie. 2015. "2016 Ambitions Seen in Walker's Push for University Cuts in Wisconsin." *New York Times*, February 16. http://www.nytimes.com/2015/02/17/us /politics/scott-walker-university-wisconsin.html.

Bosman, Julie, and Tamara Lewin. 2015. "Clinton Spurs Rivals with a Debt Plan." *New York Times*, August 14, A1, A16.

Boston Globe. 2014. "Colleges' Treatment of Adjuncts Devalues Education." April 21. https://www.bostonglobe.com/opinion/editorials/2014/04/20/colleges-treatment -adjuncts-devalues-education/VkEVK9XkLHMUEiAw92KwJJ/story.html.

Bowen, Barbara. 2012. "Austerity Education: The Real Agenda of Pathways." *Clarion: Newspaper of the Professional Staff Congress/City University of New York,* October. http://www.psc-cuny.org/austerityeducation.

Brier, Stephen. 2012. "Where's the Pedagogy: The Role of Teaching and Learning in the Digital Humanities." In *Debates in the Digital Humanities*, edited by Matthew K. Gold, 390–401. Minneapolis: University of Minnesota Press.

Burns, Rebecca. 2013. "UIC Faculty Union Flexes Muscles in Showdown over Adjunct Pay." *In These Times*, December 12. http://inthesetimes.com/working/entry /15983/uic_faculty_union_showdown_over_adjunct_pay.

Carlson, Scott. 2014. "Administrative Hiring Drove 28% Boom in Higher-Ed Work Force, Report Says." *The Chronicle in Higher Education*, February 5. http://chronicle .com/article/Administrator-Hiring-Drove-28-/144519/.

Carnevale, Anthony P., and Jeffrey Strohl. 2010. "How Increasing College Access Is Increasing Inequality and What to Do about It." In *Highlights from Rewarding Strivers: Helping Low Income Students in College*, edited by Richard Kahlenberg, 71–137. New York City: Century Foundation.

Cohen, Patricia. 2015. "Racial Wealth Gap Persists Despite Degree, Study Says." *New York Times*, August 17, B1–B2.

Commons in a Box. n.d. "Commons in a Box." Accessed September 10, 2015. http:// commonsinabox.org/.

Conn, Steven. 2015. "Welcome to Ohio State, Where Everything Is for Sale." *The Chronicle of Higher Education*, March 20. http://chronicle.com/blogs/conversation /2015/03/20/welcome-to-ohio-state-where-everything-is-for-sale/.

CUNY Academic Commons. 2009. "About CUNY Academic Commons." January 25. http://commons.gc.cuny.edu/about/.

Davey, Monica, and Tamar Lewin. 2015. "Unions Subdued, Scott Walker Turns to Tenure at Wisconsin Colleges." *New York Times*, June 4. http://www.nytimes.com/2015/06/05 /us/politics/unions-subdued-scott-walker-turns-to-tenure-at-wisconsin-colleges.html.

Eagleton, Terry. 2015. "The Slow Death of the University." *The Chronicle of Higher Education*, April 6. http://chronicle.com/article/The-Slow-Death-of-the/228991.

Eidelson, Josh. 2012. "Millionaires Tax Backers Compromise with California" *In These Times*, April 9. http://inthesetimes.com/working/entry/12999/millionaires _tax_backers_compromise_with_california_governor.

Fain, Paul. 2014. "Gaming the System." *Inside Higher Ed*, November 19. https://www .insidehighered.com/news/2014/11/19/performance-based-funding-provokes -concern-among-college-administrators.

———. 2015a. "Free Community College Catches On." *Inside Higher Ed*, July 9. https://www.insidehighered.com/news/2015/07/09/oregon-passes-free-community -college-bill-congressional-democrats-introduce-federal.

———. 2015b. "Next Phase for Gates's Completion Agenda." *Inside Higher Ed*, March 11. https://www.insidehighered.com/news/2015/03/11/gates-foundation -announces-four-priority-policy-areas-college-completion-data-system.

Fausset, Richard. 2015. "Ideology Seen as Factor in Closings in University of North Carolina System." *New York Times*, February 19. http://www.nytimes.com/2015/02/20 /us/ideology-seen-as-factor-in-closings-in-university-of-north-carolina-system.html.

Fichtenbaum, Rudy. 2015. "From the President: Politics and the AAUP." *Academe* 100, May–June. http://www.aaup.org/article/president-politics-and-aaup.

Field, Kelly. 2015a. "Obama Presses for Free Community College and Tax Reform." *The Chronicle of Higher Education*, January 21. http://chronicle.com/article/Obama -Presses-for-Free/151319/.

———. 2015b. "What Obama's 'Student Aid Bill of Rights' Will—and Won't—Do." *The Chronicle of Higher Education*, March 11. http://chronicle.com/article/What -Obama-s-Student-Aid/228391.

Fine, Michelle, and Michael Fabricant. 2014. "Solidarity at Last." *The Nation*, October 13, 18–19.

Fisher, Allan. 2014. "A Manufactured Accreditation Crisis at City College of San Francisco? The Downsizing and Corporate Overhaul of one of the Biggest Community Colleges in the U.S." (slideshow). The Committee to Save the City College of San Francisco. https://researchresourcesccsf.files.wordpress.com/2014/11 /slideshow-city-college-accreditation-crisis-09_17_14.pptx.

Francoeur, Stephen. 2014. "My Presentation on Blogging at Baruch College." *Beating the Bounds* (blog), March 28. http://www.stephenfrancoeur.com/beatingthebounds /2014/03/28/my-presentation-on-blogging-at-baruch-college/.

Fraser, Nancy. 2013. "A Triple Movement? Parsing the Politics of Crisis after Polyani." *The New Left Review* 81 (May–June): 119–132.

Gardner, Lee. 2014. "City College of San Francisco Could Get 2-Year Reprieve on Accreditation." *The Chronicle of Higher Education*, June 12. http://chronicle.com /article/City-College-of-San-Francisco/147055/.

Groom, Jim, and Brian Lamb. 2014. "Reclaiming Innovation." *EDUCAUSE Review*, May/June. http://www.educause.edu/visuals/shared/er/extras/2014 /ReclaimingInnovation/default.html.

Healy, Patrick. 2015. "Hillary Clinton to Offer Plan on Paying College Tuition without Needing Loans." *New York Times*, August 10. http://www.nytimes.com /2015/08/10/us/politics/hillary-clinton-to-offer-plan-on-paying-college-tuition -without-needing-loans.html.

Jaschik, Scott. 2015. "Killing All State Support." *Inside Higher Ed*, March 6. https:// www.insidehighered.com/news/2015/03/06/arizona-budget-deal-would-eliminate -all-state-funds-3-large-community-college.

Jones, Jason B. 2009. "Trying a Course Blog? Trying to Get Others to Blog?" *The Chronicle of Higher Education*, August 11. http://chronicle.com/blogs/profhacker /trying-a-course-blog-trying-to-get-others-to-blog/22618.

Kelderman, Eric. 2015a. "A Community College Contemplates a Future without State Money." *The Chronicle of Higher Education*, March 6. http://chronicle.com/article/A -Community-College/228273.

———. 2015b. "Tennessee's Task: Turn 'Free Community College' from a Rallying Cry into a Success." *The Chronicle of Higher Education*, February 18. http://chronicle .com/article/Tennessee-s-Task-Turn/190125/.

Klein, Naomi. 2008. *The Shock Doctrine: The Rise of Disaster Capitalism*. New York: Henry Holt.

Kreniske, Philip. 2015. "Oh the Thinks You Can Think! How the Medium Influenced Freshman Writers Cognition and INTENSITY." Unpublished paper, PhD Program in Developmental Psychology, CUNY Graduate Center.

Lessig, Lawrence. 2005. *Free Culture: The Nature and Future of Creativity*. Reprint, New York: Penguin Books.

Lewin, Tamar. 2015a. "Government to Forgive Student Loans at Corinthian College." *New York Times*, June 8. http://www.nytimes.com/2015/06/09/education/us-to -forgive-federal-loans-of-corinthian-college-students.html.

———. 2015b. "Claiming Trickery by For-Profit Colleges, Students Stage a Loan Revolt." *New York Times*, May 3. http://www.nytimes.com/2015/05/04/education /for-profit-colleges-face-a-loan-strike-by-thousands-claiming-trickery.html.

Logue, Alexandra W. 2015. "CUNY's Pathway to Shared Governance." *The Chronicle of Higher Education*, January 23. http://chronicle.com/blogs/conversation/2015/01/23 /cunys-pathways-to-shared-governance/.

Mangan, Katherine, and Beckie Supiano. 2015. "The Players Who Influenced Obama's Plan." *The Chronicle of Higher Education*, January 11. http://chronicle.com /article/The-Players-Who-Influenced/151145/.

McCambridge, Ruth. 2014. "TN Gov's Plan: Two Free Years of College for Each High School Grad." *Nonprofit Quarterly*, February 6. http://nonprofitquarterly.org /2014/02/06/tn-gov-s-plan-two-free-years-of-college-for-each-high-school-grad/.

Mitchell, Michael, and Michael Leachman. 2015. *Years of Cuts Threaten to Put College out of Reach for More Students*. Washington, DC: Center on Budget and Policy Priorities. http://www.cbpp.org/sites/default/files/atoms/files/5-13-15sfp.pdf.

Myers, Virginia. 2015. "University Inc: The Pernicious Effects of Corporate Influence." *AFT On Campus*, Summer. http://www.aft.org/node/10297.

New Caucus. 2015. "PSC Elections: New Caucus Slate Joint Statement." *Clarion*, March. http//www.psc.cuny.org/clarion/march-2015/psc-elections-newcaucus-slate -joint-statement.

New York Times Editorial Board. 2015. "Scott Walker's Effort to Weaken College Tenure." June 5. http://www.nytimes.com/2015/06/06/opinion/scott-walkers-effort-to-weaken-college-tenure.html.

Ostrach, Stefan. 2013. "Professors and Adjuncts Unite, Win Raises, Job Security in First Contract." *Labor Notes*, October 9. http://labornotes.org/blogs/2013/10/professors-and-adjuncts-unite-win-raises-job-security-first-contract.

Ovaska, Sarah. 2015. "UNC Board of Governors Moves to Discontinue, Consolidate 46 Degree Programs (List Included)." *The Progressive Pulse*, May 26. http://pulse.ncpolicywatch.org/2015/05/26/unc-board-of-governors-moves-to-discontinue-46-degree-programs-list-included/.

Picciano, A. G., C. Dziuban, and C. Graham, eds. 2013. *Blended Learning: Research Perspectives.* Vol. 2. New York: Taylor & Francis.

Porter, Eduardo. 2015. "The Promise and Failure of Community Colleges." *New York Times*, February 17, 2015. http://www.nytimes.com/2015/02/18/business/economy/the-promise-and-failure-of-community-colleges.html.

Post, Tim. 2013. "Education Gets Big Boost in Dayton Budget Proposal." National Public Radio, January 24. http://www.nprnews.org/story/2013/01/23/education/dayton-budget-plan-education.

Pratt, Timothy. 2013. "Faculty Protest Reforms They Say 'Dumb Down' Higher Ed." *Hechinger Report*, December 26. http://hechingerreport.org/faculty-protest-reforms-they-say-dumb-down-higher-ed-2/.

Reich, Robert. 2014. "Why Government Spends More Per Pupil at Elite Private Universities Than at Public Universities." *Nation of Change*, October 14. http://robertreich.org/post/99923361875.

Rhoades, Gary. 2012. *Closing the Door Increasing the Gap: Who Is Not Going to Community College?* Tucson, AZ: The Campaign for the Future of Higher Education. https://www.insidehighered.com/sites/default/server_files/files/ClosingTheDoor_Embargoed.pdf.

Ross, Thomas. 2015. "The Future of Higher Education." Paper presented at the National Public Affairs Forum, Raleigh, North Carolina, March 10.

Sailor, Kevin. 2015. "Pathways and Transfer Data: An Empirical Update." Unpublished manuscript, Professional Staff Congress of the City University of New York, Spring.

Samuels, Bob. 2013. "Making All Public Higher Education Free." Unpublished manuscript, Campaign for the Future of Higher Education, January 14.

Save CCSF Coalition Research Committee. 2013. "City College of San Francisco: The Accreditation Bullies, the Shock Doctrine and the Real Agenda to Downsize and Privatize Public Education." August 13. http://www.saveccsf.org/wp-content/uploads/2013/05/1-Sneak-Peek-4-page-desktop-version.pdf.

Schmidt, P. 2014a. "Colorado Lawmakers Take Up Sweeping Overhaul of Adjunct Working Conditions." *The Chronicle of Higher Education*, February 4. http://chronicle.com/article/Colorado-Lawmakers-Take-Up/144397/.

———. 2014b. "Power in Numbers: Adjuncts Turn to City Wide Unionizing as Their Best Hope." *The Chronicle of Higher Education*, April 14. http://chronicle.com/article/Power-in-Numbers/145863.

Scrivener, Susan, with Michael J. Weiss, Alyssa Ratledge, Timothy Rudd, Colleen Sommo, and Hannah Fresques. 2015. *Doubling Graduation Rates: Three-Year Effects of CUNY's ASAP for Developmental Education Students*. New York: Manpower Demonstration Research Corporation, 2015.

Shear, Michael D. 2015. "Obama Promotes Plan for College Affordability." *New York Times*, September 10, A20.

Singer, Natasha. 2015. "The Must-Attend for Education Technology Investors." *New York Times*, April 13. http://bits.blogs.nytimes.com/2015/04/09/education -technology-investors-converge-on-scottsdale/.

Stewart, James B. 2015. "College Rankings Fail to Measure the Influence of the Institution." *New York Times*, October 1. http://www.nytimes.com/2015/10/02 /business/new-college-rankings-dont-show-how-alma-mater-affects-earnings .html.

Stratford, Michael. 2015. "Alexander's Higher Ed Act Agenda." *Inside Higher Ed*, March 24. https://www.insidehighered.com/news/2015/03/24/alexander-weighing -new-accountability-tools-better-data-higher-ed-act-rewrite.

Strike Debt. n.d. "The Debt Resistors Operations Manual." Accessed August 3, 2015. http://strikedebt.org/drom/.

Stripling, Jack. 2015a. "The Making of a Higher Education Agitator: Michael Crow's Prescription for Colleges Divides and Inspires." *The Chronicle of Higher Education*, April 24. http://chronicle.com/article/The-Making-of-a-Higher-Ed/229619/.

———. 2015b. "Obama's Free College Plan Evokes Spirit of Higher-Ed Acts." *The Chronicle of Higher Education*, January 11. http://chronicle.com/article/Free -College-Plan-Evokes/151151/.

Taylor, Astra. 2015. "A Strike against Student Debt." *New York Times*, February 27. http://www.nytimes.com/2015/02/28/opinion/a-strike-against-student-debt.html.

Turkel, Gerald. 2006. "Financing Higher Education: Privatization, Resistance and Renewal." *Journal of Collective Bargaining in the Academy*, Vol. 0, Article 3. http://thekeep.eiu.edu/cgi/viewcontent.cgi?article=1022andcontext=jcba.

Vara, Vauhini. 2015. "A Student-Debt Revolt Begins." *The New Yorker*, February 23. http://www.newyorker.com/business/currency/student-debt-revolt-begins.

Vitale, Alex. 2014. "The Fight against Pathways at CUNY." *Academe* 100 (September– October). http://www.aaup.org/article/fight-against-pathways-cuny.

Waltzer, Luke. 2010. "The Path to Blogs@Baruch." *Bloviate* (blog), July 13. http:// lukewaltzer.com/the-path-to-blogsbaruch/.

Wittner, Lawrence. 2013. "When Education Is a Business." *The Huffington Post*, June 23. http://www.huffingtonpost.com/lawrence-wittner/when-education-is-a busin_b_3483407.html.

Wrigley, Julia. 2010. "Improved Student Transfer at CUNY." Office of Academic Affairs, CUNY, October 5.

Epilogue

Berrett, Dan, and Eric Hoover. 2015. "When Pursuing Diversity, Victory Is Hard to Define." *The Chronicle of Higher Education*. November 13. http://chronicle.com /article/When-Pursuing-Diversity/234190.

Brehe, Emily. 2015. "The Start of a Movement: Graduate Students Walk Out." *The Maneater*, August 26. http://www.themaneater.com/stories/2015/8/26/start -movement-graduate-students-walk-out/.

Brown, Sarah. 2015. "Faculty Questions U of North Carolina's Choice of Spellings."
The Chronicle in Higher Education, November 6, A6. http://chronicle.texterity.com
/chronicle/20151106a?pg=6#pg6.

Chapman, Ben. 2015. "Protesters Arrested at Demonstration over Lapsed Contract
for CUNY Faculty, Staff." *New York Daily News*, November 5. http://www
.nydailynews.com/new-york/protestors-arrested-cuny-protest-article-1
.2424023.

Eligon, John, and Richard Pérez-Peña. 2015. "University of Missouri Protests Spur a
Day of Change." *New York Times*, November 9. http://www.nytimes.com/2015/11
/10/us/university-of-missouri-system-president-resigns.html.

Gaines/Oldham Black Culture Center. 2015. "Notable Firsts." http://gobcc.missouri
.edu/about/notablefirst/.

Gall, Carlotta. 2015. "A Product of Tunisia's 1960s Resistance Continues to Protest."
New York Times, August 7. http://www.nytimes.com/2015/08/08/world/africa/a
-product-of-tunisias-1960s-resistance-continues-to-protest.html.

Jaschik, Scott. 2015a. "Iowa Faculty Group Censures Incoming President." *Inside
Higher Ed*, September 24. https://www.insidehighered.com/quicktakes/2015/09/24/
iowa-faculty-group-censures-incoming-president.

———. 2015b. "What the Protests Mean." *Inside Higher Ed*, November 16. https://
www.insidehighered.com/news/2015/11/16/experts-consider-what-protests-over
-racial-tensions-mean.

———. 2015c. "History, Words, Race." *Inside Higher Ed*, November 19. https://www
.insidehighered.com/news/2015/11/19/campus-protests-continue-princeton-becomes
-flashpoint-debate-over-woodrow-wilson.

Kelderman, Eric. 2015. "On His First Day as U. of Iowa President, Bruce Harreld
Starts in the Hole." *The Chronicle of Higher Education*, November 1. http://chronicle
.com/article/On-His-First-Day-as-U-of-Iowa/234020.

Miller, Bruce Joshua, and Ned Stuckey-French. 2015. "In Missouri, the Downfall of a
Business-Minded President." *The Chronicle of Higher Education*, November 11.
http://chronicle.com/article/In-Missouri-the-Downfall-of-a/234164.

Nelson, Libby A. 2014. "Universities Hire Politician Presidents." *Politico*, January 4.
http://www.politico.com/story/2014/01/university-presidents-politicians
-101738.

O'Connor, Emily. 2015. "MU Coalition of Graduate Workers in the Process of Unionizing." *The Maneater*, October 28. http://www.themaneater.com/stories/2015/10/28
/mu-coalition-graduate-workers-process-unionizing/.

Oide, Thomas. 2015. "Graduate Student Jonathan Butler Declares Hunger Strike."
The Maneater, November 2. http://www.themaneater.com/stories/2015/11/2
/graduate-student-jonathan-butler-declares-hunger-s/.

Pérez-Peña, Richard. 2015. "Amid Unrest in Missouri, University System Picks
Michael Middleton as Interim Chief." *New York Times*, November 12. http://www
.nytimes.com/2015/11/13/us/university-of-missouri-unrest.html.

Ruiz, Albor. 2015. "College Professors among Those Paid Shamefully Low Wages,
Demand 'Educational Justice.'" *New York Daily News*, November 9. http://www
.nydailynews.com/new-york/education/ruiz-college-professors-paid-shamefully
-wages-article-1.2427866.

Sherwin, Allyson, Elaine Edwards, and Lauren Wortman. 2015. "Swastika Drawn in Residence Hall with Feces." *The Maneater*, October 29. http://www.themaneater .com/stories/2015/10/29/swastika-drawn-residence-hall-feces/.

Sherwin, Allyson, Emily Gallion, and Lucille Sherman. 2015. "MSA President Payton Head Combats Campus Discrimination." *The Maneater*, September 16. http://www .themaneater.com/stories/2015/9/16/msa-president-payton-head-combats-campus -discrimin/.

University of Missouri. 2013. "Pioneer Professor: Remembering Arvarh E. Strickland." *Mizzou Wire*, May 1. Ahttp://mizzouwire.missouri.edu/stories/2013/strickland /index.php.

———. 2015. "Legion of Black Collegians." Student Life University of Missouri. http://mizzoulife.missouri.edu/legion-of-black-collegians-lbc/.

Vilensky, Mike. 2015. "CUNY Faculty Demand Contract." *Wall Street Journal*, November 5. http://www.wsj.com/articles/cuny-faculty-demand-contract-1446778476.

Weinberg, Tessa. 2015a. "MU Hospital Investigated for Facilitating Abortions." *The Maneater*, September 2. http://www.themaneater.com/stories/2015/9/2/mu-hospital -investigated-facilitating-abortions/.

———. 2015b. "MU's Response to Planned Parenthood Investigations Results in Rally." *The Maneater*, September 30. http://www.themaneater.com/stories/2015/9 /30/mus-response-planned-parenthood-investigations-res/.

Weinberg, Tessa, and Taylor Blatchford. 2015. "A Historic Fall at MU" (special edition). *The Maneater*, Fall. http://www.themaneater.com/special-sections/mu-fall -2015/.